River Teeth Literary Nonfiction Prize

SERIES EDITORS:
Daniel Lehman, *Ashland University*
Joe Mackall, *Ashland University*

The River Teeth Literary Nonfiction Prize is awarded to the best work of literary nonfiction submitted to the annual contest sponsored by *River Teeth: A Journal of Nonfiction Narrative*.

MICHAEL DOWNS

House of
Good
Hope

A Promise for a Broken City

For Bob McGiffert,
A good friend & a good man,
who sets the high standard
as a teacher & journalist to
which I aspire.
God. I hope I got the grammar
right.
                    Yours ever,
                        Michael.

University of Nebraska Press
Lincoln and London

Missoula 2007

Lines from "Back East Out West with Roger
Williams" by Aliki Barnstone first appeared in the
Southern Review 38, no. 3 (Summer 2002), and are
reprinted here with the permission of the author.

Lines from "A Local Man Estimates What He Did
for His Brother Who Became a Poet and What
His Brother Did for Him" by James Whitehead are
from *Local Men* (University of Illinois Press, 1979),
and are reprinted here with permission.

Library of Congress Cataloging-in-Publication Data
Downs, Michael, 1964–
  House of good hope : a promise for a broken city /
Michael Downs.
    p.   cm.   – (River Teeth literary nonfiction prize)
  Includes bibliographical references.
  ISBN-13: 978-0-8032-6012-2 (pbk. : alkaline paper)
  ISBN-10: 0-8032-6012-1 (pbk. : alkaline paper)
    1. Hartford (Conn.)—Social conditions. 2. People
with social disabilities—Connecticut—Hartford.
3. Youth with social disabilities—Connecti-
cut—Hartford. 4. High school athletes—Connecti-
cut—Hartford. I. Title.
    HN80.H37D68 2007
    305.235086'942097463—dc22   2006029420

Designed and set in Swift by A. Shahan.

for Sheri

and for my grandparents:
Walter and Helen Petry

Bóg dał. Bóg wział.

Acknowledgments

The willingness of Eric, Derrick, Harvey, Hiram, and Joshua to open their lives to my scrutiny created this *House of Good Hope*. It's been a privilege to know such remarkable men. They have my unending gratitude. Thanks, too, to their families who gave their time and good will.

Thanks to John Reimringer, Katrina Vandenberg, Mike Swift, and Stewart O'Nan, who offered important insights and who believed in this book's possibility and necessity.

Reporting requires timely assistance. Todd Fernow, director of the criminal law clinic at the University of Connecticut, provided the transcript of Butch Braswell's trial. The *Boston Globe*'s Michael Vega clarified details of Eric Shorter's college football career. Graham Brink of the *St. Petersburg Times* found criminal records out of Pinellas County. Norma Cherry of Hartford Public High School's library searched out documents important to the school's history. *Hartford Courant* journalists working during the 1980s and 1990s must be commended for their thorough coverage of the city. Hartford benefited from their work, as did I.

A grant from the Freedom Forum made this reporting possible. Thanks, too, to the people at *River Teeth*, and to those at the University of Nebraska Press whose talent is evident in this book's every aspect. Magda Chaney helped me understand the language of my forebears and to better know my grandparents. Dennis Swibold offered much needed support and encouragement. Dedicated teachers showed me the way to this book, including, from the Department of Journalism at the University of Arizona: Jacqueline Sharkey, Donald Carson, and William Greer; and from the Graduate Programs in Creative Writing at the University of Arkansas: Donald Hays, William Harrison, and James Whitehead. Jim, you are much missed.

My parents, Ed and Judy Downs, gave me everything an aspiring writer needs: books, the time to spend with them, and an audience for those first sentences.

Every page is because of Sheri, with whom the story began and continues.

When writing of Hiram Harrington at Woodland School and at Touchstone, and when writing of Joshua Hall at Weaver, I have changed the names of the children in their charge.

House of Good Hope

Practice

The teenagers ran in cleats. They chased each other, sweat-slick and panting, around the blue rubber track, some of them sprinting in the straightaways, others merely enduring the turns of the oval, pushing themselves for another lap, fighting through the bright agony of shin splints and fiery lungs and whatever misery might have writhed that day out of the city and into their individual lives. Was it pain that aged them so quickly? In Hartford, as in so many cities like it, crumbling cities where men and women on assembly lines once manufactured money but where factories now made nothing, in such cities children were teenagers and teens were grownups and grownups, if they were smart and talented and capable, had too often moved elsewhere.

My home. The city of my birth. My parents had moved our family when I was a boy. A stranger to Hartford, now, at last, I was home.

The school year had yet to start, but the Inner City

Striders commanded the track at Hartford Public High. The club was open to anyone wanting to run, jump, or throw, though most practicing through the muggy August afternoon were black or Hispanic. On the field, the bustle looked scattered and casual, like a street fair; athletes gathered here and there in clumps, strolling and chatting, a girl flinging a discus, some boys seeking distraction through the girls. Harvey Kendall spent most of his time near the jumping pit, practicing the timing and technique that had already made him the best high school triple jumper in New England, and one of the best in the nation. All the other Striders knew him, and strolled by to visit, not so much because of what he had accomplished but because of how he carried himself. Harvey was mayor of this little town of teenagers in T-shirts and shorts. They knew he might entertain them with a dance. He might ask about their workout or tell a joke. Harvey smiled and laughed often, and his joy defied the sweat and the pain, countered sore feet and defeated postures with hope and possibility. The way he fooled around, his showmanship and marquee manner, would in college earn him the nickname "Hollywood," but because he also stretched when he was supposed to, ran drills as necessary, and always demanded of himself one more inch on his jumps, he gave the Striders much of their drive and spirit.

I was there that day in 1989 to interview him for the *Hartford Courant*, the city's daily, which had just hired me away from a newspaper in Tucson to cover sports. I'd arrived in Hartford frightened and excited and in love with the city without understanding why, tingling with the romantic's sense that fate or destiny or God or whatever it was made decisions for the world had sent me back where

I began. That sense of fate intensified when I learned that of nine young sports reporters hired to cover the state's high schools, my beat would be my hometown. The other new hires found apartments outside the city, but I ended up in a neighborhood south of the newspaper plant. Within a day or so, my editor made Harvey Kendall and the Inner City Striders my first assignment. The sky was overcast and mottled that day, and though the sun was still high, the light seemed nearer to dusk when I parked my Jeep with Arizona plates in the high school's lot.

Hartford itself seemed near to dusk. For more than four hundred years, people had used this city, and though Hartford had been reinvented over and over, it showed signs of age: rusted handrails and chipped concrete steps, copper statues gone aqua; even the air felt exhausted. I didn't mind. Fresh from Tucson's unrelentingly blue skies and sleek shopping-mall palaces, I was grateful for the overcast gloom and for this familiar, grit-encrusted place. Familiar, yes, because though I had never before visited Hartford Public, my grandfather had graduated from there. My family had lived in Hartford for four generations, and I was born in Hartford Hospital. But when my parents moved I was young; I hadn't lived in Connecticut since I was nine. Now twenty-five, I knew my way around a few parts of the city, especially the neighborhoods near where my grandparents still lived. But the Hartford I knew was their Hartford, glimpsed in photo albums, a place where young men still wore overcoats and ties on picnics and where women always wore hats. Looking for apartments, I'd driven into neighborhoods I'd never seen before, neighborhoods that might have been safe or might have been dangerous, but struck me as both because I couldn't yet tell the difference between poor and criminal. I drove until I got lost, and stayed lost until I grew scared. And then I pointed myself back toward what I knew to be safe, and I drove, eyes wide and adrenaline-alert, until I recognized downtown and regained my bearings.

Harvey Kendall, who lived in one of those neighborhoods where I found myself lost, a neighborhood my grandparents likely hadn't visited since the 1950s (if even then), was to be my introduction to a city my grandparents knew only from headlines, and I knew not at all.

Though he was eighteen years old, Harvey already stood taller than my six feet two. His haircut was a low flattop; the tone of his voice disaffected, cool, quite different from the tone he used with his teammates. He looked west over my shoulder at nearby apartments called Clemens Place, named for Hartford's most famous resident, Samuel Langhorne Clemens, who wrote under the pen name Mark Twain.

Harvey started our interview by asking the questions.

Nice to meet you, he said. You from Hartford?

I've been gone a while, I said. But I was born here. My grandparents still live here.

You live in the city now? he asked.

Yes, I told him. Near Barry Square. In the South End.

So you understand, he said.

Did I nod in agreement? Maybe. I can't remember. Maybe I just asked, "Okay, can you spell your name for me?" The truth was, I had no idea what Harvey was talking about. *Understand what?* Here I was, fresh out of Tucson's desert of Circle K convenience stores and gravel-packed yards, and this kid was talking to me as though I knew his life and his city. It was as if we had survived the same burning building, escaped the same plane crash. Harvey and I. We happy few.

After Harvey established to his satisfaction that I would understand him, he spoke freely, as if he trusted me. I didn't understand but I wanted to, and I recognized a gift when I saw one. Harvey's trust made me glad that I'd chosen to live in Hartford over any of its suburbs if it meant so much to somebody. It struck me on a personal level, even as I made use of his trust on a professional level. I did my job—asking questions, scribbling in my reporter's notebook—but I found myself wanting to know what had just happened that led Harvey to trust me. Was there something about Hartford, about living here, about claiming it as home, that really did connect us? These questions would stay with me long after that first interview.

Harvey was a talker. He listed for me Hartford's problems, the mantra that afflicts so many post-industrial American cities: racism and poverty, the sirens and the blood spilled by knives and guns. He bragged on his coach, Melvin "Butch" Braswell, the founder of the track club and the track coach at Hartford Public. Butch was an unassuming man whose trim beard followed his neck down to his T-shirt's collar. He wore a pair of gray pants and shabby Nike sneakers, and his T-shirt was so thin it was nearly transparent. "Most of the coaches at the school don't even know where we come from," Harvey told me. "Butch, he lives in the city. He always tells us, 'You can do this.' He picks us up. He teaches us more than about track—like, the way of life itself."

Braswell was more modest. "I don't even consider myself a good coach," he said, but something in his words rang falsely humble. He knew what he was doing mattered. He understood that young people trusted him, that in the midst of Hartford's bad actors—the dealers and the gangbangers and the crackheads—he gave his athletes a different model of how to live. He knew that when Harvey talked to me, much of what Harvey said had first come out of Butch's mouth.

"Track can carry me on into college," Harvey told me that day. "If I get me some good grades, get me a good major, make me some good money, I can help my mom and the people I love."

People I loved, my grandparents, Walter and Helen Petry, were native to the city, the children of Polish immigrants, and had lived in the same house nearly fifty years. Hartford held them tight, where Walter had been raised in poverty by his widowed mother, where Helen had learned kitchen tips from Italian friends. They had raised their own three children—including my mother—in the city's South End and could imagine living nowhere else. It was my parents' generation that broke the ties that had bound my family so closely to Hartford.

When my parents moved out of the city, when I was three years old, they traded a narrow railroad apartment near Hartford's Royal Typewriter Factory for a Cape-style white house with black shutters in nearby rural Glastonbury on the east bank of the Connecticut River. The drive from Glastonbury would take a little less than a half hour, depending on traffic on the Putnam Bridge.

You're moving across the river? said my horrified grandparents. Why so far?

My parents eventually took us farther—from Glastonbury to Vermont, and then to Tucson, always seeking better work for my father, better opportunities for the family. It wasn't easy. My father had dropped out of high school, and the equivalency exam he'd passed and the few college credits he'd accumulated weren't enough to land him a profession. Instead he worked his way up through grease and car parts and sweat into management positions, but his jobs were vulnerable to downturns in the economy and to layoffs. The move to Arizona was meant to temper those. The economy there seemed always booming, and higher education was less expensive than in the northeast. Even if my father didn't return to college, he could more easily help his children pay tuition at one of the West's state universities. Indeed, in Arizona, I graduated high school, then college and started my journalism career. Over more than a decade in the Southwest, I learned not only a profession, but how to live through summer desert heat, how to pry cactus spines from my dog's paws, and how to eat spicy Mexican food. I suppose time and geography made me an Arizonan, and it is true I felt comfortable in Tucson's colonial, Catholic, Mexican, and Indian influenced culture. But to feel at ease is not the same thing as to feel connected. Tucson could not bind me. Some nights I dreamed that I hiked east over Tucson's Rincon mountains and there found another city, one with leafy deciduous trees and slender lanes and houses with peaked roofs. Hartford remained for me the home that should have been home, a place I knew hardly at all, a place made more mysterious, more necessary by its distance.

My old Ross ten-speed had racing handlebars and a frame painted black. I'd bought it when I was in high school with money from my grandparents. In Hartford, after I moved back in 1989 to work for the *Courant*, it became my anti-nostalgia machine. With it, I could combat that romantic perception of my hometown that grew out of childhood memories of Christmas lights arrayed at downtown's Constitution Plaza, of tobogganing with my grandfather down Goodwin Park's one big hill. In a car, that nostalgia was easier to maintain. Through the raised windows of a car, Hartford could become for me a music video, providing visuals to whatever played on the radio, to whatever memory I chose to relive.

But it was my job to cover Hartford's high school sports teams, to tell the stories of the city's children, of Harvey Kendall and hundreds of others. I could not do that honestly while harboring a sentimental fiction, or a truth that was only a fraction of Hartford's particulars. Hartford was more than my family photo albums, more than the church where my parents married, the restaurant where they met, the factory where my great-grandfather had worked. When I rode my bicycle, the city forced on me its present realities: pork kebabs and rice, the sourness of trash dumpsters, homeboys in white T-shirts driving Toyota Corollas with dashboards decorated by air fresheners made to look like gold crowns, and men pushing shopping carts full of soda cans. Hartford was more complicated, more ruthless, and kinder than I knew.

Take, as proof, the hallway marred with graffiti and perpetual dusk and the smell of piss outside an apartment where a coach lived. Or the high school girls who cradled a teammate's infant daughter and cooed while Mama ran her heat in the 100 meters. Or the young man, so in need of soccer he used a Ginsu knife to saw the cast off his leg before his doctor could say, "the bone isn't healed." The same young man, spit on during a game, spitting back. The shooting guard, coached by his father, who helped the basketball team at his Catholic high school win a state championship just before the diocese closed the school and put his father out of work. The soccer-playing twins from Puerto Rico who took special education classes and who taught a team of Laotians and Jamaicans and Poles to shout "*Mira! Look!*" whenever an opponent sprinted toward the goal posts. The teenager with dreadlocks whose name meant Prince of Peace.

Neighborhood centers. Gymnasiums. North End, South End. Clay Hill, Keney Park, South Green, Flatbush Avenue, Barry Square. Kids cried and snarled and loved each other as I watched and learned to love them. Bulkeley High School's Bulldogs. Weaver's Beavers. South Catholic's Rebels. Prince Tech's Falcons. Hartford Public's Owls. I came to know the teachers and the security guards and the fans. But it was always the kids. So many stories.

I made mistakes. There was the time I printed the bragging of a Bulkeley quarterback who guaranteed a victory over Weaver only to lose a few days later, his team scoreless, humiliated. Weaver players repeated his boast as a taunt throughout the game, and then his fellow students at Bulkeley kept the words alive, too, so that "guarantee" echoed in the halls, punctuated by laughter. His coach was angry with me. These are kids, he said. You've got a responsibility. You've got to be careful with what they tell you.

And behind his words, this message: they may act tough, but so many of them, they're frail. Beautiful, precious.

I was reminded of that—and heartened—when I pedaled through the crowded, littered streets of Hartford.

Early one morning in June, I chained my bicycle in front of Harvey Kendall's house on Oakland Terrace, a street in Hartford's North End. It was midweek, and early enough that traffic was light. Despite the street garbage and houses with shattered windows and graffiti, the just-waking city seemed washed clean, full of potential.

Harvey had enjoyed a spectacular senior year, and the *Courant* planned to feature him on the cover of its high school All-State section. While my first story about Harvey was as much about the Inner City Striders, this one would profile him alone. Harvey had agreed to let me spend the day with him at Hartford Public.

Inside the Kendall house, while Harvey finished getting ready, I met his mother: a towering woman with a face shaped by the hard years of Southern childhood, by raising eleven children, and by the death—not yet five years past—of her husband. Jessie Kendall spoke in a rural Georgia accent, lush and tangled to my ears, and I strained to make out her words. She opened a clear plastic bag full of track and field medals and let them spill onto the kitchen table as she shook her head, marveling at all this treasure, wanting to share her honest delight that God could grant her such a blessing as this child, Harvey. She showed me a trophy case and how she'd arranged his plaques and awards, dozens of miniature athletes running, throwing, hurdling, each one labeled so the Kendalls would remember how Harvey won it.

Harvey and I walked to school, taking a long route out of our way so Harvey could pick up a friend. Eric Shorter and his mother had recently moved from a ramshackle apartment near Harvey's house to newer condos a few blocks east. I knew Eric a little. He was the quarterback of the football team, a smart, good-looking kid with the remnants of a childhood hearing problem that caused him sometimes to slur soft consonants or to overpronounce words.

At Hartford Public I sat through classes with Harvey-Harv (classmates called him that), listening to unremarkable teachers say unremarkable things. I sat with him at lunch, when he ad-libbed songs to make students laugh. He laughed, too. He laughed all the time, easily, as if laughter were his normal state and anything else was an act.

After school on the steps outside, we met Eric and three others, and here Harvey's hallway make-believe ended. His demeanor changed, his star status vanished. He relaxed. Clearly these were his peers. When we came upon them, they were trading the dates—August 16, September 16, August 26—that they'd leave for college. Harvey introduced me to his friends, all seniors looking forward to graduation, each serious under the afternoon sun, backpacks full, blue jeans baggy, a couple of them paging through the new yearbooks. All around us students slipped toward school buses or gathered in cliques for the walk home.

This was the moment Harvey chose to tell me about the promise he and his four friends had made, a pledge to each other and to their city, not just to give something back, but to give everything back, and then to give more. Hartford needed them: not just the money they'd someday earn, not a part-time commitment, but an effort that would last all day, every day. "I'm not the smartest guy," Harvey said, "but in August I'm going to college. I'm going to do the best I can and come back and help this community." The others nodded—yes, yes, all of us, we'll all come home.

As they talked, as I wrote what they said, I became struck with the possibility that Harvey had opened up to me that first day we met because he thought I would understand this pledge. Because I'd been born in Hartford, because now I lived there. Because I'd gone away and come back. We were a team after all—the sons of a city that needed us.

Harvey recalled the trophy case from that morning, the plastic bag of medals. "All the awards don't mean nothing," he told me, "until our mission is accomplished."

There are assurances, and there are promises, and there are oaths. Harvey spoke with a zealot's belief, a belief strong enough to reverse reality, to make two plus two equal five, to change the color of the sky. He and his friends could even change Hartford, make it right. But he was nineteen then. In ten years he would be changed, as would his friends, as would Hartford. In many ways, the city would be worse. Hartford would demand more of Harvey and his friends—and yes, of me—than any of us expected on that afternoon in June. Who knew whether they would return, whether I would stay, whether we could make lives to keep faith with this place and its people?

This, then, is how those five young men began to teach me about the city of my birth and what we owed it. Their lessons would be compounded by those of other Hartford teenagers. But those five in particular—and their stories and their pledge—would stay with me, posing a challenge and raising questions. Over the next decade and beyond—when my grandparents, old and in failing health, needed family the way old, failing Hartford needed people like Harvey and his friends—those five and I would work to understand the answers. What do we owe the people and places who made us? And how much must we sacrifice to pay that debt?

Then, times would come when each of us would choose: to stand by Hartford or abandon it.

one

I want to go back East away from the new,

where the sky is small, domestic as a tablecloth
smoothed pretty by God's unbearable lucent hands,
to go to the old city where I was young,
and the Atlantic wind pinched my cheeks . . .

ALIKI BARNSTONE
"Back East Out West with Roger Williams"

1

Busted for drugs?

Naw, man. Beefin', and he got shot.

I heard it was a knife, yo.

The freshmen traded rumors. Something from Hartford's streets had crept into football practice and snatched away a teammate. The players let the news drag their attention from blocking drills and wind sprints, so the coaches blew their whistles to end the workout and call the freshmen for a speech. Derrick Walker, fifteen years old, unsnapped his chin strap and lifted off his helmet, then bent to rest one knee on the dirt. Most of the freshmen took a knee, and they made a three-deep circle around Coach Ferguson.

They called their coach Homer. When he wasn't coaching Hartford Public's freshman team, he was an assistant with the varsity, and when he wasn't doing either of those things, he was a security guard at the school. He liked to laugh with students in the halls, teasing them with good-natured insults as they bumped and dawdled in the sally between classes. He joked so often that when he wanted them to take him seriously he had to say, "All jokes aside" or "In all seriousness." They thought of him as a chubby kind of Cool Daddy, with his slicked-back hair and dark skin. He rode a chopper.

Now Homer was about to give a speech to his freshmen. Something bad had happened; they'd lost someone.

All jokes aside. He began.

You are lucky to be part of this team! Look around you. Years from now, some of you won't be here. You'll be incarcerated. You'll be dead. You'll be on a sidewalk strung out. So what you've got now is special. And I'm not talking about football. Football is football. No big thing. But life is life. You've got friends here. Teammates. You have to enjoy this, start making the right decisions. Make football a tool. Use it. Build on it. The things you learn here can carry over and make you a better person in life.

All around him was the staleness of adolescent sweat soaked into shoulder pads and jerseys. A few guys flicked dirt off their cleats; others watched rush-hour traffic thicken on Farmington Avenue. Some didn't pay Homer any mind. City kids, they couldn't step off a sidewalk without somebody giving a speech, wanting to save a life.

But Derrick Walker heard Homer and listened hard. Here was a coach sounding like a parent, caring about something more than how to read a play or break a tackle. The speech made sense to Derrick, the same way the counter-trap made sense. That was Derrick's play. When it worked, Derrick ran with the ball ten or fifteen yards into the other team's territory. But if a blocker failed to spring the trap, some moose from a suburban school might drop Derrick on his rear before he gained a foot. After a busted

16

play like that, some fellas would come back to the huddle full of red-eyed fury. Mother this and mother that . . . ! But that wasn't Derrick's way. He'd get down on himself for his own failures, but clap and cheer for any other guy who needed a lift, who'd messed up, blown a play. Derrick would give him a hand, help him up, even if it was Derrick's butt that had been ground into the turf when this guy missed his block.

That's what Homer meant. Forgive each other. Rely on one another. Don't go it alone. Set a common goal and work for it. Derrick knew a little bit about teamwork, and was only now beginning to understand what a strange miracle it was, all those separate brains and separate bodies somehow meshing the way a thousand-thousand blades of grass come together to turn a field green. For it to work, each player had to be aware of what he could do and what he couldn't. Running backs ran. Linemen blocked. Quarterbacks passed. Quarterbacks didn't block. Linemen didn't pass. You used whatever part of you helped the team, and you put aside everything else (even that anger at another broken play). In that sliver of time between referees' whistles, you attended to your own work, acted as an individual, and yet something more happened. You pushed a man out of the way, and the team scored a touchdown.

That was how Derrick heard Homer's message: *together, you change the game.*

Homer ended his speech; the players jogged back to their basement locker room, and, surrounded by his team, Derrick felt comforted and grateful. He was young. He didn't yet know how Homer's message would guide his life; maybe it was only that Homer put words to the way Derrick already knew he wanted to live. It was 1986, Derrick was a freshman, and soon, steered by the truths he'd known and Homer had named, Derrick would join with friends to make a different sort of team, a different sort of street gang.

They numbered five.

Eric Shorter played quarterback and hated to lose. When the Owls were down, Eric chewed his lip and squinted. Sometimes he cursed out his teammates. He was Derrick's best friend and had been since middle school, and to see one without the other was like seeing Batman without Robin. Neither had a father at home. Derrick's had left when he was young. Eric lost his to prison when his father killed a man.

Harvey Kendall joined them, too; Harvey who even in helmets and bulky padding could move with frightening grace and speed. Striding downfield, catching passes no one else could, it was as if he had skipped adolescence, pulled a man's body on with his uniform. He was the tallest on the team, and the best athlete, splitting time between the freshman squad and the varsity.

And there was Hiram Harrington, a punishing running back who made the most of the play they called "The Gut." He'd run straight into a crush of tacklers, and though he ran nearly upright, anyone who tried to stop him was offering himself as a sacrifice. Off the field Hiram seemed lethargic, slow-moving, observant. A comedian, too, always bantering, snickering about somebody's bad hair or new sneakers, anything to mess with your mind.

Come basketball season, they would be joined by Joshua Hall, a baby-faced, serious kid who played without the street fury other Hartford teenagers brought to the court. In fact, he stood out at Hartford Public because he wasn't street. Joshua had grown up——and still lived—in one of

Hartford's gentlest and most picturesque neighborhoods. His childhood was one of block parties and yards without fences, in a place that had been a model of integration in the 1970s until more and more white families hammered "For Sale" signs into their lawns.

The five became friends gradually: after football practice; in the loud cinder block hallways of Hartford Public; during classes; at a city park, lounging on the hood of an '87 Chevrolet Celebrity, watching girls in tight pants and high heels, girls who bared their shoulders and wore earrings loud as Christmas tree ornaments. Mostly their friendship found its cement on treks home after school. Walking together shortened the distances. They joked, and they complained about homework and argued about sports, and by traveling in numbers they were less likely to draw the attention of gang members who were always preying on youngsters, taunting them, demanding allegiance none of the five friends wanted to give.

They talked about that, too, and about what else was wrong with Hartford. They knew who was hungry in their neighborhoods, knew what hunger meant, because some of them—like Harvey—had come home to the bald white light of an empty refrigerator. They recognized racism because some of them—like Joshua—hated how they frightened white people just by being young, male, and black. They heard gunshots echo off abandoned buildings, and they watched friends turn—as Homer, the coach, had warned—into gangsters, into addicts, into prisoners, sometimes into corpses. So many kids gone wrong, the list so long, they'd remember the faces but forget the names, ask each other, "Who was he, that guy Homer gave the speech about?" Shake their heads. Breathe deep. Nope. Nope.

The five talked, but their repeated stories and complaints circled round and round, frustration underlining what they already knew, anger putting fresh exclamation points on the ends of old sentences.

In 1986 Hartford was badly broken, small and hard and well past its Golden Age. It was a city of broken street lamps and blaring car alarms and people shouting at each other from tenement windows. Sirens. Sirens at any time of day. In any neighborhood. That fall of 1986, on Laurel Street and on Kensington and even in the governor's mansion, people were talking about this new drug—crack—making its way up from New York City, and how it would change everything, make all the rape and robbery and violence worse. Already in Hartford too many people lived in crumbling fortress-apartments behind brick walls and steel doors marked with spray paint.

Long a home to immigrants, such as my Polish great-grandparents and my Irish great-great-grandparents, Connecticut's capital city had become a city of emigrants, too, a place where people came to live until they could leave for someplace better. When neighbors arrived, they came from everywhere: the American South, the Caribbean, Europe, Asia. Together they made a city rich in all the signs of sidewalk culture—a Turkish restaurant near a Greek social club, reggae music and salsa, calzones, kielbasa, do-rags, and tricked-out sedans. When neighbors left, it was often because they could now afford to live in a town that had less need for deadbolts and door chains and first-floor window bars. What Hartford's people had in common was addresses in a city that was to be survived and endured, then—oftentimes—abandoned.

The exodus repeated itself on a small scale every day at rush hour, and the five friends noticed and were troubled by it. After school, after practice, they often caught a city bus on the E line, riding it over pothole-filled roads with oiled seams and broken curbs and littered with bags from Dunkin' Donuts or McDonald's. They rode the bus east into downtown, past Marshall Street where it seemed crack had visited every door and turned the buildings hollow. The bus bumped and shook past the national headquarters of Ætna Insurance and then past the spot where a grander, Gilded Age version of Hartford Public High School once stood, an elegant building that had been torn down and was replaced now by a patch of weeds and an interstate highway.

Downtown at the turn of the twenty-first century was not so much different from the downtown the five friends knew more than a decade earlier. When I visited the city center in May 2000, I walked along streets that cut deep canyons between office towers, many of the skyscrapers built on the strength of the city's insurance industry: Phoenix Mutual Life Insurance, Hartford Steam Boiler Inspection and Insurance, Traveler's, and Ætna, and dozens of others. There was little sun. The skyscrapers stood too high, the streets ran too skinny to allow direct light except for the few midday minutes when the sun reached overhead. The lack of light washed downtown in a perpetual gloom. At the workday's end, people crowded the sidewalks. Suburbanites—mostly white—walked grim-faced to parking garages, quick and determined, as if nothing, not man nor God, could prevent their escape from the city. Darker-skinned people—mostly Hispanic and black—waited at the main transfer site for buses that would carry them a dozen or more blocks. Some would ride home to small houses with yards and cyclone fences that kept garbage from blowing off the streets into their neatly tended rose beds. Others ended the day in apartments with dark hallways where light bulbs that weren't smashed were burned out, or at Nelton Court or Stowe Village or Dutch Point Colony or some other treeless public housing project where outside at basketball courts kids bounced off broken box springs to dunk on netless hoops.

Today was a Wednesday, and there was a silence to the rush-hour bustle. If someone laughed, others turned to stare, to accuse. An ambulance honked its way through tight traffic. In the distance, a man played a trumpet: "From the halls of Montezuma to the shores of Tripoli" was the only phrase he knew, and he played it over and over. A boy walked alongside the high wrought iron fence that surrounds the Old State House, Connecticut's first capitol building. He ripped a sheet of paper into bits and let them drift with the wind, littering the littered sidewalk. People ignored him. He acted as alone in the crowd as if the streets stood empty.

A bus stopped at the curb, and the crowd shifted forward, swaying side to side as each person took child-steps toward the bus doors. Among them was a teenage boy wearing a backpack, its strap marked in glittering paint: "RIP Quanny." It was a reference to a fourteen-year-old boy who, after a night of joyriding and troublemaking, was shot to death while fleeing Hartford police. Quanny was black, the officer white.

Not long after, the rush was over. City buses had filled and driven away. Cars in a line heading for the suburbs had fought their way to either of the two interstates that join near Hartford's center amidst a series of on- and off-ramps that look from above like the ribbon on a concrete gift. Now the downtown traffic was so light a stray cat crossed the street with no sense of urgency. Of the few people left on the sidewalks, some looked as if they might sleep in doorways.

Eric and Derrick, Harvey, Hiram and Joshua saw this retreat from the city over and over again: white people rushing to their cars, fleeing to the suburbs, trying not to be the last to escape. Most of those white faces belonged to strangers, but what particularly hurt was how many of them belonged to teachers and coaches. Or bosses at the office supply store where Eric and Derrick worked. Or people who did business with Hiram's father. Or police officers. Or firefighters.

Each of the five friends caught a different bus home. When Harvey stepped off in his neighborhood and walked past a corner where drunks gathered around a telephone pole, he wondered what it would be like to have neighbors who were teachers or police officers or bosses at a supply store.

He wanted to be that neighbor.

"Harvey was always the one who always talked about coming back," Joshua told me years later. "He always talked about coaching or starting a rec center. He always felt it was his obligation to do something like that. I think we all just took that on."

"We all had a vision," said Eric, "and we talked about that vision."

They felt blessed. Not all of them enjoyed easy lives; the electricity might be shut off for a month, now and then a neighbor threatened violence. But unlike so many of their schoolmates, they each had parents who loved them, and they each knew adults—like Butch Braswell—who recognized their young talents and encouraged them. The five friends felt obligated to share what grace had come to them, and so, while still in high school, Eric and Derrick, Harvey, Hiram and Joshua pledged their lives to their city.

They made their pledge with the naiveté of youth and the wisdom of the street, and they made it because they loved justice and their neighbors. The promise emerged not in one moment with a secret handshake, fingers cut and blood mingled, but instead out of those hours spent together and out of their complaints, which they could make only so long until a solution revealed itself.

They would leave home for college, but the pledge required that they come back with their degrees, live within Hartford's limits, wrestle with its wrongs, love the city and make things right. It was a serious promise, and they made it not only to Hartford but to each other.

"We felt it was our duty to come back here and clean some of this nonsense up," Harvey said, nearly a decade after he and the others began their mission. "Take any inner-city kid. Our life expectancy is short. We're supposed to be a statistic. We're supposed to be in jail or working a low-paying job. Ten different children by ten different mothers. We're supposed to either be not doing anything in our lives or not making a difference in nobody's lives."

The five friends wanted to defy the statistics. Or maybe they wanted to be a different kind of statistic, the kind nobody counts.

2

Q: Now, had you seen your husband walking towards the door?

A: Yes.

Q: Did you see the gun in his hand?

Deposition of Linda Shorter, recorded by Cowan, Cheryl B., court reporter, Circuit Court for Pinellas County, Florida, November 15, 1973.

August along Florida's Suncoast usually means sunny mornings and muggy afternoons until the building thunderstorm breaks, dropping the temperature and raising the humidity so that the stickiness index is always about the same. Saturday, August 4, 1973, was different. It was well past thunder-shower hour when Robert Shorter arrived home from a sweaty day of work, and there hadn't been a drop of rain. All day long he'd worked wires and fuses as an electrician, with help from his cousin and best friend, James Cooper, the two of them hustling all over Pinellas County. Now that he was home, all Robert wanted from his wife was dinner and a cold beer.

Robert was a good man. Linda believed that. He was the oldest of nine children, and when his own father left, it fell to Robert to support his mother and siblings by working as a field hand. He spoke with a difficult-to-understand, rural Florida dialect, and he didn't have much formal education. Put an electrician's blueprint in front of him, he could read that, but you couldn't expect him to do as well with the evening paper. This didn't make him unusual among the young people in Marianna, Florida, where he was raised and where many kids dropped out of school to work. The family story was that when Robert and his relatives moved from Marianna, they chose St. Petersburg instead of Tampa because in St. Petersburg the streets were numbers, not names, making it easy to get around without reading.

In St. Petersburg he met and married Linda. They had a good life with their children, Candy, Gerald, and Eric. Robert provided a comfortable house on 35th Avenue South at the edge of ritzy, mostly white Lakewood Estates, next to a country club. Robert and Linda could afford to go out nights. The children wore nice clothes—no hand-me-downs—and they loved their father. Once Eric had learned to walk, he ran to his father every time Robert came home.

Robert was a good man. Linda wanted to quit her marriage anyway.

Because, as far as Linda was concerned, if Robert Shorter Jr. had developed any flaw in his thirty-five years, it was jealousy.

She believed that jealous rage changed her husband. He argued then. Drove crazy if he was behind the wheel. Accused her of little infidelities: flirting with this guy, looking too long at that one. Drinking only made it worse.

Once she planned on leaving him. Then she found out she was pregnant and maybe from some combination of hope and fear, she decided to stay. Even then they had words over naming the baby. If it turned out to be a boy, Robert wanted a junior, another Robert Shorter like he'd been to his own father. Linda said no. She wanted her son to have his own identity. But Robert insisted, as if he knew she could walk out, take the children, and leave him with nothing. He wanted at least the name.

They compromised. He'd get his Robert Shorter, but the middle name would be Eric—the name Linda wanted—and that's how they would call the child: Eric.

That was nearly two years past, and now Linda again wanted to take Candy and Gerald and Eric and leave her marriage. She just didn't know how or when, and sometimes she doubted whether it would be the right thing.

That steamy August night, she and Robert had plans to go to a club with friends, but there was little festivity or anticipation. She and Robert didn't say much to each other after he came home from work. Around eight thirty, another couple picked them up. Robert and Linda left the children with aunts to baby-sit while they spent a night of dancing at the Executive Lounge.

At the club, they met Robert's cousin James, and the lot of them camped around a circle table. They all ordered drinks, Robert ordering the Tom Collins that Linda would nurse through the evening. One of their friends had brought a bottle that he kept in a bag at his feet to sneak from now and then to refresh their empty glasses. The band played, and the Shorters danced and drank and smoked. Robert kept ordering drinks. Five or more, Linda later estimated.

> Q: How was his condition that night? You kept saying that he had been drinking a lot.
> A: Yes. They had been drinking a lot.
> Q: Can your husband hold his drink? Did he seem drunk that night?
> A: No, my husband, he can't hold his drinking.

Robert was talking more than usual, and he wanted to dance and dance—both signs to Linda that he was drunk. Song after song, he pulled her out onto the floor. The band kept up an exhausting pace, its first set lasting nearly three hours, and the sweaty dancers kept up, too. Eventually, around midnight, the band took a break, and Linda left the table to buy more cigarettes from a machine. She plugged the machine with enough money for three or four packs, but when she pulled the knob, dollars worth of change cascaded onto the floor. As she knelt to collect the coins, a band member offered to help. Robert stepped out of the nearby men's room and saw his wife talking with a musician.

Robert asked her right then to take that wedding ring off her finger and give it back to him. If she wasn't going to treat him right, he wanted no part of her.

No. No. No. Linda didn't want that whole jealousy thing anymore. She and Robert argued, and then were quiet until last call. The Executive Lounge closed up, and Linda and some others walked a friend to her car. "Hurry up," Robert called after her, but she must not have been quick enough, because when she returned, he was gone. James,

Robert's cousin, had come that night in his father's car, and he offered Linda a ride home.

When they parked outside Robert and Linda's home, they saw Robert come to the door armed with a 12-gauge shotgun that he had borrowed months before from his brother. James told Linda to stay outside. He would go talk to Robert, calm him down.

Candy was still in the house. Gerald and Eric, too.

Linda was afraid. She walked to a neighbor's who she knew was on vacation and sat on the stoop to wait. She pulled her knees up to her chest, and when the gun went off she covered her ears with her fists and curled into a little ball.

The police came with sirens and lights, and they arrested Robert, charging him with murder. The ambulance took away James Cooper's body, minus the left side of his face that had been blown away by the shotgun blast. He was later buried in his hometown of Marianna, after a service at a local AME church, survived by his wife and his son.

The trial was scheduled for mid-November. Robert pleaded not guilty to murder in the second degree. His attorney argued that the killing was no act of sudden rage but instead an accident, that James and Robert wrestled over the gun, and it went off. The gun blast could have just as easily killed Robert. They had been drinking. It was late. It was an accident.

Linda never could remember much about what happened that August night in the hours following the shooting. She couldn't remember after a while whether she'd been to the police station. She couldn't forgive herself, either. She felt responsible for James's death. She felt responsible for what her children saw, especially Eric, who had run into the room as he always did to greet his father and who had his arms wrapped around Robert's leg when the gun fired.

Linda could not remember much, but even that was more than she wanted. She hated to be in the house on 35th Avenue. Didn't want to cook in it. Didn't want to watch TV there. By Halloween she'd found another place and moved the children away from the ghosts, out of their father's house.

In November the state called on her to make a deposition. The prosecutor prodded her about Robert's jealousy. She tried to answer the questions truthfully without incriminating her husband.

> Q: Well, at the Executive didn't he accuse you of running around with another man or other men?
> A: He didn't pinpoint nobody that I was going with.
> Q: Well, I mean even though he didn't name a particular person, did he accuse you?
> A: He was drinking that night.
> Q: Will you please answer the question?

The jury delivered its verdict on November 20. Guilty. In February, a circuit court judge sentenced Robert to life, less the eighty days he had already spent in Pinellas County Jail.

The actual time Robert served would amount to about eight years, but by then Linda would be gone from Florida. He was mistaken if he thought she would wait for him, because even from prison he accused her of infidelity and threatened her if she saw another man. The hell with this shit, she told him. So she divorced Robert, saw another man, told Robert she planned to remarry, and did. She moved with the children to Inglewood, California, but that marriage didn't work out, either. Her new husband was like Robert in too many of the wrong ways, and Linda showed no patience this time. The split left her with nobody in Inglewood. Not friends, not family. She needed help if she was to raise her children alone. She had family in Florida, but she couldn't face St. Petersburg. Too close to Robert. Too close to everything. But there was family in other places. In Hartford she had an aunt and cousins. She could find work there, too, her cousins told her. So in November 1975, Linda packed up a rented moving van and drove across the country. In Hartford, she took back her maiden name. Linda Stills got a job processing claims with the Ætna Insurance Co., and she settled into a new life. But try as she might, she could never get comfortable in Hartford. People there seemed as cold and gray as the weather. Nobody said hello, not even the neighbors. Though she would live in the city more than twenty-five years and though her youngest, Eric, would call it his hometown, Linda would never get used to that New England reserve. But she could live with it. What choice did she have?

II

Young Eric Shorter possessed serious powers of concentration. That boy was as bullheaded as Linda had been when she was a child. As she still was. Eric would watch cartoons on television, lying on his belly, staring at the screen, and she'd call to him.

Nothing.

Call to him again.

Nothing.

Finally she'd walk over and touch his shoulder with her toe.

But Eric's powers of concentration, though truly formidable, weren't the only reason he ignored his mother. She didn't know it, but her baby boy couldn't perceive the world the way other children could, a lack that might have led to his sharp concentration, that powerful focus developed to compensate for all those distant and vague sounds. Linda got the news one day from people at Martin Luther King Jr. Elementary School, where Eric was in first grade. They had run tests. Eric couldn't hear out of his left ear.

She blamed the shotgun blast, and she blamed herself, relived the shooting and every act she might have taken to change the unchangeable horror of that night. Learning from doctors that the hearing loss was more likely the result of an infection when Eric was an infant didn't lessen her embrace of guilt. Shotgun blast or ear infection, she believed she had failed to protect her child. She would not fail him now.

Eric transferred from MLK Elementary over to Rawson, a school equipped to teach children who suffered from hearing loss. He started to wear a hearing aid, an expensive, bulky chunk of metal that extended far out of his ear. Other kids teased him. He'd come home and cry in his mother's arms, and she'd cry, too, and tell him, Baby, don't let them kids bother you.

She worked two jobs to pay for the hearing aid and the tests and the treatment at a children's hospital in nearby Newington, so she wasn't home as often as her children needed. She'd have preferred to be two people, the worker who could provide and the mother home to protect, because no sane mother—and Linda was sane—wanted to leave her children to fend for themselves on Woodland

Drive, a short dead-end road near train tracks, filled with squat, brick apartment buildings where the neighbors included people so hopped up on drugs they couldn't stand straight or get their eyes to focus. Cousins looked in on the children, but what kind of life was that? Why was the best she could do such a struggle? Why did she have to call her children together one December to tell them there would be no Christmas tree and no presents? But she did tell them. Impossible as those words were to speak, she spoke them. What she didn't say was that Eric's hearing problems had drained her ability to pay for anything. She cried and told her babies "maybe next year."

Eric was seven years old. His father was gone. His mother worked so many hours. He couldn't hear out of one ear. Not yet in third grade, he had already suffered taunts that he was a freak, that his skin was too light, that he was less than, that he was unacceptable. Crying to his mother hadn't changed any of that. She couldn't protect him at school. So he fought back. With his fists, if he had to. Angry and fierce, he became a handful in classes, a child punk. Month after month he hung out with the wrong kids on Woodland Drive, kids whose lives were models of how to survive, how to bite and tear and claw, how to wound the people who wounded you, how to wound the people who didn't. He stole bicycles. He repeated the fourth grade. A little monster, Linda called him, but she called him that with sympathy and sorrow and a mother's perfect understanding of how her baby suffered.

Then came Quirk Middle School. Sixth grade. Having worked his way up at Rawson, he was at the bottom again. And worse than the bottom. Students at Quirk were segregated by ability, not just by grade level. Eric, with his poor report cards and his repeated year, ended up in the class with the dummies and the troublemakers. But he was smart enough to notice that all the pretty girls were in the other class.

Nope. Wasn't gonna happen. Low grades that only he, his mother, and his teacher saw were one thing, but to have every pretty girl at Quirk believe he was stupid?

He couldn't punch his way out of the class. He couldn't steal his way out of the problem, couldn't goof off and lose that "dummy" label. There was only one answer. In his sixth grade mind, he came to realize that surviving and thriving were different things. His mother worked long hours, sacrificed in the hope that someday her family would do more than scrape by. That's the model he would have to follow. Math, history, English. Time for Mr. Eric Shorter to worm his way into books. So as his old crew spent time outside making mischief, he stayed in, turned the pages, and, that's right, teachers at the school recognized the change. Moved him so he got to sit in the pretty-girl class. Smiles all around. Hi, I'm Eric.

But boy that he was, he couldn't spend all day with books. He needed to run and shout and sweat. But not with the troublemakers. That time was past.

The shoulder pads and the football helmet transformed Eric's adolescence, turned him into a weapon. On those autumn days at Keney Park, after school, on weekends, wearing No. 27 with the Northwest All-Stars, Eric could slam his body into someone else. Knock some kid off his feet into the wet grass and fallen oak leaves. Hit back and get praised for it. Midget football, they called it. The NFL for the littlest men.

On offense, the coaches named him the quarterback. He made their choice easy. He could throw and run, sure, but what was more important was that he had the spark, the fire that drew other boys to him, that made other boys take note when he spoke. Eric was beginning to learn what it meant to win, how life made it easier for you when you were on top. Get a good grade on a test, and the prettiest girl didn't snicker when you sat next to her in class. No football player teased you if you brought a whole world into his rib cage. Nobody laughed at you when you scored more touchdowns. So every play became a must-win. He'd yell at his teammates if he had to. Slap their helmets. Get face-to-face and shout. And they'd listen, too, listen to the kid with the hearing problem. He might tell that tall kid, Harvey Kendall, this pass is coming to you and you better catch it! He might tell Kamala, who lived near Eric in the Woodland Apartments: It's our neighborhood against theirs!

All that bad boy aggression. It was almost more than those little Midgets could stand.

But the Northwest All-Stars won and won often. When they lined up for the team photo—Eric, Harvey, Kamala, even dimple-chinned Kevin Hicks who would one day cap his front teeth with gold—they believed they mattered. They could stand side by side, dressed in tattered jerseys and scuffed helmets, and know that together they had asserted themselves on a world that wanted at best to ignore them and at worst to destroy them, and by force of will alone made spaces through which they could run and through which they could win.

Eric played soccer, too, and basketball, though neither of those meant as much to him as football. He worked as hard at one sport as the other, but scoring on a layup felt nowhere near as good as knocking someone down. He liked the fellas on his teams, though. Guys from his soccer team and his football team hung out together, and Eric hung with them. He was becoming less the outsider. Chief among those guys was Derrick Walker, who played basketball with Eric at Quirk Middle School. Derrick could play some *ball*. He scored 29 points in one game against ninth-graders from the high school. But he had an easy attitude. Quick to smile. He and Eric just hit it off. They had the same goals, the same attitudes. Derrick had been raised by his mother, too, and as Linda did with Eric, Derrick's mother raised her boy to be proper and polite. Even when Derrick and his buddies from the projects bought beer illegally at that little corner store, El Placito Dulce, Derrick was the kind of kid to say thank you when the clerk handed the bottle over the counter.

He and Eric became best friends. Each made the world easier for the other to bear.

III

Hartford's borders shape the right half of an hourglass, and it's not a spacious city: only a few square miles. Hartford is, in fact, more a collection of neighborhoods gathered around a small downtown than a city in the sense that Boston or New York is a city.

By the time Eric Shorter entered Hartford High in 1986, his home was a city long divided by race and economics and geography. Its origins lay in a squabble between peoples. The Dutch arrived first, in 1632, and named the place after songbirds they found, calling it *Kievit's Hoek*, or "Lapwing's Point." That lovely name gave way when the Dutch decided the spot, at the confluence of two rivers, would serve well for a trading post and fort. A new name better expressed the Dutch plan for commerce: *Huyshope*, translated as "House of Good Hope."

Within a few years the Dutch had rivals. By 1636 the Puritan minister Thomas Hooker had led the establishment of a farming village and allowed its borders to reach to the walls of the Dutch fort. The Puritans and Dutch argued and scuffled over plowlands for nearly twenty years until an English captain led a force that seized the House of Good Hope. Though the site of the fort would later be called Dutch Point, the city would thereafter be called Hartford.

It would undergo many transformations. From farming village to nineteenth-century New England port city (whose sea-captains and merchants were known as "River Gods") to manufacturing center and insurance-industry capital. The geography would change as well. In the 1930s the rivers flooded twice, spilling over banks and into downtown, crippling the city for days. My grandmother worked as a clerk at the time, and she often told how she had to hang her firm's money from makeshift clotheslines to dry out the bills. The flood so devastated the city fathers' sense of invulnerability, so threatened their manufacturing livelihoods, that they fought back against nature, constructing levees to keep the Connecticut River within its channel and burying the smaller river, the Park River, that flowed through the center of downtown into the Connecticut. But the levees and the burial also separated Hartford from its most significant natural features, the rivers that with their sounds, sights and smells had defined the city for more than two hundred years. By the 1960s, the north-south corridor of Interstate 91 was squeezed between downtown and the river, adding another barrier to further alienate residents from the natural flow of water that had spurred the early Dutch to choose the site for their *Huyshope*. Hartford, once fought over because it was a place of rivers, now, effectively, had none. Only the factories and insurance companies remained. For most Northeasterners, Connecticut's capital city is no more than a skyline to look at as they push speed limits between Beantown and the Big Apple. Interstate 84 crosses Connecticut from New York to Massachusetts, and neatly partitions the city into north and south. By 1986 the part of town north of I-84—the North End—had for decades been considered the black part of town. Hartford's Jewish population had lived there years before, along with Italians and Irish. But as black migrant workers from the American South and the Caribbean filled the North End to work in the city's factories or in nearby tobacco fields, the neighborhood's whites moved to the suburbs or into other parts of Hartford. White real estate agents encouraged the segregation by steering black families away from other areas of the city. As a result, men play cricket at Keney Park, or soccer, and eat Jamaican beef patties after games. Baptist churches have replaced the North End's Catholic parishes, and AME Zion churches have moved into abandoned synagogues. Albany Avenue, the commercial center of the North End, sounds loud and boisterous with R&B and reggae and hip-hop and rap.

Some black people do live in the South End and even a few whites live in the North End, but in general, Hispanics and whites live south of Interstate 84. Seldom do the whites from the South End find reasons to visit the North End, and vice versa. Sometimes the reasons are racist, as with a great-uncle of mine from the family's Irish side who argued that someone ought to bulldoze the North End with Army tanks. Other times, it is a matter of convenience and distance. Other neighborhoods seem as alien and impossibly unnecessary as Saturn. Eric and his friends no more considered attending the South End's Columbus Day parade on Franklin Avenue, or the Puerto Rican Day parade down Park Street in the Frog Hollow neighborhood, than my grandfather thought of playing golf at Keney Park.

If Hartford is separated from within by race, it is separated from the outside world by wealth. The city's economic elite has a long history of moving farther and farther away from the center of town. In the late nineteenth century, real estate along Bushnell Park near downtown had been choice property for homes of the wealthy. But as nearby ghettos filled with immigrants—mostly Irish and Italians—the wealthy moved away from their new, undesirable neighbors. South to Washington Street, then west out near Nook Farm where Mark Twain lived for seventeen years, then north to the Blue Hills neighborhood, and to the West End and Prospect Avenue where the governor's mansion still sits high and back off the road, lording over those who drive by. By the time Eric and his friends entered high school, Hartford's wealth had, for the most part, moved into surrounding suburbs with names hearkening back to the English colonists' roots, names such as Avon, Simsbury, and Farmington, names that over time have come to mean "wealth" to those who live in Greater Hartford. Given the ring of moneyed suburbs surrounding it, Hartford was sometimes described as the empty hole in the middle of a richly glazed doughnut.

Left behind were a few middle-class families, retirees who remembered Hartford's better days, a new generation of immigrants, people on public assistance, people in poverty, and all the blight that poverty breeds: abandoned housing and rats, garbage and drugs, gangs and murder.

Seeing Hartford now makes it hard to imagine what

a magnificent city it once was. Seeing Hartford Public High School, it is difficult to imagine its regal predecessor. But in Mark Twain's day, Hartford Public High School had been a glorious, gabled palace of towers and spires on Hopkins Street, a work of architectural arrogance befitting its status as the second oldest public high school in the country, in what was then one of the richest cities in America. Originally founded as a grammar school in 1638, Hartford Public's Hopkins Street building was first constructed in 1885, then enlarged in 1897. My grandfather, Walter Petry, graduated from this Hartford Public. But some three decades after his commencement, when the time came to build a new interstate through the city, the once-glorious palace was just a crumbling edifice, expensive to maintain. So what had been Hartford Public for nearly eighty years fell to the wrecking ball in 1963 to make way for I-84, the highway that would so neatly bisect the city into black and white.

The new Hartford Public was ugly, built at 55 Forest Street in the early 1960s, when the city was not as wealthy as it had once been. The school district built the new Hartford Public as an institution in the worst sense of that word, a building that was functional but not at all inspirational. From the front the school appeared boxy and flat-roofed and numbingly symmetrical. Classrooms and offices benefited from dozens of windows, but the windows rested in skinny metal frames and had been laid out with all the excitement of cars in a parking lot. Around the section of the school that housed the gymnasium, the walls were vast expanses of brick, uninterrupted by any variety except, perhaps, a door. Over the next quarter century, the building took a beating and the Board of Education failed to find money for upkeep. The yard out

40

front wore to dust under the tread of so many sneakers. Students in class stared out windows made of scratched, clouded Plexiglas. The school's doors were heavy steel, a reminder to the teenagers who attended that they could be considered a threat (an insult and a source of power), and those doors had been painted over dozens of times to hide graffiti. Gym lockers were crumpled and dented. The sky-blue paint on the outside faded and flaked. The football team played at Dillon Stadium—a city-owned field a few miles from campus—because the high school field was filled with gravel. In November 1900, Mark Twain had given a speech at the Berkeley Lyceum in New York City, in which he had said, "Out of the public schools grows the greatness of a nation." Ninety years later, someone looking at Hartford Public might have wondered whether Twain knew his words could serve as both compliment and warning.

The new Hartford Public High School, only a couple miles from the site of the old one, was still the most central high school in the city, and thus the most integrated. In 1988, when Eric was in school, the *Hartford Courant* reported that the school's population was 57 percent Hispanic and 34 percent black. Whites and Asians made up the remaining 9 percent.

When Eric and his friends walked through the school's doors, they entered a world in which classrooms were a Babel of languages: Spanish, English, Vietnamese, Laotian. The school was dynamic, and it could also be dangerous. Members of The Avenue and other North End gangs sat in class with members of Asian or Hispanic gangs from nearby Park Street. Worse, gangs were no longer just a means for vulnerable kids to find support. Now they acted more often as mini-cartels in the drug trade. The money flowed, the stakes were higher, the violence more prominent. The gangs kept tight hold on their turf. When Eric and his friends walked out of the school's doors at the end of the day, they traveled home through one gang territory after another, taking care to wear neutral colors and avoid the insignias that marked you as a member. No matter whether you liked the New England Patriots or the New York Giants, sometimes it was better not to wear a team's ball cap in a particular part of town.

For too many Hartford kids, gang life proved tempting. It offered money and glamour, and both of those led to respect, the only hard currency worth anything in Hartford's poorer neighborhoods. It didn't matter how old you were, or how straight your friends were, the pull remained strong. When Kevin Hicks was barely fifteen years old, he had already been drawn to that life, embraced it, just a few years after scoring touchdowns with Eric and Harvey and the Northwest All-Stars.

From all this brokenness, Eric Shorter—a freshman at Hartford Public High School—intended to draw an education.

IV

A young man of serious intent had to keep busy. That was the rule of city life. Staying occupied, Eric and his friends believed, kept you out of trouble. Too much time on your hands, you'd get bored, start looking for things to do. And too much of what Hartford offered wouldn't get you anywhere.

So there was school, and after school there was practice. Football in the fall, basketball after that, track and field in the spring. Summertime proved the most dangerous. Summertime meant too much time. How many kids had Eric known who left school in June walking on the right side of life, then came back in August striking a pose, with expensive new clothes and fat gold chains around their necks?

Part of Eric's summers involved long trips to Florida. He never doubted that his father loved him, even as Robert Shorter served his time. Somehow Robert would figure out ways to send child-support money. Linda always told Eric that his father was a good provider and that he loved his babies. Eric believed her, though he still didn't tell friends about his father. Some friends didn't even know he had one. After Robert Shorter was released from prison, he resumed his career as an electrician. With the money he earned, he sent checks during the school year. In the summer he sent for his children, and gave Eric another way to avoid Hartford's deadly time.

There was work, too, to make summer fly by. With Derrick, Eric stocked shelves at Hartford Office Supply Co., or at the Stop & Shop grocery store. Girls helped occupy their time, too, girls who were frequently sisters (even twins: Meribel and Marisol). Because Eric and Derrick spent so much time together, their names became one word. "E 'n' D." Like brothers. Better than brothers! Inseparable. If teachers or friends saw one without the other, they were shocked. Derrick even took to calling Linda Stills "Mom."

But what most helped them survive the summer was Upward Bound, a federally funded program that gave them six weeks together at Hartford's Trinity College, a small and private liberal arts school, away from trouble, with opportunities to improve themselves and prepare for college. Every year, Upward Bound recruited a new batch of freshmen, and it was the job of a guidance counselor at Hartford Public to recommend students for the program.

When E 'n' D were freshmen, he had suggested they apply. But the process was competitive; Eric was accepted, Derrick was not.

Uhn-uh, Eric thought. Not happening that way. Furious, he tracked down a Hartford Public teacher who also taught at Upward Bound. "How can I get into Upward Bound and Derrick didn't?" he demanded to know. Hadn't they taken the same classes? Hadn't they earned the same grades? Eric said, "I'm not going to this program if Derrick isn't going." The teacher listened, then appealed to the people at Upward Bound. The next summer Eric and Derrick moved into dorm rooms on the Trinity campus.

They'd go home on weekends, but they would have stayed forever at Trinity if they could. The college, founded in the 1820s by ecumenical Episcopalians and later to become a member of "The Little Ivy League," was an island smack in the middle of the South End—a peaceful haven with Gothic towers, a movie theater, a library, and sloping fields of rich grass. Compared to Woodland Apartments, life at Trinity was luxurious. Three squares a day. Bathrooms with hot water and plenty of water pressure. No addicts sliding along the hallway walls. Windows without duct tape to seal the cracks. Windows without cracks!

Yo, Eric thought. If this is college life, bring it on.

The next summer they returned, and this time Joshua Hall joined them. The three were assigned to the B quadrant: four bedrooms that opened into a living room. They called themselves B-Side, and Derrick later turned the name into an acronym: *Brothers Striving together, Independently Demonstrating Excellence.*

Students took classes during the day, and ever-competitive Eric even turned that into a contest: the Hartford Public students against students from the other Hartford high schools. He'd work late at night while the other guys were joking around, then be on them the next day about their test scores. "Josh, you got to represent Hartford Public!" B-Side had become a neighborhood gang, and Eric was the gang leader, but his gang dealt in essays and theorems and hypotheses rather than crack and marijuana and guns.

At night the B-Side boys worked out in Trinity's weight room. Hartford Public didn't have a weight room, and E 'n' D and Joshua were like kids with new toys, bench pressing, squatting, enjoying sweat and the noise of metal weights colliding. They worked mostly on their upper bodies, or as Derrick liked to call it, "massaging the anchor." They talked, too, about their goals and visions for the future. Taking two steps forward, but always making sure they'd take that step back. They were the fortunate sons, they knew. People invested in them, and they had to give back. They had to! Because there were others who got lost—guys like baby-faced Kevin Hicks, that one-time Northwest All-Star who had crossed over, and whose body was found during their sophomore year in a field in nearby South Windsor, two bullet holes in his head. Hicks was fifteen years old then, and, the *Hartford Courant* reported, so decomposed police could identify him only by his four gold-capped front teeth, engraved with a K and an H and a dollar sign and a star.

v

Years later, Coach Jack LaPlante loved to recall how Eric came to football practice one day with his eyes all swollen to little slits.

Things happen at a school like Hartford Public. Kids fooling around in the locker room can lead to all sorts of trouble, sometimes tragic, sometimes comic. Jack had seen worse than Eric's eyes in his years coaching and teaching at the Pub. Yeah, he'd seen worse. But little had impressed him more.

Eric had been messing around with a kid who was a Silver Mittens boxing champ. They knew and liked each other. In the hallways between classes, Mr. Silver Mittens would fake like he had the football tucked up against his body, throw out a straight arm, juke around Eric like E couldn't tackle him. Later, in the cafeteria, Eric would shadow box, bob and weave, like he could take Mr. Silver Mittens with a quick combination.

But this day, Silver Mittens must have been in some kind of mood. Teacher took away his Walkman or something. Eric didn't even know something was wrong. He and Silver Mittens were in the locker room in the basement—laughter echoing off all the metal, all that stink of stale uniform—and Eric, he does his bob and weave routine. Mr. Silver Mittens whips around, fists flying. Wham! Bam! Next thing Eric knows, his face is mushy and he's leaning against a locker.

Later his eyes are like baseballs. He can barely see, the lids are all closed up. Even so he's walking across the school parking lot with his pads on. Football in his hand. LaPlante meets him in the school parking lot. LaPlante thinks, My God.

Let's go, Eric says, his words small and mean.

Tough kid. LaPlante won't forget that about him. Tough. Smart, too. The offense Hartford Public ran had a lot of movement, players going here and there. You really had to know what the hell you were doing. And Eric could do that. He could handle it. He had a plan for success, too.

Not many of LaPlante's players had something like that. An actual plan, like: I'm going to do this, then this. Step one. Step two.

Eric was all of those things.

Gifted young man.

The year that the five friends were juniors, all of them earned starting positions on offense and defense. If LaPlante had his way, he would have enough kids so each could play either offense or defense because to play both wore a kid down as a game and a season dragged on. But LaPlante always had a tough time filling his roster. He could identify all kinds of reasons: indifference to the sport, injuries, trouble at home, discipline cases, grades. But in the suburbs, coaches could start twenty-two guys, eleven on defense and eleven other players on offense. Not at the Pub. It was part of the reason the Owls had suffered so many losing seasons. Every kid played every exhausting down.

Derrick played running back and defensive back. Harvey Kendall, wide receiver and defensive end; Hiram Harrington, fullback and linebacker; Joshua Hall, he played tight end and defensive end; Eric, cornerback and, as always, quarterback, yelling at players in the huddle, exhorting them, barking profanities until Hiram would chuckle, shake his head and say, "Hey, probably you need to calm down."

That year they were juniors HPHS won its first two games, a feat unheard of in the school's recent history of loss, so miraculous that the *Hartford Courant* made special note of it.

Wouldn't you know it, the Owls lost their next game, 20–7, to suburban Enfield.

It wasn't easy, going out to the suburbs to play. Too often, Hartford Public—outnumbered, outsized, outmanned in every way—got served up as the homecoming team. The Owls hated that. Sitting through homecoming festivities was bad enough, all that self-congratulatory "aren't we the best school ever" bull crap, but there was the obvious insult, too. No school wanted to lose its homecoming game, so administrators always planned the party for when they played their weakest opponent. Away game after away game, the Owls faced homecomings.

And there was racism. Sometimes it was overt: some fan shouting something about niggers. Other times it was more subtle. One cool October night, the Owls rode a school bus east on Interstate 84 to Vernon where they were to play Rockville High School. They went through their usual routines, warming up on the field, listening to introductions, the national anthem. Rockville was always a powerhouse, so the Owls were particularly hyped, bouncing on their sideline, cheerleaders behind them chanting, "You . . . Can't . . . Rock the Pub! Say! You can't rock the Pub!"

Rockville received the kickoff. On the first play after, the Rams ran a sweep to the right, blockers forming a human wall of momentum and aggression to mow down the Owls and make room for their running back, who carried the ball. Aaron Fisher, a Hartford Public junior who was quick as a siren and strong as asphalt, dodged the blockers and tracked the running back, tackling him near the sideline. As Aaron hopped up, he tapped the running back's helmet with an open hand and offered congratulations on a good run.

Whistles. Flags. One of the game officials ran to Aaron, told him he was out of the game for throwing a punch.

Some Owls shouted their protest. Others stood stunned. But every kid on Hartford Public's bench thought the same thing: Zebra saw what he expected to see. One of those terrible Hartford kids. All a bunch of crack dealers and thugs. Probably stealing stuff from the locker room before the game.

The ejection carried an automatic suspension of one game, so Aaron would, in effect, miss two. The next day, Hartford Public appealed. Rockville's coach, an old friend of LaPlante's, wrote a letter to league officials.

"The tackler slapped him on the helmet and congratulated him on a nice run," Coach Tom Dunn wrote. "Apparently the officials misinterpreted this attempt to show good sportsmanship as a punch and ejected the tackler.

"This has been verified by members of the chain crew, who were on that spot on the field. They said there was no malice or harm meant. It was a sportsman-like gesture.

"We feel that an injustice has been done the player and that he should not receive a one-game suspension under the 'ejection' rule."

A committee of league officials reviewed films from the game, called them unclear, and decided to back their game official. Aaron sat out the next game.

Aaron came back to the team, no worse for his time away. But when Derrick left the Owls that same season, it was for good.

The end of his season began in a Thursday practice, the week after the Owls' fourth game. Rain fell the day before, and left the practice field nothing but mud and gravel. The coaches blew their whistles and called for tackling drills.

I'm not doing tackling on this field, Aaron told Derrick. I'm not doing this.

But Derrick had never been one to backtalk coaches. That's how he became LaPlante's favorite, because he never complained. Some of those Hartford Public players would cry if the wind blew, but not Derrick. He never wanted to disappoint people, never wanted to let anyone down. Not his school. Not his team *(a thousand-thousand blades of grass turn a field green)*. If LaPlante asked, Derrick did. Change his field position. Play one more down. "No problem, coach." Respectful young man. Polite. That nickname of his, "D. Nice," fit him better than his shoulder pads. If coaches said "tackling drills," Derrick lined up to tackle and be tackled.

It was the being tackled part.

Guy wrapped his arms around Derrick, tried to push him over, wrestle him down. Derrick fought him to a standstill. Refused to be tackled. A coach blew a whistle to end the play, and Derrick let up. The other guy didn't. Derrick's foot sank into the mud as his body twisted toward the ground. As he hit, he heard a strange sound, and he felt something funny, not just in his ankle, but throughout his body. When he looked down, the ankle had blown up, like there was a tennis ball tucked inside the sock.

Probably just a sprain, one coach said. But Derrick didn't think so. Later, at home and in bed, the pain grew fierce. Teeth-gritting, fist-clenching pain. He put pillows under the ankle to keep it elevated. Wrapped it with an elastic bandage. Moms came home from work. Is that ice under the Ace bandage? she asked.

No, it's just the Ace bandage, he said.

That night he stayed at St. Francis Hospital until 2:00 a.m., when the swelling finally subsided enough for technicians to take X-rays. The next day, he stayed home from school, telephoning LaPlante to explain why he had to miss practice.

Hey, big guy! LaPlante said. How's the ankle?

Not good.

What's not good?

I have a splint on it. When the swelling goes down they'll put on a cast.

He didn't watch practice after that. It tore him up seeing the guys go on without him. Strange that he felt so left out when his teammates hadn't wanted to make him feel that way, hadn't chased him off, hadn't turned on him like wolves against the pack's wounded and the weak. No, they'd just kept playing. They themselves stayed healthy. Just kept telling jokes and sharing bus rides and walking home (walking!) after practice. Left him behind with only a pair of crutches and his longing for company. How much can you want a thing that means so little in the daily drama of the world? With all that was wrong in Hartford, how could a few high school football games break your heart? But to savor victory in an Owls' uniform had been Derrick's dream as long as he'd been capable of dreams. It was what he had in a city where disappointment was habit, the hope upon which he relied. Being an Owl placed him in a family tradition. Most of his brothers and one sister had attended Hartford Public. As a boy he'd sat in the stands and cheered the Pub. Even when his family moved into a Weaver neighborhood, he insisted on staying with Hartford Public. He fantasized about the games he'd play as an Owl, and once he stepped into that building full of blue he never wanted to leave. He had scored perfect attendance as a freshman. Now, with his worthless ankle, he missed games and missed his teammates. They had set a goal, he and Eric and Joshua, that previous summer at

Upward Bound. They would capture that elusive winning season, the first at Hartford Public in a long time.

But now he wasn't blazing across a field alongside Harvey, hitting wide receivers so hard they'd drop the ball. He wasn't under those Friday night lights, crouched low, fingers in the dewy grass, waiting to take a hand-off from Eric. He wasn't hanging out with the guys after practices, getting teased by Hiram. He was home, willing his bones to knit, and praying: Next year.

For the rest of the Owls, the junior season was going well. With one game to go, Hartford Public, at six-and-four, had assured itself a winning season, the first since LaPlante took over. Aaron Fisher piled up startling statistics as a running back: 122 yards in this game, 246 in that. Eric threw with great accuracy: seven of his ten passes caught in one game, five of six in another. And Hiram, all 215 pounds of him, wrecked offenses from his position at linebacker. In a victory over Manchester, he made thirteen tackles, hurling his big body at top speeds and knocking down anybody who dared carry the football into the center of his field. All the Owls played that way. Full of city-bred fury, they were eager to hit and to hit hard. That's what opponents noticed about Hartford Public. Even if you beat them, your ribs reminded you the next day that you'd been rocked by the Pub.

For the season finale, the Owls traveled to Dillon Stadium in Hartford's South End for the annual Thanksgiving Day game against archrival Weaver. They called it the Turkey Day game, and it was all things that a rivalry can be: the team that won put an exclamation point on the season and owned bragging rights for a year. Hartford Public had started the season with a win against Bulkeley, its other city rival. Beating Weaver on the season's last day would make the Owls the city champions.

It didn't happen. Weaver triumphed, 22–14, and though the Owls finished the season 6–5, they ended on a losing note. But they took from that loss one necessary thing: a taste for the year to come. Because if they were all juniors now, think of what they would do when they were seniors. Hell yes, they'd take Weaver. Maybe even a state championship.

After the season, the *Courant* named Aaron Fisher an all-state running back. Hiram won all-state at linebacker, one of only two juniors on the all-state defensive team. He had finished the season with 140 tackles and six sacks, and he'd even scored seven touchdowns when playing offense. Recruiting letters filled his mailbox after he was named all-state, some from big-time football schools. Phone calls came at all hours of the day from coaches at schools such as Syracuse, Tennessee, Southern California, Maryland, and Texas Tech.

He'd made a reputation, as had the Owls. They weren't yet champions of anything, but nevermore would Hartford Public play the dismal part of homecoming rollover.

They talked to Aaron. What more could they do?

After practice, he would sometimes walk home with Eric and Derrick. Like them he had no father waiting for him, and they understood what tugged at him. Easy money. Quick respect. And with no big man to guide him, to push him away from all that street stuff, to tell him no. So they spoke up instead, asked him, pleaded with him to stop hanging out with those homeboys on the corner. Everybody knows those dudes are dealing, they'd say.

In the cafeteria at lunch. On the bus to an away game. Hanging out in front of the school before the morning bell. Joshua feared for him in a quiet, fatalistic way. He talked to Aaron, too, looking into his face and all the while thinking, "It's only a matter of time." Harvey talked to him. Hiram, also. They recalled for him the fate of Kevin Hicks, and mentioned once more the two bullet wounds in his decomposed skull.

Fisher, man, you got a future. You're all-state. Colleges wanting you to come play ball. Why you want to mess around with these other people? All this negativity. Yo, they dragging you down, man!

They tried. And as long as they caught a glimpse of him at school in the morning, as long as he arrived on time to practice, that was good. But one day that spring of their junior year, Aaron didn't show up for school. Derrick noticed him missing in English class. Hadn't Derrick heard? another student asked. Police made a raid that morning. Found drugs. Found Aaron.

Damn.

Aaron hadn't been dealing, but he'd been involved, and he got locked up. He spent three months in jail, and those three months so unhinged his life that he wouldn't return to school for more than a year more. Eric struggled against the news, against the sense that he'd failed his friend. Since his days with the Northwest All-Stars, he'd heard grownups tell him, "You're the leader." LaPlante told him, "You're the leader." At Upward Bound, he heard it, too. But he hadn't led Aaron anywhere. And he felt the loss. Sudden. Irrevocable. A pass dropped. A ball fumbled away, bouncing farther and farther. Right into the arms of the other team. Gone.

54

In the summer Eric and Hiram attended football camp at Boston College. They learned new tricks, new skills, new plays. They lifted weights. Got trim. Got tough. They sweated through drills, and sometimes they'd catch each other's eyes.

Yo, yo. We got the nucleus. Yeah, we lost Aaron, but look at all we got coming back next season. You. Me. Derrick. Harv. Josh. Some good young kids. Nobody's gonna mess with the Pub. Yo. Look out Rockville. Look out Enfield. Look out Weaver cause Turkey Day gonna be a different story, baby.

Gonna be ours.

3

Something about life made Bo Kendall run. Harvey's older brother would sprint across the street to meet a friend for an evening stroll. Run paths into the grass around the schoolyard if recess lasted long enough. He'd have even run to church if his mother let him. He loved that smooth jerk of legs and arms that felt like ground-flying, made running a habit the way other kids made habits of pinball or television or chocolate ice cream. So of all the kids on Oakland Terrace in Hartford's North End, of all the Kendall brothers, Bo was the perfect choice to run an errand.

That June Tuesday of 1984 was sunny and pleasant, the kind of day that surprises people with its perfection, draws neighbors out of their houses to their stoops, to the sidewalks, to lean over fences and chat in the clarity of the afternoon. A little after lunch hour, a neighbor of the Kendalls called to Bo. She gave the sixteen-year-old money and an errand: get me some oxtails and neck bones, she said. Be quick.

Bo sprinted up Oakland Terrace past neat two-story houses and past others that had been neat once but were now mostly in need of the care only money could give. He ran over sidewalks where crabgrass and dandelions grew through sprays of broken glass, past yards with blooming hydrangeas and past houses where the paint peeled off every sliver of trim. He glided down the easing grade to Albany Avenue, then turned at the package store where sodden men sometimes wasted time on the corner. Zipped into a nearby grocery store. Zipped out with a brown paper bag in hand and headed home, legs still churning.

Bo didn't hear the police car until just before it hit him. Tires skidded, and then the cruiser swerved onto the sidewalk, slamming into him, launching Bo through the air and against a chain link fence. More skidding, then cops shouting at him, jabbing nightsticks into his rib cage and his back. Cops everywhere, and Bo on his back like an overturned beetle scrambling on the sidewalk, trapped between concrete and the chain link and the nightsticks—the oxtails and neck bones forgotten.

The cops shoved him into one of the four cruisers now clogging the street. They drove him a few blocks away, and it was a couple of hours before they admitted their mistake. He was not the black teenager who had stolen a woman's purse. The woman herself said so.

The police seemed to understand the ramifications of their mistake. "They told me not to say nothing to nobody," Bo told a reporter from the *Courant*. "When my mother came, they let me go."

Bo was scraped and bruised. At nearby St. Francis Hospital, doctors examined him, made sure nothing inside him was damaged nor any bones broken. Then they returned him to the care of his family: mother Jessie; father Albert

Sr. for whom Bo—Albert Jr.—was named; three sisters and seven brothers, including thirteen-year-old Harvey, who now saw something dissonant in his older brother. Bo was still Bo, but he had changed somehow, the easy run of his life interrupted. He'd been bumped off his spot in the world, and where he'd landed the air hung heavy and quiet. Or maybe it was not Bo's spot alone but the family's. For the Kendalls, for Harvey, what happened to Bo on that loveliest of afternoons made all other things new in the ugliest way.

For as long as the Kendalls lived there, Oakland Terrace never was a pretty street, combining the occasional well-kept home with the sort of house that one day might have a mattress in the front yard and another day a television with its screen shattered. The Kendalls kept their shades pulled and curtains drawn, so whether you were a passerby on the way to work or an addict casing the house, you'd never know that the entry hall was decorated with pictures of Jesus Christ at the Last Supper and of Martin Luther King Jr. The house became a refuge against the ugliness, and the ugliness became worse and more frightening following the assault on Bo. Yes, dealers and addicts skulked through the neighborhood, thieves and kids in gangs who preyed on people trying to make an honest life. But now, the Kendalls needed to fear Hartford's police, too.

The family filed a lawsuit that didn't yield anything for years and then not much. But once that suit was filed, it couldn't be taken back, and the family worried that filing the suit was like beating a Rottweiler into a corner. The dog might bite back. Vengeful cops could make up some reason to hurt you. Or maybe on that day you needed them most, they'd drive smack into a traffic jam. Stop with a flat tire.

It was an unhappy time, one that would grow unhappier still. Less than a year had passed since the police ambushed Bo when Albert Sr. suffered a stroke. A few weeks later, heart problems damaged him further. He fell in and out of a coma. On Father's Day, 1985, he opened his eyes only long enough to close them one last time.

He was sixty-two years old when he died. He had grown up an adopted son in the South during the Depression and served as a soldier in World War II. He married once and it took. He worked as a bricklayer to raise eleven children, sometimes suffering through a month or more out of work when business slowed. When he could afford the cheap seats, he'd bring his boys to watch professional wrestling and laugh with them and cheer. He stood five foot six, and for most of his life weighed 130 pounds. He never owned his own home. His family buried him in Griffin, Georgia—his hometown. He left sons not yet old enough to live away from home.

When he turned fifteen and was a freshman at Hartford Public, Harvey—with height from his mother's side of the family—already bumped up against six foot four, and he had earned a spot on the Owls' varsity basketball team. He was a deer on the court, a quick leaper who could rip rebounds away from taller boys. Long-armed, long-legged, a fierce defender. And he played with flair. His high school coach would one day say of him, "If the dunk is punctuation, Harvey's are exclamation points."

He had learned the game at Sigourney Square Park playing alongside and against his brothers in pickup games, a bruising education that refined his jump shot, toughened

60

his defense, and taught him the game-face snarl of a competitor. The games helped off the court, too. Every city kid needs something more than wisdom to survive the streets, some charm that protects him special. An alliance with a gang can do that, but so can a story in the newspaper that celebrates a young man's accomplishments in chess or on the football field (one reason, perhaps, why as a reporter for the *Courant*, I always found Hartford kids willing to talk). Being unremarkable for a street kid is like being broke.

For Harvey playing basketball with his brothers gave him street currency. Brothers Rick and Jimmy qualified as playground legends at Sigourney Park, winning again and again and somehow avoiding trouble in a world of rattling backboards, game-stopping explosions of profanity, and the occasional dispute that could end with a guy jugged in the neck with a knife. In the Asylum Hill neighborhood, basketball *made* the Kendall brothers, and the Kendall brothers made a basketball-playing gang. Harvey lived protected by their reputations, their street smarts, and their wisdom. But as his brothers grew older, they took jobs that kept them busy. They moved away from Oakland Terrace. They married. Started families. Moved on to new problems and new challenges. They left Harvey to handle city life more and more on his own.

So he was alone after the Owls finished basketball practice one night during his freshman year. He stuffed his duffel bag with schoolbooks and his rank practice jersey and shoes, and he slung the bag over his shoulder, then pulled up his hood to protect against the chilly winter rain. He wanted to be home, and he kept up a quick pace just short of running, hustling across dark streets, dodging cars that hissed and splashed through puddles, the light from their headlights absorbed by the cold wet dark. It would be easier to get home if he cut through the St. Francis Hospital parking lot, so he did, but as he zigzagged between cars someone yelled at him to stop.

A police officer. A white police officer.

Harvey stopped.

He knew what the cop saw—a tall black man. It didn't matter that Harvey was only fifteen. Size and skin color made him suspect in the cop's eyes, he knew that, and here he'd been caught running through a parking lot full of cars owned by night-shift nurses and doctors. Guilty until proven innocent.

The officer drew near but kept a safe distance.

"Where are you coming from?"

Harvey looked at the cop's nightstick, his handcuffs and gun. The cop could do anything. He had the weapons, the badge, the authority. The dark night. The rain.

"Basketball practice," Harvey said.

So quiet in the parking lot. Dread silencing Harvey's breath, silencing even the rain. Harvey slowly unzipped the gym bag, showed the officer his sweat-wet jersey, his schoolbooks.

The cop let him go.

When Harvey reached home, he unlocked the front door, then locked it behind him, heart and stomach and head all telling him that he should still be running, that even here he could not rest, that he shouldn't stop until so much ground lay between him and that parking lot he couldn't ever go back. He had feared that cop, expected death or worse, and Jesus and Dr. King on the walls didn't change that. Basketball could protect him from the 20-Loves or The Avenue, but it didn't matter with cops. No charm, no spell, no plea protected you from their arbitrary whims, their eruptions of violence. More than two years had passed since Bo's sidewalk encounter with police, and the apprehension and outrage Harvey first tasted then had remained. It would stay as long as Harvey lived in the city's North End, as long as he was young, as long as he was black, as long as those descriptions meant that some people would always assume the worst of him (and of Eric and Derrick, and Hiram and Joshua, all in their own places and times). Store clerks would watch Harvey, and white women on downtown sidewalks would switch their purses to the other side if they saw him draw near. Cops would assume the worst, too. Cops late at night in dark parking lots.

Each assumption those strangers made was a fresh insult that squeezed Harvey's heart and pumped him full of the old fear and outrage.

Harvey-Harv! Only a freshman, already a star. Playing varsity basketball and the team on a fast track toward the playoffs. One afternoon he's wasting time in the Owls' gymnasium waiting for the bus to arrive—the rattling chariot with torn upholstery that will deliver the team to its game against Hillhouse High School of New Haven. Girls watch from the bleachers so he shows off. Dribbling between his long legs. Dropping in a casual, easy dunk. Passing the ball to the girls so they can pass it back.

The girls like him. He's tall and he's got pretty teeth on a wide, happy face. He's shy. When he smiles you can see it's a shy smile. But he talks a lot because he's shy, and what he says is funny.

Now comes this guy through the gym on his way to the locker room. The man stops. Calls to Harvey. Says, "Hey. Hey you, come here. Kendall."

Who's this? Harvey wonders. Who's this scraggly guy wearing raggedy cotton sweatpants and dirty sneakers? Some dude from the streets? How'd he get in here? How's he know my name?

"Hey. Hey you, come here. Kendall."

Harvey walks over, but takes his time, checking the man out. This guy, what is he? What's he about? Unshaven. Yellow eyes. Wearing a bandana wrapped tight around his skull. A baseball cap sitting crooked on his head. Harvey can't even tell how old the guy is, except that he's older than Harvey.

The man talks. His words fly fast. He mumbles with such speed it's as if he's afraid the world will end before he gets out everything he hopes to say. Seen you play football, he says. Seen you play basketball. You've got that look great jumpers have. I like how you compete. You're gonna come out for track, right?

Harvey knows the question isn't a question.

I don't know, Harvey says, because he doesn't. He's never run track before. I don't know, he says. I guess.

The guy introduces himself.

Butch Braswell. I'm the assistant track coach. I've been watching you, he says. You've got good legs for a jumper. Good speed. You've got a jumper's walk. You could do great things in the triple jump. You'd be state champion. Compete nationally.

Harvey's thinking: State champion? I don't even know what the triple jump is!

Harvey says: Okay, Coach. I'll think about it.

Don't call me Coach, says the man. No need to call me Coach. Call me Butch. I don't want to be an authority over you. Just call me Butch.

And when the man in dirty sneakers—when Butch—

walks away, Harvey wonders what just hit him. He's never known a coach who didn't want to be called "Coach." Coaches are all about discipline, aren't they? All about "I'm the boss" and "you do what I tell you to do" and here was one who said, "I don't want to be an authority over you.

Harvey dribbles the basketball again. One bounce. Two. The ball smacks the floor and the sound echoes off the powder-blue walls. The girls wait to catch another pass.

But Harvey takes a moment and decides: All right. I'll try track. See what this man is about.

The first day of track practice, Butch led Harvey to the jumping pit, set him up at the end of the rubber runway, and aimed him toward the sandpit more than 130 feet away. The triple jump is one of the most technically complex events in track and field. It involves five major movements. The sprint down the runway, which generates momentum and is called the approach. The take-off, which must be calibrated given the length of the approach to put the jumper's toe as close to the take-off line as possible without going beyond it and making the jump illegal. The hop, with its one-footed landing that allows for the step and then, off the same foot as the hop, the jump for the final distance. Hop. Step. Jump. The world record in the triple jump when Harvey took his first was 58 feet 11 1/2 inches. A good high school triple-jumper in Connecticut could travel forty-five feet with the hop, step, and jump.

Harvey jumped about eighteen feet.

After practice, Butch drove his future state champion home.

Okay, yeah, he told Harvey. You're doing good. The only thing you got to do is concentrate.

He started explaining things about the jump, things

about Harvey's body. In order to get here, he said, you have to do this. Then this. Thrust that leg out and up. Use its momentum to help your jumping leg.

He broke down the event. Made it easy for Harvey to understand. If Harvey had questions, Butch answered them. Harvey had known other coaches who saw questions as challenges, but not Butch. Butch still dressed shabbily. Sometimes, he showed up for track practice wearing his uniform from his work as a deputy sheriff. But Harvey had learned not to judge people at first glance.

On the second day of track practice, Harvey triple-jumped forty-five feet. Walked through the sky. Just as Butch promised.

Melvin D. "Butch" Braswell had a long and colorful history in Hartford. Many people knew him, and many had no idea what to make of him.

A devout Seventh-Day Adventist, he touched neither pork nor spirits and never uttered profanity. He had been a radical in the early 1970s, espousing black power as president of Hartford's Black Stone Rangers, an affiliate of the Black Panthers, and he was once arrested and later cleared of attempted murder in connection with a shooting directed at Hartford police officers. He was a skilled jumper who insisted people in Hartford had purposely fouled up paperwork at a track meet and cost him a shot at the United States' trials for the 1984 Olympics. He worked as a deputy sheriff whose job was to help maintain order at the Lafayette Street courthouse, escorting prisoners to their trials and back to lockup. He was a black belt in Kung Fu. A father of one son and adoptive father of another. A man who lived with his mother in one of Hartford's roughest neighborhoods, in a ramshackle home he owned with the address numbers spray-painted on the sideboards of his porch next to a "No Trespassing" sign. A part-time employee of parks and recreation who organized midnight basketball games to keep teenagers out of trouble. The founder of a summer club—the Inner City Striders—that helped inner-city *and* suburban kids learn the nuances of track and field. A fisherman who loved the quiet of a stream. A foster parent. A teacher without a classroom. A man who once said he was "angry most every day." A fellow respected by businessmen and gang members alike. A man who some people in authority didn't trust. A man who didn't trust the people in authority, be they in the schools or the city government or the police department, and who didn't hide his contempt for corruption and his belief in conspiracy. A neighborhood presence who told kids that he hated drugs. A caretaker who would hand a twenty-dollar bill to a street bum who'd asked for ten. A man who sought purity of body, mind, and spirit.

He stood nearly six foot four, with rangy, thick arms and strong, spidery hands. His brow seemed permanently furrowed as if from the effort of forever balancing love and anger. When he spoke, his habit was to look up and away from the person he talked with, especially when talking of weighty matters: God. Racism. Poverty. Justice.

He was born at home in North Carolina on July 2, 1950, or maybe on July 22—he had two birth certificates, each with a different date. His family moved to Hartford when he was a boy, and in Hartford he remained, living in the neighborhood he sometimes called "Chocolate City."

He had jumped competitively in high school and college and thereafter, winning national recognition, but by the time Harvey met him he competed less and coached more. Butch knew jumping, and he could pick out jump-ers. He joked that all he had to do was stand in the school cafeteria. The sprinters came through the door first, the ones who were fast and who needed to cross that line as if salvation awaited on the other side. The weight men fol-lowed, the giants who threw the discus and put the shot and who ate trayfuls to maintain their bulk. Then came the jumpers. Long lazy walkers. Tall guys. Denim jeans hanging low, showing their boxer shorts. You could divide those jumpers into two groups: speed jumpers (who had the momentum to carry them great distances) and power jumpers (who had the leg strength to defy gravity).

But Butch hadn't seen many like Harvey. Neither speed jumper nor power jumper, young Mr. Kendall embodied both.

By his sophomore year, Harvey had jumped 49–7. By his junior year, he was competing nationally against the best high school triple jumpers at meets in Utah, California, and New York. Twice he had been invited to the Golden South Invitational track meet in Florida, a meet attended by a few hundred of the nation's best high school track athletes. He won the Junior Olympics national triple jump for boys aged fourteen to sixteen. He owned bags full of medals and trophies. He attributed all his success to his coach.

He credited Butch's workouts, which stressed flexibility and strength, and which made bodies suffer. Half an hour of stretching, followed by a ten-mile run. Then another half hour of stretching. Sprints up the North End hill they called Lookout Mountain. Three hundred sit-ups. Trips across the Connecticut River to East Hartford, to a pond posted with No Trespassing signs around its beach-sand hills, signs Butch ignored to make Harvey and the rest run up and down until their bodies were coated in sweat and sand and their thigh muscles felt ready to peel away from the bone. With most coaches, Harvey might rebel against such brutal drills, but how could he argue with Butch? If Butch said "Run ten miles," he didn't punch his stopwatch and wait for you to get back. Naw. Butch ran, too. When he said "sprint," he climbed that hill as fast as he could go, those thirty-eight-year-old legs hustling, and he expected you to keep up. When he said "three hundred sit-ups," he crunched out every one.

Harvey credited Butch's lessons in technique:

If Harvey missed the board: "Take a half step back and chop that first step." If Harvey wasn't getting enough extension: "Raise the angle of your leg." There were lessons in landing, lessons in twisting, lessons in concentration. And if Harvey still wasn't getting it, then Butch would launch himself from the board and pop off a forty-five-foot-plus jump to help Harvey see and understand.

He credited Butch's heart:

A kid needs to believe that he is part of his coach's agenda. That was Butch's credo. In summer and fall, spring and winter, in season or out. Butch looked out for Harvey. He gave him five dollars for lunch if he needed it. Bought him new sneakers when Harvey's wore out. Paid for his first plane trip so Harvey could compete in a national meet in Utah. Raised money for other trips. He took Harvey to church sometimes, and other times took him fishing in eastern Connecticut. And Butch treated others the same, whether they could compete nationally or not. When he organized midnight basketball tournaments, he paid for the trophies. He let neighborhood teens who had trouble at home watch TV at his house and eat out of his fridge. One time, he even helped get Hiram out of jail. Hiram's crazy neighbor, burdened by some kind of hallucination, had called police and said Hiram threatened to murder him. Hiram denied it, but the police arrested him anyway until they could sort things out. That night in his cell, poor Hiram couldn't sleep for the roaches and the stink of urine that choked his breath. But the next day Butch explained to the judges and the police, to everyone he knew from his job as deputy sheriff, that Hiram couldn't have made a death threat because he had been at track practice that afternoon. The confusion cleared up, Hiram walked free. See, Butch was whatever you needed him to be: coach, older brother, father, guardian angel. Harvey's mother, a woman of faith, had prayed, and Butch was an answer to her prayers. "I thank God for a young man like Butch," she told me that day I visited her and she spilled a bag full of medals across her kitchen table. And because Butch cared so much, his athletes wanted to win for him. They ached for victory with every nerve twitch and muscle contraction—for him. Every time Harvey sprang from that board, he wanted the gold medal. He wanted to be the proof of Butch's genius.

He credited Butch's mission:

You can change the world with a victory. Butch told this to Harvey. And he told it to Bobby Torres, his whippet, a wiry youngster of Puerto Rican heritage who was Hartford Public's best sprinter and long jumper and Butch's other national contender. Look at the two of you, he said. A Hispanic kid and a black kid. This city's getting torn apart because Hispanics and blacks won't get along. Not in the streets or in the schools or even in City Hall. You show them what we can do together. Against all odds. A Hispanic kid and a black kid. Park Street and Albany

Avenue. You show the city and the school board and the newspapers. Make them notice all the way to the state capitol building. Show those teachers in your classrooms who believe you're too dumb to learn. We can be better than they think we can. Right here in Hartford, even here in Hartford, we can rise above. You can be born in the ghetto, but that doesn't mean the ghetto's born in you. We can transcend.

He spoke to them as a prophet to a people. They believed.

Come the end of their junior year, Harvey and Hiram, E 'n' D, and Joshua had arrived at their solution to Hartford's problems. They alone could not fix everything. Not the potholed roads. Not corruption at City Hall. They could not lower taxes to lure new manufacturers. They could not rescue all the Aaron Fishers of the city let alone the one. But if each of the five returned home after college, if each of them chose—like Butch—to live in the city, they could contribute something. And if others followed their example, pretty soon Hartford would be a city of Butch Braswells and Harvey Kendalls and Derrick Walkers and Hiram Harringtons, filled with positive people, and all the negativity would get squeezed so deep underground it would bury itself.

Eric hoped to practice law, Joshua wanted to teach history, and Harvey wanted to concentrate on kids. Hartford's youth needed more ways to play, more alternatives to the asphalt and concrete. Harvey imagined himself back home from college, his new degree in marketing tucked in a desk drawer, opening up a bowling alley in the city. In his spare time, he would volunteer to organize a youth football league. He saw himself emulating Butch, on the streets gathering children about him, calling them away from the drugged-out zombies and away from the gun-toting menaces that lured children (as Hicks had been lured) and then left their decaying child-bodies in a grassy, distant field.

Harvey explained this to me that August afternoon I first visited Hartford Public's track and met him. We were both, I suppose, naive. Harvey was young, and though wise beyond his years, could still picture himself as Hartford's hero, an image that might fail as he aged and accepted his own limitations and those life forced upon him. As for me, I didn't fully grasp the origin, scope, or ramifications of Harvey's dream. Having grown up in a place Harvey would call the suburbs, I knew too little of the pain Hartford visited on its children.

I didn't know on that August afternoon that Hicks was dead. I didn't know that Fisher was gone. I didn't know that Harvey attended a school with ten security guards, or that some of his fellow students were homeless while others lived in dark and broken apartment buildings haunted by junkies. I didn't know that his teachers by Connecticut law were among the highest paid in the nation, and that they lived in safe suburban homes, yet some fell asleep at their desks and others had just given up, deeming their charges unteachable. I didn't know that Harvey wondered whether I was like those teachers, whether I was another white guy from the 'burbs, assigned to a city, a job, I didn't care about. When that afternoon he asked me, "You live in the city now?" and I answered yes I spoke the truth, though I was by my demographic history closer kin to the people Harvey didn't trust than to Harvey himself. But naiveté so often depends on sincerity, and Harvey and I, despite everything that made us different, held that in common. He wanted to live a story that mattered. I wanted to tell one.

"It's better to be out here to train," Harvey said, "doing something positive, than standing on a street corner doing negative stuff."

Always deliver the message, like Butch said.

It was the August before their senior season, and football practice had already started. Players laced their cleats and sweated and spit mouthfuls of water into the grass and gravel. But Harvey wasn't with them. He suffered from a painful growth, a bump wedged between the lower socket of his knee and the ball joint, and he didn't want it to become any worse. It couldn't get worse, not if he was going to be healthy for track season. He might love football more than any other sport for its fall weather, its grass stains, the crunch of helmets and pads, the camaraderie, but track would pay his college bills. Harvey had dreamed his dream of a happier Hartford and made his pledge with Eric and Derrick, with Hiram and with Joshua. Fulfillment of the pledge depended on college and college depended on a fifty-foot triple jump. The jump depended on the knee. The city depended on it all.

So. No football.

II

Joe Harrington, insurance agent and entrepreneur, was a self-educated man. His son Hiram would one day call him "the smartest man I know." Joe had finished at Dudley High School in Greensboro, North Carolina, in 1956 as the top boy in his class. Though accepted at five colleges, he opted for the Air Force, and while working as a freight traffic specialist, took courses in his spare time at colleges near the bases where he served. He even won the service-wide short story writing contest. After the service, he took additional college classes and in 1968 completed the course work to become a Chartered Life Underwriter; as far as he knew, he was the youngest black CLU in America at the time.

But if Joe got some education from the classroom, he received degrees more from his own reading. He swallowed books. He once drove from Newark to a bookstore in Manhattan to buy a recently released copy of *Doctor Zhivago*. His basement was home to William Faulkner, Robert Frost, James Baldwin, Tennessee Williams, Vladimir Nabokov, Paul Laurence Dunbar, and Shakespeare. He was particularly fond of quoting *Macbeth*: "It is a tale told by an idiot, full of sound and fury, signifying nothing." He enjoyed the gift of retention, and much of what he read stayed with him. Consequently he owned a diverse and precise vocabulary, and he peppered conversations with words as varied as *sagacious, macrocosmic, matriculate,* and *rat hole.* He often ended sentences with "and so on and so forth," a habit picked up by Hiram, the second of his two sons.

Joe Harrington knew a lot, and he was certain of this: Hiram and his older brother Herman would attend college.

That's why words nearly failed him one August day in 1989 when Hiram, the family's all-state linebacker whose talent drew the daily admiration of college recruiting letters, came home with the news that his grades had sunk too low, and he wouldn't play football his senior year.

How did this happen? Joe sputtered. What college will look at you now?

Joe would later recall that day: "Parents, in spite of all their best efforts and all they know and so forth, on some occasions are simply broadsided by the antics of their progeny."

Hiram arrived in Hartford on June 1, 1972, as a six-month old baby. He had been born in Newark where his father owned an insurance agency that lost much of its business following the devastating riots of 1967. Countless buildings burned in the rampage, and rioters sometimes stoned Newark firemen trying to put out blazes. As a result, insurance companies canceled policies neighborhood by neighborhood. The notices came to Joe's office in two-to-three-inch-thick piles every day for weeks. And when the companies were through, the value of Joe Harrington's insurance agency had shriveled. On a business level, he understood. Insurers usually don't calculate neighborhood-wide mayhem as part of their risk assessment. It didn't make sense to throw good money back into such communities—a truth that applied to Joe as well. When, a few years later, he was offered a federally funded job in Hartford helping minority entrepreneurs start businesses, he said yes.

The family—Joe and wife DeLois, sons Herman and Hiram—moved into the Blue Hills section of Hartford's northwest side, a peaceful, clean, racially integrated neighborhood. They enjoyed the quiet, the friendliness of neighbors, the neat yards and the middle-class comfort. But rent was expensive, far beyond what the family had paid in Newark. The Harringtons moved three times in Blue Hills looking for better deals until Joe found a building he wanted to buy: a brick three-family house at 22 Sanford Street off North Main Street on the northeast side of town. There was a drawback. The property sat at the nexus of public-housing projects, nearly equidistant from

Nelton Court, Stowe Village, Bellevue Square, and only a little farther than the others: the South Arsenal Neighborhood Development project, better known as SAND.

DeLois protested. Why should they move their children to such a questionable—even dangerous—part of town?

Because the house was a bargain, Joe argued. He could buy the house out of probate court for cash, and he believed he could make money renting out two floors while he and his family lived on the remaining floor. Better to be a landlord than a tenant. It made economic sense.

So the Harringtons changed their address for the fourth time in ten years.

Eight years later Joe had lost $7,000 and abandoned the brick house on Sanford Street.

High taxes. Improvident (as Joe called them) renters. A decaying neighborhood. These forces combined to make it unfeasible for the Harringtons to raise enough in rent to cover expenses at 22 Sanford Street. With money and sweat, Joe and his young sons worked to make their building livable. They spent hours repairing drywall, installing flooring, cleaning stairways. But a property is only as attractive as its neighborhood. And this building over here was falling apart. In that house drug dealers practiced their trade, their customers stopping by at all hours. Kids from the projects tagged neighborhood walls with graffiti and harassed tenants at 22 Sanford. Loud music. Sirens. And when the neighborhood was at its worst, the occasional soul-cracking report of a handgun. Joe Harrington had to keep rent low even to attract tenants. The tenants themselves became less and less stable. One day a mentally ill tenant left a hot clothes iron on her living room floor. She lived on the third floor, and the iron burned through to the second. A fire spread. Firefighters saved the structure, but the damage was severe.

Joe Harrington brought the house keys to City Hall and dropped them on the desk of a lawyer-bureaucrat he knew there.

I've had it, he said. Here's the keys. You take it.

The lawyer protested. The city didn't have the resources—

That's your problem, Joe said. I don't need it. I am not going to continue to pour money down this rat hole.

Young Hiram studied all of this. Like his father, he had sweated for that house. Given summer days to it. He was barely a teenager, and already he had learned an important lesson about the city. Economists would have called it disinvestment, the phenomenon by which people withdraw their funds from a community. Hartford, and particularly its North End, would suffer from disinvestment through parts of two decades. Disinvestment would do such damage that in April of 1993, the *Hartford Courant* would report that the city was saddled with 371 vacant, tumble-down buildings, most of them apartments, and another 150 properties considered blighted.

For Hiram, statistics could only underscore the truth he learned from 22 Sanford Street. When neighbors don't care, not even the smartest man in the world can save property on a city block that wants to eat itself alive.

When they moved the family from Sanford Street, Joe and DeLois chose a house on Westland Street, a better neighborhood but only a few blocks away.

Hiram could keep friends he'd made, many of whom were kids who lived in SAND, a sprawling project of blocky, small-windowed, white buildings that from the outside were more reminiscent of Soviet-bloc military barracks than of apartment buildings. Hiram and his friends—Derrick Walker among them—played near railroad tracks and watched older people steal groceries, cereal boxes and the like, out of parked freight trains. The kids played football on SAND's dirt and grass yards, tackling each other in the summer dust, passing and catching as people streamed into a nearby second-floor apartment to buy drugs.

Sometimes the boys met with trouble. Kids from Bellevue Square used to mess with kids from SAND. Once when Hiram was in eighth grade, he and Derrick and some of their friends were chased by older kids with golf clubs wanting to roll them. Another time older teenagers sucker-punched Hiram's friend Dukie because of a spat over a girl. Hiram was four or five years younger, but already gifted with the size that would make him a ferocious linebacker in high school. He offered to pit his 190 pounds and two fists against them. But fists weren't how the older boys planned to fight. One pulled out a broomstick. And another showed a sawed-off shotgun. Hiram learned that day how fast he could run.

After that he avoided SAND. And no matter where he went in the city, he made sure never to wear dress shoes or sandals. Only sneakers.

Joe Harrington knew his son played with kids from the projects, but he didn't worry because Hiram's friends weren't bad kids, just poor, and it was just like Hiram to pick friends who came from tough backgrounds. Joe's youngest had always been one to rescue a stray kitten from the middle of the street, bring it home and feed it milk. He treated neighborhood kids the same way. He'd bring home the bedraggled, the troubled, and if he couldn't solve their problems, he'd ask Joe to help.

It wouldn't have surprised Joe if his youngest son grew up to become a minister or a teacher. Hiram, for all his joking and seeming lethargy, was calculating and dedicated when it came time to care for others. He loved the underdog. And so he loved Hartford, too, that underdog of cities.

A statue of Mark Twain stands amidst shade trees outside the Hartford Public Library's main branch. Engraved on the pedestal that upholds the statue is a Twain quote that suggests Hartford was not always an underdog.

"Of all the beautiful towns it has been my fortune to see, this is the chief. You do not know what beauty is if you have not been here."

What might Twain have seen that so impressed him?

At the time, he would have walked Hartford's wide boulevards decorated with elms and oaks, past opulent homes that he called "private hotels," each sitting on "an acre of green grass, or trees." The city boasted its commercial success by building public palaces and temples of business in neoclassic and late Georgian styles, and city residents enjoyed the well-trimmed lawns of the nation's first public parks. If Hartford was beautiful, it was beautiful with money. The city contained more money amidst a smaller concentration of people than a Mississippi River urchin, even a world-traveling urchin, had likely ever seen. Hartford's Gilded Age wealth prompted *Scribner's Monthly* magazine in November 1876 to report that the city of 40,000 enjoyed a greater proportion of money to population than any city in the country. Of all business taxes paid to state government, Hartford at the time accounted for about one dollar of every three.

The money came from a marriage of two major industries: manufacturing and insurance. Or as sharp-tongued Twain put it in a speech: "the Colt's Arms Company making the destruction of our race easy and convenient, our life insurance citizens paying for the victims when they pass away . . . "

Along with Samuel Colt's revolvers, Hartford was home to manufacturers of steam engines and bicycles and motor carriages, typewriters built by Underwood and Royal, rubber, textiles, books and the printing presses that made them, horse nails, and much else that could be forged. As a city of manufacturers, Hartford prospered amidst the carnage of the two world wars when factories retooled to build weapons. Hartford factories after World War I employed 31,000 people in a city with a population of 138,000.

Insurance, however, defined Hartford and led to its nickname "The Insurance City"—a dull and apropos title given how Hartford has made a habit of avoiding risk. Insurance companies benefit from their customers' fear of fire and death, but themselves do not fear the future. They manage it. They calculate odds and spread risk, then charge money to become bearer of the fears of their customers. If the company is well-managed, hardly any risk exists. So it is an optimistic and practical industry. Hartford provided the industry with a sensible home, furnished with all the necessities and none of the frilly curtains.

The city is the capital of "The Land of Steady Habits," as Connecticut is called, and its Puritan founders laid a practical foundation long before the insurance industry blossomed. A story, perhaps apocryphal, explains that the Puritans' first graveyard in the city's Statehouse Square no longer exists because early residents used the cemetery's headstones to make foundations for new buildings. That unsentimental Puritan ethic lived on in the attitudes of the great insurance companies and helped them and their city thrive, each in the other's image. The practical city helped create the practical industry, which in turn bolstered the city's controlling ethos. Eventually practicality permeated Hartford's civic life.

That is not to say Hartford has been a timid city. When it has had money, it has also had confidence, and the city's leaders have made bold moves. But more often than not, those bold moves carried the weight of common sense rather than the air of romance. In the early 1800s, Daniel Wadsworth, the scion of one of Hartford's early famous families, wanted to build an art museum. More practical city fathers argued that something so frivolous as paintings and sculpture alone would not draw practical-minded donors. Why not make a small art museum, they suggested, but add a library and offices for historical societies? Daniel followed their advice, but it was long after his death before his Wadsworth Atheneum became the kind of art museum he had first imagined.

When the Park River, the river that bisected the city and which served as a garbage dump and sewer, flooded in 1936 and 1938 and turned much of downtown Hartford into a lake, the city buried the river and its conduit. Combined with the levees built to contain the Connecticut River, the burial of the Park effectively removed Hartford for decades from enjoying natural running water. In the 1960s, when Hartford business and civic leaders razed a lively ghetto in the name of urban renewal, the concrete plaza they built in its place was sterile—with a few small trees—and uninviting to most downtown workers looking for a lunch oasis. It was, however, easy to maintain. Practicality also ruled when the city bulldozed its exquisite public high school, rather than pay for renovation and find an alternative route for Interstate 84.

When Hiram Harrington and his friends attended Hartford Public High School, such practical decision-making had helped diminish the city. Factory owners had made pragmatic decisions to move operations to other states where taxes and labor cost less. Middle- and working-class residents of Hartford moved away to West Hartford and Rocky Hill and Manchester and other suburban towns where better schools and safer streets made the decision seem easy and sensible, even if the move was sometimes an escape from black and Hispanic neighbors and therefore tainted with racism. Department stores opened in suburban malls near where customers now lived and where parking was abundant, and closed their downtown stores. Try as it might, downtown failed to lure them back. Expensive parking, the violence and robbery connected to the drug trade and prostitution, and the belief that "there's nothing to do in Hartford anymore" combined to give suburbanites reasons to stay away. To many citizens of Greater Hartford, the capital city was like a ripped screen door in their comfortable house, one that could be left ignored and unmended as long as no flies came through.

That was the attitude offered by a man from Wethersfield—the town on Hartford's southern border—vacationing in North Carolina on a gusty day in June 2000. On vacation, too, I met him atop the Cape Hatteras Lighthouse where we enjoyed the view of a churning Atlantic Ocean. He told me that since his retirement from Travelers Insurance Co., he had refused to go into Hartford. He would sooner drive to Florida than the few miles into Hartford's South End, into the neighborhood where my grandparents still lived. "The scum line has moved down there," he said, "and it keeps moving south."

Nothing could pull him back. Not the delicate cannoli or the earthy veal marsala on Franklin Avenue in Hartford's Little Italy. Not the Hartford Stage where famous names still performed national-class theater. Not exhibits of Picasso or impressionists at the Wadsworth Atheneum. Not outdoor concerts at Bushnell Park. Not the minor-league sports or the games played by the University of Connecticut's nationally ranked basketball teams. Implicit in the decades-long abandonment of Hartford by suburbanites is the idea that the city's benefits are not worth the hassle—or, more importantly, the risk—of touching "scum."

At the time of Hiram's high school years, Mark Twain's beautiful town—once one of the nation's wealthiest—was now one of its poorest. The citizens of Greater Hartford proved themselves too practical for their capital city's own good.

The Hartford Public cafeteria is loud loud LOUD, and some girl over there with a big voice shouts to another girl over here and trays clatter and somebody raps to a song on his Walkman and it isn't pretty. Security guards in blue uniforms stand or lean against the cinder block walls and watch the students charge the air with all that adolescent energy. The guards also keep track of the tension levels, and they take mental notes so as to know whether some sideways glance in the cafeteria could lead to something bloody after school.

It is spring of their freshman year, and the five friends eat together. E 'n' D. Harvey. Hiram. Joshua. They share much: strong families, goals, and the desire to think and to talk about what they think (though not always to study). They know somehow that they are different than their classmates. When, in the football locker room, senior players came to haze the freshmen, to toss them in the showers, this group of friends just looked at them and said, "No. We don't do that." And the seniors moved on, chose other victims. It wasn't that the seniors feared a fight with Hiram or Eric or Harvey (though these freshmen could fight), but because they sensed that this group wouldn't play the game. Maybe that's what distinguishes and bonds them. The five friends understand the unspoken rules of city life but refuse to follow them. So they stick by each other, even though there are times Harvey would like to knock Hiram's smile down his throat. Hiram will make you crazy any way he can, making fun of your mother, or sticking his thick finger in your mashed potatoes. Quiet as you please. No showboating. Just stick his finger in there and smile like a Hartford Buddha.

The others giggle. Harvey says, Man! Who elected this clown freshman class president? A guy who puts his fingers in your mashed potatoes? What's that all about?

Which was true. Hiram was freshman class president, this guy who was so unserious that "Class Clown" would one day be written next to his name in the high school yearbook. This guy who had received report cards since fourth grade that read: "Hiram doesn't apply himself." Hiram could laugh about those, too.

But every now and then, Hiram's face acquired another look, one that suggested a cool surface necessary to contain the furnace underneath. On those walks home after school, between chatter about girls and music and sports, between goofing and using that city sixth sense, the one that tells them when a rental car is a dealer or when it's just a rental, when screeching tires mean show-off and when they mean drive-by shooting, when a siren belongs to an ambulance or to cops, or when the noise vanishes and the sudden silence means something is about to go wrong, Hiram and the others would step lightly through the city and watch kids only a few years younger toss a football near graffiti-tagged projects or dribble around fast-food containers dumped from a trash can across the asphalt. They remembered themselves at that age, and they imagined the lives of those kids. Maybe there was no father at home, like at Harvey's house, and at Eric's and Derrick's. Or maybe it was worse and Pops was home, but he beat Moms. Or maybe an older brother was dealing, or using, and keeping the household awake all night long while he got high with friends and watched TV infomercials. Hiram and his friends worried about those little kids. Then their teenage bluster failed, even Hiram's. And here's where that cool-furnace face showed itself. Hiram might say: You know why Hartford suffers? Because people don't know each other and can't trust one another. He'd recall what his father had said about an apartment building owned by a friend, how tenants stole water pipes out of the walls to sell for scrap. How that owner gave up and abandoned the building to the flies and the junkies and the squatters.

The five would swap theories. Stories. Harvey might recall the story about Bo or about that lonely winter night when he met the police officer and came to know the city's brittle, frightening edge. He'd wonder aloud: How can people think I'm dangerous? Or Eric? Or Josh? Look at us! C'mon man. We're just kids.

They talked about these things because they had to, because you couldn't make a life talking only about girls or music or sports.

Hiram Harrington loved all sorts of sports. He wrestled on Hartford Public's team. He ran track with Butch and trained with him in the summer. On the golf course, his drives from the tee flew sweet and long, and he worked a summer job as a starter at the Keney Park course in the North End. He later became a lifeguard at a city swimming pool. But it was amidst the controlled chaos of a football field that he excelled.

Hiram defined muscle and speed. In track he ran the 100-meter sprint and sometimes the 200-meters, the two swiftest races in the sport. In the weight room he bench-pressed 350 pounds with hardly a grunt. Translated to the football field, that muscle and speed made Hiram a sledgehammer tackler and a cannonball running back. Years after Eric Shorter played alongside Hiram he could not remember a time Hiram ever gave ground. You could tackle him. You could tangle up his legs or throw him off balance. But knock him backward? No way. On defense, a runner on his way north—no matter how big—would smash into Hiram and get thrown south. Nobody flattened Hiram. Nobody rocked his world.

He wore Number 34, like his favorite running backs: Herschel Walker and Walter Payton. Of the two, Hiram ran more like Walker. Payton danced, lithe and quick, switching directions in mid-stride to make tacklers grab air. Walker, like Hiram, was a human pile driver who attacked the line of scrimmage with short, choppy steps that made it seem he wasn't moving when he was, in fact, using the ground as a springboard, all that leg-strength pummeling would-be tacklers *bam! bam! bam! bam! bam!*

Like Walker, Hiram followed plays to their diagramed conclusion. If he was supposed to follow the right tackle, Hiram followed the right tackle. If he was supposed to dive behind the left guard, he dived behind the left guard. And if someone from the other team dared get in his way, well, bring him on. Hiram would always—*always*—get yardage. Maybe tacklers could hold him to three or four yards a carry, but they'd pay.

Yet, for all his ferocity, Hiram could have gained even more yards and made even more tackles. His full capabilities showed themselves only in glimpses, when by some strange momentary alchemy Hiram's effort matched his physical gifts and a kid from Rockville or Manchester paid for it, Hiram lowering his shoulders and smashing the kid so the clash of their pads echoed through rusted, nearly empty Dillon Stadium. More often Hiram did what needed to be done and little more. On the field, as happened in his classes, Hiram could have received a report card that read, "Hiram doesn't apply himself."

Come the summer of 1989, however, Hiram's football work ethic changed. He'd made all-state as a linebacker the season before. The recruiting letters had started to arrive. Down at Dunkin' Donuts at Laurel and Farmington, flirtatious girls behind the counter gave him freebies. Success sweetened the world, and Hiram wanted more. So that summer he trained hard with Butch and the Inner City Striders; he shaved his time in the 40-meter dash—the distance used to measure football speed—from 4.7 seconds to 4.5. He trimmed fat and gained muscle, weighing in at 205 pounds. With Eric he pounded against some of New England's best at the Boston College football camp; he learned tricks and techniques that he believed could help him repeat as an all-state linebacker and maybe even win him the same status as a fullback.

For once, he applied himself. The dividends showed in his quick step, his agility and power. Now all he needed were the games.

It was August and humid that morning before Hiram's senior year—the first of twice-a-day football practices in what was called "Hell Week." Hiram parked his mother's black 1985 Toronado in the school parking lot, then strolled toward the gravelly field and track where the players had already gathered. But Coach LaPlante met Hiram before he could reach his teammates.

LaPlante wasn't smiling. He spoke softly.

Hiram, he said. How you doin', big guy?

Hiram waited.

Bad news, LaPlante said. There's bad news. You're ineligible. You can't play this season.

Hiram heard the words and didn't. LaPlante could have said, "Hiram, you've been elected mayor of Hartford" or "Hiram, we'll wear flip-flops this season instead of cleats" and Hiram would have understood as well. The message hit Hiram like mud against a wall. It splattered but didn't penetrate.

Ineligible? Hiram said. How? How's that possible?

LaPlante wasn't sure. Hiram's grade point average was off just a few tenths of a point. He suggested Hiram talk to his teachers once school started in September. See what happened.

Hiram looked past LaPlante to the field. The guys already stretching, already jogging. Laughing. Now the earth under his sneakers seemed part of somebody else's life, as if this was not the Pub's football team out here, because Hiram played for the Pub, and if this was that team, then he would be out there, too; therefore, this was not Public's football team.

And so on.

And so forth.

He marched back to the Toronado and drove to his girl-friend's house. When she asked why he wasn't at practice, he told her he had made the greatest mistake of his life.

He had failed at something. He had coasted through so much, but never had he failed. And failure hurt, not only for its own sake, but because it took away the game, and he had never lost something so fundamental to who he was.

His mother's face showed her disappointment. His father's failure to find words showed his bewilderment. They revoked privileges. His father told him: Come to terms with the reality that the whole purpose for going to school is to get an education. It is not to play football.

For years Joe Harrington had told his boys about the southern rural roads in his home state of North Carolina, how drainage ditches ran along either side of the roads, filled with grass and gravel and mud. Steer too far left or too far right, you end up in a ditch. If you steer properly, you will meet curves and hills, but you'll keep on toward your destination. "Hey fellas," he used to say when his boys were in trouble. "Keep the car on the road."

Hiram had totaled the car.

Hiram wasn't the only one ineligible that year. Joshua didn't have the grades, either, but Joshua hadn't been all-state. So on the first day of school, it was Hiram who be-came the center of attention—for all the wrong reasons. Students stopped him in the halls to ask why he wasn't playing. Teachers, too. One older teacher, a rare enthusiastic fan, pinned Hiram in a hallway.

What did you do, Hiram? the teacher spit. What did you do?

Years later Hiram could still see the teacher's hands waving too close to Hiram's face, taunting him, demanding to know, wanting—what? An apology? He could still hear the words denying reality: Hiram, you cannot be ineligible!

Hiram grabbed the teacher's wrist. He squeezed. He was stronger than the old man. He had never felt more angry.

You know, he said. Could you just stop it?

The second day proved no easier. Or the third. Hiram's autumn afternoons had long centered on 1:54 p.m. and the start of practice. Now, left behind, the last bell that marked the end of class time left him disoriented, aimless. He tried watching practices, but that forced him to see a sophomore wearing his number. He made it to a game, and Hartford Public lost, and Hiram saw precisely where he would have made a tackle that his replacement didn't make, where he would have gained yardage his replacement didn't gain. He watched Eric and Derrick struggle. And afterward he couldn't face them. Years later he might be able to say to his old friend Dukie, "Remember that time at SAND and those dudes with the shotgun?" because he had stood up for Dukie. But what if he'd left Dukie alone, fled to a safe place then watched while Dukie got beat on with broomsticks and the butt-handle of the gun until his skin broke and bled? What then? He'd never be able to look Dukie in the face. It was like that now, seeing the guys. Hiram had been unwise and selfish about his success; having neglected his books, he had betrayed his best friends. Underdogs all, he had abandoned them.

He let himself drift for a week or two, realizing that all his old distractions—girls, sports, hanging with the fellas—only made him feel more the Judas. Meanwhile, his father's words stayed with him. *The whole purpose for going to school is to get an education . . . Come to terms with that reality.* All right. Okay. Hiram might have failed to play his way into college, but he could change those old ideas about what mattered. After school, while his teammates ran buttonhook pass patterns and sweeps to the left and to the right, Hiram would board the city bus for downtown. There he would find a table in the Hartford Public Library where he could spread out his schoolbooks, then work.

III

Jack LaPlante grew up in East Hartford, a tough factory town across the Connecticut River from Hartford. He'd been a good schoolboy football player and had played a year at the University of Bridgeport before joining the Army. After that, he finished college, then returned to Greater Hartford as a social studies teacher at Hartford Public. He never taught anywhere else but first coached high school football as an assistant in Glastonbury, a suburb southeast of Hartford where he lived. Glastonbury's team was a perennial powerhouse, so when Amado Cruz, Hartford Public's principal, needed a head football coach, he turned to LaPlante. He saw in LaPlante a tough, compassionate man who could bring suburban discipline to inner-city kids. Cruz didn't believe the suburbs offered all the answers, but he thought LaPlante's strictness could complement the quality Butch Braswell fostered: inner-city fire.

LaPlante was a slight man and not tall, but he loomed large. His broad face played host to a crooked smile, and his voice was big, too, a tough blue-collar blast that echoed in the locker room when he needed kids to take care of fundamentals, like locking up their shoulder pads and helmets after practice. He could also quiet that voice, until it was just above a whisper: a soft, slow, well-balanced mumble that kids sometimes heard more clearly than the yelling.

LaPlante inherited a football program as battered as the city's streets. For years, the team had lost far more games than it had won. For a home field, the Owls shared with other city schools the rickety Dillon Stadium, where sections of the bleachers might sometimes be marked off in caution-yellow tape because they teetered near collapse. Dillon sat miles away from the high school, exiled to an industrial neighborhood near the old Colt Arms factory, and at some games fewer than forty people spread out through the stands. Worse, sometimes the Owls' games drew students who came not to cheer but to laugh and heckle.

In those years Hartford Public students cheered for basketball, not football, and LaPlante had to compete with the pervasive attitude that football didn't matter. He had to build enthusiasm for a game that in recent seasons had done little for its players but wound the confused mix of manufactured dignity and bravado that was often all Hartford teenagers had. That alloyed psyche was loud and brash and necessary to hide the inadequacy so many kids felt, but it was fragile, too, and few students dared risk it for the weekly humiliations—the body-crushing, mouthful-of-turf losses—Hartford Public had suffered for so long.

Somehow LaPlante managed to recruit freshmen. The next problem, then, was keeping them, and to do that he pitted himself against an overwhelming menu of social problems: kids without parents, kids who were parents, kids who worked to buy their family's milk and eggs and potato chips, kids who were addicted, kids who had siblings who were addicted, kids who suffered beatings at home or from rivals on the street. It wasn't unusual for LaPlante to receive a note that read something like "Please excuse Eduardo from practice; he was hit yesterday in the back with a baseball bat." So, in his soft voice, LaPlante tried to balance compassion with discipline:

Okay. I know your mother's car had its battery stolen, but don't you live just two blocks from here? Can't you walk to practice? Okay. Now, where's your jersey? Why did your sister sell your jersey?

These were not problems faced by coaches in Glastonbury.

And there was one more major obstacle: grades.

Many, many kids couldn't keep their grades high enough to compete. Not just because Hartford teenagers had to deal with every societal scourge before they even opened a book, but because Hartford's school board—in an effort to improve academics—required higher grades for athletes than did other school districts in the state. In Hartford the school board had made it so a kid taking five courses could earn four Cs and one D and still not play. In Glastonbury—and at most high schools in the state—a kid could play with four Ds and an F. Those schools followed the minimum eligibility requirements set by the Connecticut Interscholastic Athletic Conference, the state's governing body for high school sports. When Hiram and the others were in high school, only one Connecticut school in every seven used the higher standard of a C average, and Hartford's three high schools were among them. LaPlante liked the theory behind the C Rule: that athletes should prove themselves as students before receiving the privilege of play. But he hated the result. He worried that for some Hartford kids the only thing that brought them to school was the promise of practice later in the day. What happened when that kind of kid saw his average drop and watched sports drop away with it? Did he transfer to Glastonbury to play with his low grades? Not a chance. Some Hartford educators, LaPlante among them, worried that taking away football or basketball was the same as casting that kid into the street. As one Hartford vice-principal told the Board of Education, "I would rather have a student with a D average in history, science, and arithmetic than an A average in drive-by shootings or drugs."

Not every Hartford teenager enjoyed Hiram's good fortune: a stable home with two parents who worked and who would encourage a child kicked off a team to study instead. For those kids, LaPlante wanted two changes in the C Rule: he wanted the school board to pay for teacher-monitored after-school study halls for athletes, and he wanted athletes to receive fair warning that their grades were slipping before they lost their eligibility. He wanted no more demoralizing surprises for players like Hiram or for the coaches. He wanted fairness, too. It wasn't right that schools played by different rules. Look at the result, he'd say, then point to the losses. From 1982 through Hiram's senior year, Hartford's three high schools had won 49 football games and lost 168.

"Eighty percent of our kids were taken out by the C Rule," LaPlante told the *Hartford Courant* before the start of Hiram's senior year. "It was supposed to be the culmination of a four-year building experience, and instead we go back to square one."

Square one meant losing. With Hiram and others on the sidelines, LaPlante and the Owls lost their first game that season. And their second. And their third.

Butch saw that Harvey missed football. He saw how it troubled Harvey to watch as Eric and the few others who remained once again became a homecoming team.

How's your knee? he asked.

Better, Harvey said.

Do you want to go back? If you do, then go. Nobody will think less of you either way. Do what you need to do.

Harvey rejoined the team in time for the season's fifth game. But his presence made little difference in how games turned out. Maybe Hartford Public scored a touchdown or two more or kept other teams from scoring as many, but, aside from one game that ended in a tie, the Owls kept losing. A fifth game. A sixth . . .

But Harvey was back where he belonged, and if the crippled Owls still lost at least they lost with the school's best athlete catching tight spirals from Eric, running pass patterns with Derrick, proudly wearing his football jersey to Hartford Public's own Homecoming dance. With Harvey at their side you couldn't call them losers. At that dance, yearbook photographers took pictures of them: Eric, Harvey wearing his blue football jersey, and Derrick. Especially Derrick, who won the title of Homecoming King—what better reward for staying true to the blue, what greater thrill—and who danced that night in the school gymnasium, wearing a medallion around his neck and his velvet crown perched loosely over his flattop haircut.

Hiram? Hiram was missing from those photos. But LaPlante hadn't forgotten him. A few games remained, and LaPlante had a plan for Hiram. Come back to the team, he said to him one day. Let's make a point. Put a face on what's unfair. Turn losing into some kind of victory. Harvey's a captain, and so are Eric and Derrick. Let's make you one, too. The heck with the C Rule.

As juniors, Harvey and Hiram and the rest had lost to South Windsor badly. Harvey would never forget how South Windsor's fans had flayed the Owls with a chant from the stands: "No score, no brains! No score, no brains!" It hurt. Oh man, it hurt. LaPlante planned Hiram's return for South Windsor.

He warned Cruz and a vice-principal, but told no one else.

The Pub was still the underdog in LaPlante's mind, even with Hiram on the team. LaPlante played only a dozen or so seniors. Most of his players—freshmen and sophomores—made the varsity just so Hartford Public could fill the sideline with uniforms, so its weaknesses wouldn't seem so apparent. Nevertheless, with Hiram and Harvey added to the mix, it was the best team LaPlante had fielded all season.

And when the final second ticked away, Hartford Public had tied the Bobcats. Not as good as a victory, but not as bad as the humiliation of the year before. It would do.

As his players headed for the team bus, LaPlante met the South Windsor coach at midfield for the ritual handshake between coaches. He took his opponent's hand and said, Ralph, we had an ineligible player. Our tie should be forfeited. It's our loss.

The next day LaPlante notified the Connecticut Inter-scholastic Athletic Conference.

And then an angry Board of Education almost fired him.

But LaPlante had grabbed the board's attention, and he used it to make his arguments about the C Rule. He wasn't alone, either. Administrators and coaches from Bulkeley and Weaver joined him. They wrote letters, attended board meetings, and lobbied the board's members. It was too late for Hiram, who having played one game in violation of his eligibility would not play in another. It was too late for Hartford Public in 1989, which—having lost Aaron Fisher and Hiram, Joshua and others—would win only one game all season. But eventually the lobbying worked. By 1992 the board had changed its C Rule to allow for probationary periods and study halls. A few years after that, Hartford Public accomplished the unthinkable and won a state football championship, the first ever for a city school, beating Southington High School on a crisp night at Southern Connecticut State University in New Haven. LaPlante still worked the sidelines, and in the crowded stands a one-time homecoming king grinned through the whole game, watching the Pub rock to the state title, feeling so good that nothing in life had ever come close, so good that the only way anyone could understand was to cut him open and see all that sky blue radiating out of him. Of the five friends, he was the only one there, and at the end of the game Derrick visited the field where Hartford Public players and their families celebrated, and LaPlante hugged him, one of his favorite players ever, and LaPlante yelled with that big blue-collar voice.

You guys! You guys were the icebreakers! The pathfinders! Because of you guys, we're here now!

Hartford Public versus Weaver in 1989 was no state championship game. Though a rivalry, it didn't carry a whisper of the gridiron shout that was Oklahoma versus Texas, UCLA and Southern Cal, or Auburn and Alabama. It was the last game tagged on the end of two teams' losing seasons. Thousands of fans would not pack Dillon Stadium on Thanksgiving Day, not even hundreds. Reporters would not crowd the press box. Marching bands would not take the halftime field. Fireworks would not shower over the team that at game's end could proclaim, "We weren't as bad as they were."

So maybe neither team would leave Dillon Stadium for the state playoffs, and maybe the game didn't matter in a world that hardly ever noticed Hartford, let alone its high schools, let alone what might happen between their football teams one holiday morning in November. Even so the coaches and players headed with passion and expectation toward Thanksgiving Day, armed with the truisms that have become cliché when archrivals meet:

Records don't matter; this game is in the family, and family fights can't be predicted. We want bragging rights for next year. Our seniors want to go out winners . . .

But coaches and seniors never dwelled on the flip-side cliché: to lose the final game against the archrival—the team that is most like you—is to lose it forever.

The day before the Thanksgiving Day game, Hartford Public staged a pep rally in the gymnasium. Fight songs! Speeches! Cheerleaders! The players wore their jerseys and received carnations while a student in an Owl costume waved furry wings and danced across the hardwood floor, sweeping away the sting of seven losses. It was a one-game season now, and the gym shined bright with possibility. Derrick Walker smiled behind his sunglasses, holding his carnation with two hands, his head covered by a winter sock cap with "Hartford" knitted into it.

The snow that fell early Thanksgiving morning robbed the players of their grand finale. All week they had aimed toward Turkey Day, and then Dillon Stadium filled up like a bowl of ice cream and the game was postponed to the weekend. For some players the finale lost its oomph. How could you call it the Turkey Day game if you played on Saturday?

With the game postponed, Thanksgiving became for me a day off, and I spent part of it with my grandparents enjoying the usual holiday fare in their dining room, which doubled as their den. Walter and Helen Petry in many ways embodied what I had known to be Hartford. They lived in a two-story, one-bathroom house on a rise above one of the city's main avenues and across the street from a public park. As a child I had played concealed by the rhododendron bush in their yard and enjoyed the damp mystery of their basement, the entry to which doubled as a coat closet so any trip downstairs first required a parting of rain slickers and winter jackets. Their house seemed to me as much a Hartford icon as did the Traveler's Insurance Company Tower and the blue onion dome of the Colt factory. The names of my grandparents' friends, names such as Winialski and Carbone, belonged among Wadsworth and Bushnell and Twain and others I associated with Hartford history.

But my grandparents' Hartford, a realm that once reached into every corner of the city, was shrinking. Though they had yet to suffer the most debilitating injuries of their old age, they had acknowledged some limitations and seldom drove outside their neighborhood, fear-ing, in what seemed like equal measure, other drivers, the lack of parking, and the abundance of crime. Their Hartford was now no more than St. Augustine's church, the South End senior center, the grocery store and the bank. At the same time, my Hartford was expanding. As I reported the stories of Hartford's youth, I was seeing the city through those young eyes. By living in Hartford, I saw, too, through my own. Together, these points of view crashed into an enormous, confounding, energetic picture of a city. I wanted to understand how it all fit together, how the Hartford of my childhood could be the contemporary Hartford of Walter and Helen Petry and also the Hartford of Harvey Kendall. What remained of the old in the new? How had one led to another? Was one Hartford mine alone, separate from the others, or could I live, somehow, in a Hartford that contained them all? Where did the multiple Hartfords intersect? In me?

I noted tangential connections of geography and history, such as the fact that my father had once worked in the Colt factory next to Dillon Stadium where Harvey Kendall's Owls faced Weaver and where I walked the sidelines taking notes. I recognized how lives lived in Hartford followed repeated patterns. Harvey and his friends faced racism in the city, as decades before so did my grandfather who changed his name from Petrykowski to Petry so as to find work without the burden of the dumb Polack stereotype. Eric Shorter grew up poor in a single-parent family; so did my grandfather, whose own father likely drank himself into a kidney disease that killed him six days after his thirty-first birthday, leaving his widow to feed her children with sacks of beans handed out by the welfare office. But I also acknowledged the particulars of different eras, that racism of language was not the same as the racism of skin color, that prohibition gin was not crack cocaine, that polio was not AIDS, and how these particulars made for different lives. But the patterns remained.

I noted how even generations intersected, how a fellow coaching at South Catholic knew a cousin of mine who had been a cheerleader there. A coach at Bulkeley might have known my uncle, my mother's brother, who had been at the top of his class as a senior. These educators, these mainstays of the city, remembered Hartford's past and worked daily with its future.

And yes, many Hartfords did intersect in me. My presence at the Weaver-Hartford Public football game connected Walter Petry's Hartford with Harvey Kendall's. I didn't know the nature of that link, or what it meant, or how it worked. But it existed, and if I were ever to fulfill Harvey Kendall's charge ("So you understand," he had said), then I needed to nurture that link.

So on that day when Hartford Public did not play Weaver, I prayed the Catholic grace and ate a Thanksgiving meal with my grandparents, and knew that somewhere in the city Harvey Kendall shared bread and meat with his family, and his friends did the same. We shared our meals in a broken city, yes, but it had lasted long and still contained so many lives. The city, our city, endured. In the midst of all its chaos, this tenuous place somehow felt solid in a way no other place I ever lived felt solid. I believed this centuries-old city had room for me. Between Harvey and my grandparents, it had welcomed me. In it, I believed I could belong.

Saturday morning, the players suited up for the Two-Days-After-Turkey-Day game. Seniors tugged on their Hartford Public jerseys, snapped the helmet straps around their chins, and tried to remember each ritualized action as they completed it for the last time. The snow—tinged now with gray—had been plowed into banks behind the end zones and far beyond the sidelines. On the field before kickoff, the seniors stood as their names were announced over the loudspeaker and their parents summoned from the stands. The sons honored their parents—Linda Stills, Emma Walker and James Treadwell Greene, Jessie Kendall, Joe and DeLois Harrington, Edrick and Sonja Hall—by giving each mother a rose, and then the small crowd in turn honored the seniors, the dull clap of mittened hands, for their service to the school.

I wrote in my notepad, the only reporter in the stadium.

Neither team played well. The players blew steamy breath into their fists to warm stiff fingers and stamped their cleated feet to keep the blood circulating in their toes. The field was hard and slippery, and Hartford Public's young running backs could not handle the ground as Hiram or Aaron Fisher might have. The youngsters slipped, tripped, stumbled, piles of green Weaver jerseys atop them. When the Owls could gain yards against Weaver's defense, it was usually because Eric had found Derrick or Harvey or someone else with a pass. But there weren't enough of those, and Hartford Public's first touchdown came when the Owls were on defense. Harvey, playing defensive end, batted a Weaver pass out of the air, caught the tipped ball and sprinted with it to the end zone.

For much of the game, the teams played tied, and then with a little more than a minute and a half left, Weaver scored its second touchdown. The Beavers missed the extra point, but still led 12–6. Now, Weaver players could tell that their opponents felt the threat of another loss, felt every bruise of spirit suffered in the first seven. The Owls began to squabble. They cursed each other, assigned blame loudly for broken plays.

Hartford Public had little over a minute to score a touchdown and tie the game. If the Owls could reach the end zone, then score the extra point, they'd win.

Eric believed. He always believed. He began the drive, barking orders. There wasn't enough time for a running game even if Hartford Public had one. The only way to the other end of the field was through the air, and so what if the Owls' offense hadn't scored a touchdown yet? We gotta do it now!

A pass caught here. A pass caught there. The drive was only a few plays old when Eric dropped back, then tossed the ball to his right. But a Weaver player reached the ball first, caught it, and sprinted past stunned Owls. Eric watched. He saw it all: the Weaver jersey, the ball captured then cradled against green and white fabric, the Weaver player hurtling past Eric who was the only one near enough to make the tackle, but who at the end of this season-long tribulation could not bring himself to give chase. Spent, Eric could only throw his hands high and let them drop just as quickly. The Weaver player celebrated with his teammates in the end zone. The final score: Weaver 18, Hartford Public 6.

In his last high school game, Eric had passed for 109 of Hartford Public's 131 yards, creating almost all of the Owls' meager offense. With every sweaty, steely bit of his spirit, he had pushed the Owls to win not just that one game, but a whole season's worth, and they had failed. Now in the gray twilight of this cold Saturday, with his mother watching from the stands, Eric wept in frustration.

Weaver coach Wil Jones saw his young opponent's distress, and he nodded in Eric's direction. I kept writing. Wil Jones told me that Eric was an outstanding athlete and an outstanding gentleman. "I know he's going to go someplace," the coach said.

IV

Spring.

There's Bobby Torres sitting in the patchy grass alongside the jumping pit, savoring the sun and blue sky and the warm argument they make that anywhere—even in Hartford—there can be a perfect day. He's wearing sneakers and Hartford Public-blue sweatpants, headphones covering his ears, and he's holding in one hand the tape cassette player. Maybe he's listening to something by Commission. Maybe something by Snap.

"I've got the power! Whooo, yeah! I've got the power!"

Dance floor music. That's what they call it. A mix of German machines and American street rap. Bobby listens, taps his foot. He watches as Harvey charges out of the golden day down the pebbly rubber of the runway, cleared for takeoff . . .

A man's voice rapping: *"Like the crack of the whip I Snap! Attack!"*

That's how to hit the board. Snap! Attack! Like a whip-end jerked forward, your body launches, drives through air until gravity finally tugs it back. Harvey splashes into the sand. Bobby's music keeps on. Menacing chords drift along like a sedan creeping down Park Street, backed by jackhammer rhythms and rap tough as asphalt. And above it all, a woman's angel voice of celebration, Phoenix-like, rising over the street and the jackhammer, over the jumping pit filled with sand, up there in the blue . . .

104

"I've got the power!"

The sky. The street.

"So please—stay off my back or I will attack . . . and you don't want that!"

"I've got the power!"

Bobby makes a triangle of his legs—one extended, the other bent at the knee—and stretches so his forehead nearly touches the ground. Harvey's brushing off sand, and Bobby nods toward him. Harvey and Bobby, both of them born of the street and grabbing at sky. Isn't that what jumping is about? Taking strength from the earth in order to leave it, if only for a moment?

It's been a good spring. The two have jumped across the Eastern Seaboard and beaten all comers. In Florida, Bobby launched himself twenty-three feet and seven inches to win the long jump at the Golden South Invitational in Orlando, a meet where only the best high school athletes compete. Harvey traveled fifty-one feet, three inches in the triple jump, the best he's ever jumped at a meet, and the best jump anybody has ever made at the Golden South. Then came the Connecticut high school meets. Harvey won the triple jump at Class LL, the meet for the largest schools in the state, setting a meet record in the event and outdistancing his nearest competitor by more than four feet. He won the high jump, too. Bobby won the long jump; Harvey placed second. In the next day's paper, the *Courant* called Harvey, "the state's triple jump king."

Now comes the State Open, the meet for the best finishers in all the events statewide, no matter how big the school. Colossal Glastonbury against rural schools so small it takes three towns to make them. The State Open. The best versus the best. It was what Harvey had aimed for all along. For four years.

That Tuesday in New Britain's Willow Brook Stadium, athletes in their kaleidoscope of uniforms mingled in the grassy infield and the stands. The twelve lettermen from Staples High School in Westport—champions of both the State Open indoor track meet and autumn's cross country running meet—wore their navy blue with the big white S on their jerseys like Superman. Weaver's ten competitors wore green. There were athletes in the bumblebee yellow and black of East Hartford, the gold of South Windsor, the brassy orange and blue of Bloomfield, the red and white of Norwich Free Academy, the purple and white of Prince Tech Vocational. Harvey and Bobby wore blue and white, the only Owls on the field, the only competitors from Hartford Public to qualify for the open. But if Weaver and Staples brought numbers, Hartford Public's duo brought distance and speed. Bobby won the 100 meters and the 200, and though he could muster only twenty-two feet, six inches for second place in the long jump it was all right because no one but Harvey jumped farther. Then Harvey won the high jump.

Butch Braswell scratched out the numbers on paper. Ten points for every victory. Eight points for every second place. He added the other teams' totals. Of Harvey and Bobby's events, only the triple jump remained unfinished though it was already decided; Harvey had set a meet record with his third attempt, four feet better than anyone else had leapt that day. Butch felt comfortable with the math. Hartford Public's pair had beaten the state.

Bobby sprinted off to the jumping pit, shouting "Word Up! We won the State Open!" He slapped hands with Harvey. "You're the man!" he said.

"We're the man," Harvey said, and he laughed.

The next morning their victory was headlined in the top right corner of the final edition of the *Courant*'s front page. In only his second year as a head coach, with athletes he had nurtured since they were freshmen, Butch Braswell had won the state's most important high school track and field championship. "We wanted to win this state title for Butch," Harvey was quoted in the *Courant* as saying. "He's done a lot for us in the past four years, giving himself 365 days a year. He's like a second father. We wanted to do it for him."

Butch bought jackets for his champions to commemorate the victory, and he offered to have a message embroidered on them. Harvey and Bobby wanted hip-hop phrases: "Can't touch this!" "I've got the power!" "You can't rock the Pub!" But Butch shook his head. "Naw," he said. "I want to put on there, 'Against All Odds.'"

And when he explained why, when he recited again for them all they had overcome—even to have lived to age eighteen—Harvey and Bobby had to agree.

Later, when the *Courant* featured Harvey on the cover of its spring all-state special section, he used the forum to convey the message on his jacket, and to expand its reach to every child in his city.

"We all is in a war," he said. "And we're battlin' a lot of odds, and it's not pretty."

To: Harv

Yo, you are one of my best friends in life, you have made me very happy and humble to know and share so many good times together, so many ranks yo it was just a bunch of fun. Too bad we aren't going to school together. Yo I will miss you and everybody. Please stay silly cause you know I'm going to. Also, please I said please keep in touch cause we all we have. Your good friend for life, Hiram Harrington, # 34.

Graduation nears. The five friends—their backpacks full, their jeans baggy—hang out on the steps of Hartford Public one afternoon, and they exchange dates. August 16. September 16. August 26. The days that they will leave Hartford for college. Harvey to Blinn Junior College in Texas. Hiram to Livingstone College in North Carolina. Joshua to Norfolk State University in Virginia. Derrick to Virginia State University. Eric to Boston College.

Phase one, complete. Mission accomplished. Phase two about to launch.

Some carry in their backpacks their copies of the 1990 yearbook, white with a sharp-taloned blue owl perched on the cover. Inside are photos of a school full of kids "do'n the 90 thing." The five friends are featured prominently. Under Joshua's senior picture reads Malcolm X's quotation: "The Ballot or The Bullet." Under Eric's: "Success is hard to accomplish, so those who work hard are the ones who achieve it." Under Derrick's: "We are the dreamers. School has taught us history now we must create the future."

On page 22, beside principal Amado Cruz's portrait, sits his message to the graduating student body. It reads as if written specifically for those five who made the pledge:

"Since 1638, Hartford Public High School has produced outstanding classes which have set the future course of life at home and abroad. Their leadership and guidance has challenged the odds, persevered and achieved for the benefit of humanity, not merely for self interest. Yours is a generous tradition of caring and of helping those less fortunate and deprived. Take that humble banner of love and service to your future . . . What investment will you make for a better, healthier and safer world?"

To My Nigger Harvey,
Now that it is our senior year and we are happy to get outta here. But it is also sort of a sad time because we have been friends for about eight years and now we are going on to college and we won't be around to have fun together, but we always be friends.

E. *Shorter*

c/o 90

The day of the graduation ceremony, Harvey stands with his mother in his front yard and someone snaps a picture of him wearing his blue robe and mortarboard, his arm around Jessie. Behind them a neighbor's white house is washed in sunlight. They both smile and squint into the glare, the son who has made it and who will leave soon, the first in his family to go away to college, and the mother whose faith has maintained her through eleven children. She has taught her son to walk in that faith; he believes and has used that belief to temper the anger that grows as naturally out of the city and into him as crabgrass from a weedy lawn into a sidewalk crack. He has worked to make sure his anger never twists into despair. With faith, there is always hope. That is what Jessie has taught him. That is what Butch proved to him. Against all odds. Anything can happen. Anyone can win. It is true for Harvey. It is true for Hartford. There is always hope. There are five friends to prove it.

To Josh Malik Hall (the fighter for the "B" people)

What is there to say? You have been such a good friend through the years. Let's not lose touch with one another because friends like you are hard to come by nowadays. Let's keep striving for the promised land. I know you will make it so I won't stress it.

The Brothers

For life.

Good luck in all future endeavors.

D. Nice

c/o 90

V

A damp sheet lay over Harvey's sweaty skin. He couldn't sleep. The window hung open but fresh air didn't help. Outside was no cooler. If he could stretch himself out on a bed of ice maybe then he could sleep. But not now. His older brother Rick—recently divorced and home again, temporarily—suffered the same in his own bed. The two lay in the room and listened to themselves breathe. It was only a couple months since Harvey's high school graduation. It was August.

Gunshots! Damn, those were gunshots next door!

The sound yanked the brothers out of bed. They gathered at the open second-story window and saw two men in the yard next door, the yard of the white house. One man aimed a handgun. The other fled. From above, Harvey and Rick watched one man hurling himself around a corner, the other leaping a fence. Then the two men met and the pursuer once more took aim. Harvey could not count the shots. He heard more than two. Beyond that, he would not remember. He saw sparks from the gun. He watched the wounded man knocked back into the iron banister on the porch steps of the white house. He saw the gunman flee. He watched the wounded man stumble.

Harvey and Rick rushed downstairs. From their front porch, the brothers could hear the wounded man say something. He spoke with a West Indian accent, and they couldn't understand him. Rick rushed back inside to call the police. Harvey stayed.

The West Indian man bled. He mumbled. Harvey watched as the wounded man fell forward to his knees, then to his hands. The man held himself that way a moment. He gasped for air. Then his arms and legs gave in, and he fell on his face. He sighed. Drew a long breath. Exhaled. It was over.

The police cars' swirling lights lit the neighborhood red and blue. Harvey watched the officers with their heavy flashlights step toward the dead man. As if they feared a trap, as if they suspected the man wasn't really dead, they toed his body, then kicked it—hard enough to roll it over. They waved their flashlights over the corpse. Harvey, standing nearer now, helped by the light, recognized the man from the neighborhood. Now the man was sopped in blood. He wore Champion suede sneakers. Harvey would always remember the sneakers. He would remember, too, how the police yanked up the man's shirt to show bullet holes and his bloody chest.

Oh. That's what Harvey said. He said, oh.

The police examined the porch banister, bent from the force of the man slamming against it. The police asked questions. But it had been dark. It was after midnight. There were no lights. The shooter ran that way; the brothers couldn't see his face. Not what he was wearing, either, no.

And even if they had, they would have lied. You don't

want to see anything in Hartford. You don't want to become the next victim.

Back in bed, Harvey shut his eyes but still he saw the body, the smeared blood; he heard the last breath repeat itself. He had never watched someone die before. He had known violence. He had seen stabbings and once watched a man get hit by a chicken truck, but in his eighteen years he had never actually seen life exhale and leave.

Only weeks before he had boasted in an interview with me that he would come back to Hartford, that he would make a difference. Now Harvey lay on his mattress and felt the new, terrible weight of that night and thought to himself, "I am ready to go to college. I am ready. I need to get away from here."

4

I

For Eric nights brought doubt.

He was a freshman at Boston College and frustrated. At Hartford Public he had grown accustomed to the buoyancy that confidence gave him and how hard work helped him stand out because, as he liked to say, "There is no traffic jam when you go the extra mile." Now there came hushed, bleak nights in his dorm room in Fitzpatrick Hall when he felt no confidence, when it seemed Boston College would kick his work ethic and his inner-city self back to Hartford.

He had taken advanced placement courses in high school; now, on a campus called "The Heights," he struggled in classrooms where often his was the only brown face staring up at a professor who addressed the class in Latin, or in some kind of English that sounded like Latin. He despaired when his classmates seemed able to easily change verbs based on tenses and to recognize the cases of nouns, to explain the role of the Constitution in the

113

working of the federal government, to synthesize research into hypotheses, to exist lightly in this world in which Eric felt so leaden, so alien. He had wanted this school because it *was* alien: predominantly white, wealthy. Such a place, he believed, would help him focus, provide fewer distractions (fewer friends, fewer young black women) and more discipline, more resources to help him succeed. But he would spend hours crafting papers or studying, and his grades made it seem that he had no idea how to study. In the hallways of his dorm, he listened to students talk about vacations they had taken to places with names he didn't recognize. Other students argued about world events, and he wondered, *Israel? What's going on in Israel?* He watched others spend a hundred dollars on a Friday night while he sometimes needed to ask friends for money to buy lunch. Expensive cars in the parking lots had window decals advertising private boarding schools like Taft, Phillips Exeter, Choate . . . schools beyond Eric's understanding of city and suburb, schools that didn't fit the schematic he'd made of the world.

Football no longer offered solace. He had quit the team. What scholarship help he received had nothing to do with sports, but he had volunteered as a walk-on and become a defensive back for Boston College's Eagles—the best college team in New England. No matter how hard he worked that fall, Eric spent each game watching from the sidelines. Practices took hours away from his studies. He had to ask, Why am I in college? And he answered, To become a lawyer so that I can practice law in Hartford. That answer led him to quit the team after the fourth game and rededicate himself to his studies, but still his grades didn't improve.

Maybe Boston College was a mistake. Maybe he would

never fit in at a private Jesuit school. Maybe he would have been better off had he chosen a historically black college as Derrick, Hiram, and Joshua had.

More than once he knew these doubts, and often all at the same time. On the nights when he came closest to quitting school, he would telephone his best friend on campus, Mike Reed, also a defensive back on the football team who had gone through freshman orientation with Eric, and he would ask to borrow Mike's Toyota Camry, the "Brown Bomber." Mike would give him the keys.

During those two-hour drives back to Hartford, Eric thought about all the people who helped him get to college, all the positive role models, people who invested time to show him what he could be. Eddie Griffin was one, who had been a high school basketball legend in Hartford in the 1950s and who now taught in the Hartford school system and worked as an assistant coach with the Hartford Public football team. Coach Griffin, a man with a sandpaper voice and a snow-and-gravel beard, had sometimes brought players to his house in South Windsor to let them see what high aspirations could bring a kid from Hartford: a big kitchen that opened onto a family room; a riding lawn mower; so much space in the backyard that the Griffins debated whether to build a swimming pool or a tennis court. Jonah Cohen was another positive, a counselor at Upward Bound who was white and Jewish and in college then, and who tutored Eric in math and let him know—by attending his games, by telephoning him at home—that he believed in Eric's potential. And there was the barber who encouraged Eric to apply to West Point and win a nominating letter from a Connecticut congresswoman, even if he didn't want to go, just to show that it could be done, that Hartford kids could dream of such things. And Uncle Lenworth, who gave Eric two hundred dollars to pay for his school books. And, of course, his mother.

But come two a.m. or so, when he left Interstate 84 at Sigourney Street in Hartford, Eric wasn't looking for people to emulate. He steered Mike Reed's Brown Bomber north, then turned left on Asylum Avenue, right on Woodland, over the railroad tracks and then right again past boarded-up buildings on Homestead, then back down Sigourney past his mother's new apartment. He cruised his old neighborhood and looked for the prostitutes and the drug dealers and the junkies. They were easy to pick out. After midnight, there was no traffic, no children's voices, no teenage lovers entwined and propped against a lamppost. The life that crowded the streets during the day was gone now, tucked in, asleep. Eric drove slowly through the Asylum Hill neighborhood and saw what remained: predatory shadows leaning against brick walls, the tips of their cigarettes aglow. Other shadows, too: tattered ruins of people that searched dumpsters, screwed license plates off cars, stared through iron bars into shop windows, kicked crushed beer cans into the street.

When Eric drove back onto the highway, he wanted Latin and hypotheses and Israel if that's what would lay distance between him and Hartford's shadows.

II

The Brothers of Fire and Brimstone.

The Sons of Kush.

The Blue Riders of the Camel which Crosses White Sands.

The Technicians of Step.

The Men of the Dove.

The Brothers of Phi Beta Sigma answered to all these

116

names. They conceived of themselves as the inheritors of majesty.

But it was the fraternity's motto, "Culture for Service and Service for Humanity," more than its lyrical titles, that attracted Hiram, now a freshman at Livingstone College in Salisbury, North Carolina.

At Livingstone, founded by the AME Zion church in 1879, Phi Beta Sigma seemed to Hiram more eager to serve than any other fraternity on campus. Members worked as Big Brothers, providing company and role models for fatherless boys. They ran canned-food drives. They organized all-night camp-outs to draw attention to homelessness. They learned stepping acts—energetic evocations of military drill lines, Motown moves, and African ritual dancing—and performed these at elementary schools to gain students' attention so that the young people might listen to a message about studying and college.

Hiram pledged Phi Beta Sigma as a freshman, and in doing so became Phi Beta Sigma for life. He slept outside to draw attention to homelessness. Asked people for canned food. Learned to step.

Nearly four years later, after he had become a captain of the football team and was about to graduate, there would come a night when Hiram rubbed frozen hamburger over his left biceps. A fraternity brother bent a wire clothes hanger into the shape of the letter Σ and heated it on the burner of a stove. When Hiram gave the signal, a fraternity brother pushed the burning brand into Hiram's skin.

The sizzling flesh stank, but the pain lasted only a few seconds. Later, the wound leaked pus, but the work was done. In all the years to follow, that sigma-shaped worm of ash-dark skin would remind Hiram of how he meant to live. Culture for Service. Service for Humanity.

III

Joshua Hall recalled Canterbury Street in Hartford as a children's story, as a gliding bicycle with fluorescent streamers; a squirt gun filled from a garden hose; a kindling fire set in a garage by mischievous, curious boys and extinguished by an alert neighbor; tulips in May; cherry bombs in July; leaf piles in autumn. In his memory, Canterbury Street grownups leaned out of open screen doors to forever call boys and girls home.

He was born on that street, in that big yellow house with evergreen trees in a southern row.

No, that's not right.

But that's what he *told* people. Relatives. Friends. He said, "That's the house where I was born."

His mother would sometimes set the record straight.

As much as Joshua wanted to have been born in that two-story house, he had been born instead in the usual place, a hospital, and when Sonja Hall carried him home for the first time it was not to Canterbury either, but to a different house in another part of Hartford. It wasn't until Joshua was sixteen months old that the Halls moved to Canterbury Street. But for Joshua the distinction didn't matter. His truth remained that he never knew another home, and he felt Canterbury Street so deep inside him that the neighborhood might well have been born out of him.

A bicycle with streamers. Squirt guns. Distant voices calling him home.

His friends from tougher neighborhoods teased Joshua about living in "The Suburbs," but Joshua looked at Canterbury Street as an example of what Hartford was once and should be again: a place where parents held good jobs and children were safe when they played outside, where gentler rhythms guided life. What had ruined all those other streets (ruined Woodland and Mather, Oakland Terrace and Sanford) was an aberration. Canterbury Street sustained Hartford's true self. Anybody strolling downtown at night could see the sleepy and peaceful old soul of the city. No raucous clubs and shows, no sparkly nightlife of neon and perfumed young women and men showing off their shiny cars. For a lot of people—people like Joshua's older siblings—that sleepiness might have been a reason to leave Hartford for fire-breathing cities like Baltimore or Washington DC or Atlanta. But not for Joshua. Hartford's quiet nightlife only proved his vision of the city and filled him with nostalgic longing for its rebirth.

No wonder, then, that he chose to attend college in Norfolk, Virginia, a quiet, mid-sized city that sat across Chesapeake Bay from Newport News. Norfolk State's 120-acre campus wasn't ivy-covered old; most buildings sprawled with wings and corridors like corporate offices in a suburban business park, designed for use rather than beauty. In that way it was a practical campus. Maybe at first Joshua couldn't have said why he felt so comfortable in Norfolk. But later, while taking a course in urban geography, he listened to Dr. Jesse Pendleton—a long-time professor and the kind of man who would have owned a house on Canterbury Street—compare Norfolk and Hartford. Dr. Pendleton had studied urban geography at Clark University in Worcester, Massachusetts, and in the 1960s he'd often visited Hartford, a city of interest because of its efforts at urban renewal. Dr. Pendleton had heard stories that some of the people who led Hartford's urban redevelopment in the 1950s and the 1960s had eventually landed in Norfolk and plied their trade there. These were only stories, of

Connecticut, came to see about the rent, Buddy barked as if the dog smelled Yankee. Despite Buddy's manners, Derrick Walker took the room.

Short-sleeve days of sun and clean skies. People who smiled and chatted with strangers. Safe streets quiet enough to allow the work of songbirds to fill a young man's ears. What Hartford boy wouldn't love living in Petersburg, or spending time at Virginia State? Not even loneliness plagued Derrick, who happened to have family nearby. One of his brothers lived close enough for weekend visits, and that brother also owned a janitorial business. He hired Derrick to clean office buildings and gave Derrick a little spending cash. Good thing, too, because school bills demanded most everything Derrick had. Tuition, paying rent to Mavis, buying food, the quarters to clean his clothes at the local Laundromat . . . the whole package cost around ten thousand dollars a year. Student loans helped, and so did federal grants. His mother, who had retired as a nurse's aide, went back to work as a housekeeper at a hotel so she could help pay her son's college bills.

For two and a half years, Derrick worked his way through courses in vsu's Department of Engineering Technology, analyzing circuits, writing technical reports and working with electrical control systems. He took liberal arts classes, too, and math. He was learning to organize engineering projects, to manage workers, materials, and equipment.

But one day, in the middle of his second semester as a junior, Derrick answered a phone call at Mavis's house. The caller was a brother who still lived in Hartford with bad news about their mother. She had hurt her back at work. She's in a little pain, Vincent said. A few days later

Derrick got a second call from home. The little pain had grown into something worse. His mother needed back surgery. She needed to have two disks removed from her spine.

He caught a train right there in Petersburg, transferred in Richmond, and rode that train home to Hartford. A friend picked him up at the station.

When he first saw his mother he could tell by the cast of her face that she was suffering, and her expression struck him as a call for help, and he was glad to have come home. He stayed through her operation and even after that, helping around the house to prepare her meals and wash dishes and answer the phone when it rang and bring in the mail. He missed classes and more classes until he could miss no more. Then he kissed Moms and boarded a train at Hartford's Union Station for the trip back to Virginia. He needed to make up the work he had missed and take his final exams.

When the semester ended, he again boarded the train out of Petersburg for the eleven-hour trip to Hartford. Again he moved in with his mother. Her health had improved, but the recovery came slow. She still couldn't return to work. And that remained the case when Derrick returned for his senior year. He paid the bills he could, but without help from his mother the debts mounted. Food. Rent. Quarters for the Laundromat. He left school in October, unable to afford the luxury of education, and left Petersburg by train, and never returned to Mavis Cupid's house.

V

Oh, that long, tall triple jumper had beautiful teeth. Whoever that man was, his teeth made Carma Robinson gush.

In the stands at Odessa Junior College for the 1991 National Junior College Track and Field Championships, near the finish line, she stood with her father watching that man with the beautiful teeth.

How could anyone not notice him, wearing the jersey of Blinn Junior College, raising his arms over his head, trying to lift the crowd to its feet to applaud for him before he launched himself down the runway.

Arrogant man! Just like all those athletes from Blinn. Most arrogant track team in junior college. But look at his teeth!

He stood nearly a hundred yards away, and still she could see him smile. Carma Robinson ran the quarter-mile and sprints for the host team, for Odessa Junior College—not the most arrogant team, but their women were known as the best athletes and the best-looking women running junior college track in Texas. She was proud and smart and admittedly spoiled, and she had always preferred men with pretty, straight teeth.

Oh Daddy, she said, to her father who was standing beside her. I'm going to marry that man.

Who? said her father.

Him! She pointed.

You can't even see him, her father said.

But I see his teeth. I'm going to marry him.

Her father shrugged and with his camera snapped a picture of Harvey Kendall, though he did not yet know the jumper's name.

Nearly a year passed before Carma again saw that jumper from Blinn. Again it was at the national championships, but this time she noticed him at a party for the athletes. Carma was gabbing and laughing with girlfriends from her high school days who had made the trip to cheer for her. It was late in the evening, and she saw him resting against a stair rail. She hadn't forgotten him, and, being bold, she approached. She talked to him a little. He played it cool; Blinn had just won the national championship, and he affected the air of casual success. She flirted. Then she offered him a ride to the hotel where all the athletes were staying.

Naw, he said. Thanks. And turned his attention elsewhere.

"Just totally blew me off in front of my girlfriends," Carma recalled years later. "He just blew me off."

But Carma Robinson wasn't through with Harvey Kendall. She didn't know it, but she would get one more chance at the triple jumper with perfect teeth.

VI

Butch Braswell arrived at the Superior Court building the morning of Dec. 11, 1992, at about quarter to nine, his usual starting time as a special deputy sheriff. Butch's station stood near the rear of the second-floor lobby, and his responsibilities centered mostly on Courtroom 3B. As captain of the deputy sheriffs, he earned $110 a day to keep order in the court, escort prisoners back and forth to the lockup in the basement, answer questions from people passing through the lobby, and run errands for lawyers and judges. That morning he worked mostly youthful offender cases; things stayed busy a while, but during a quiet moment in the sheriff's booth, he opened the newspaper. About that time a small, soft-spoken woman approached. She wore dungarees and a jacket and a baseball cap, and she wanted to talk. She may have asked his name. Butch didn't know her, but the two spoke for a little while, then walked to the lawyer's lounge on that floor. The room was locked and intended for privacy; Butch punched in the code on the keypad beside the door, and then he and the woman stood alone in the brightly lit room.

She told him she wanted to deliver a package to an inmate who was coming to court that day, a prisoner named Gary Ortega. Butch told her he didn't know the name, but he and the woman returned to the lobby to check the day's docket. Not finding the man's name, Butch told her to wait, that he'd look around, and he left the second floor lobby.

He returned well over ten minutes later and said he couldn't find any Gary Ortega. He and the woman talked a while longer, then returned to the lawyer's lounge because she said she wanted again to talk in private. She said Ortega had told her to seek out Butch, to ask for him, that Butch would deliver the package. At some point while in the room, the woman showed Butch a green balloon, knotted at its neck, filled with something that gave it a little weight and heft. Butch said, "That's not my style," and turned to leave, put his hand on the door handle, had turned the handle, but she stopped him.

She reached into her jeans pocket. "He told me that he'd take care of you," she said.

"Take care of me?" Butch asked. "How is he going to take care of me? I have a family to support. Who is going to support my family? I don't do things like that."

She dug two twenties and a ten from the pocket and held out the money. Butch's demeanor changed. He came away from the door. Then she handed him the green balloon.

"You'll get this to Gary Ortega?" she said.

"Yeah," Butch said, and he took the money and the balloon.

More than a year later, the woman would testify in a courtroom in that same building that she told Butch as they left the lawyer's lounge that inside the green balloon was "a little coke." Her name was Regina Rush. She had been a trooper with the Connecticut State Police since 1987, though her encounter with Butch was her first undercover assignment.

That afternoon after Trooper Rush left Butch holding a green balloon, Butch left work early—around two o'clock—as he often did so he could be at Hartford Public promptly for the start of track practice.

VII

Two blocks east of Hartford Public was the intersection of Farmington Avenue and Laurel Street where, in a second-floor corner apartment, lived Sheri Venema, a Michigan native with swimmer's shoulders and a gray-white cat named Pequot. Years before, Sheri had broken away from the close-knit Dutch evangelical Christian community where she was raised and seemed now unable or unwilling to settle on another home. For her the world offered too many places to want just one. Her list of former addresses included zip codes in Baltimore and Minneapolis and Norwich, Connecticut, and now she worked as a bureau chief at the *Courant* and lived in Hartford. We met a year after I started working for the paper and began dating six months later. One day to come, she would agree to marry me.

Her building at Farmington and Laurel was called the Willoughby, a grand old gathering of apartments now converted to condominiums. Four stories high, its ground floor included a Chinese restaurant and the public library's Mark Twain branch. Inside, the Willoughby's elegant lobby offered wide, gently rising stairs, a vaulted ceiling and floors of polished stone. The elevator had an accordion gate and a sliding door with a windowpane etched in early twentieth-century flourishes. Sheri liked how her condo felt private at the end of its hallway, and also cosmopolitan in a way that cities do—cramped and spacious at the same time. The apartment had only one bedroom and a narrow kitchen, but light shined through tall windows, adding to the bustle and energy when she welcomed friends for a party or a Sunday brunch.

But in the early 1990s, Marshall Street, a short block from Sheri's condo and half the distance between the Willoughby and Hartford Public High School, had become one of the city's most notorious drug alleys. And its influence spilled beyond its sidewalks. The changes emerged over a year or two, obvious shifts in the psychology of the neighborhood, manifested in the day-to-day. A nearby drugstore bolted bars over its windows. Across the street at the Dunkin' Donuts parking lot, drug dealers—young men carrying walking canes as a sign of their trade—used the outside pay phone at all hours to set up buys.

One afternoon, in preparation for a few days vacation, Sheri had carried groceries and luggage downstairs to put in the trunk and backseat of her dented and scraped Nissan Sentra. Needing to make two trips, she locked the car's doors and headed upstairs for the second load. Up, down, and back again. But vacation had already ended. On the sidewalk and on the seat cushions of her car lay pebbles of window. Her bags were gone. First, a bite of anger as she swept glass out of the car onto the street; then a slow, fear-filled recognition. Someone had been watching. Someone had watched her and waited. A scavenger. A predator.

Now came handwritten signs from the Willoughby's condominium association taped beside the building's entrance warning against letting strangers inside. Each night coming home from work, Sheri hurried from her parking spot to the Willoughby's door where those signs hung. Working the locks required two hands. If she carried groceries, she put them down, opened a lock, picked up the groceries, stepped into a vestibule, then opened a second set of locking doors to reach the Willoughby lobby. Security applied to guests as well, who could no longer be buzzed in. They needed to call from the Dunkin' Donuts so that Sheri could come down to meet them.

Somehow danger found its way past all those precautions. Robberies of storage stalls and the coin-operated laundry machines in the basement made Sheri's trips downstairs eerie and threatening. One time Sheri listened as two men quarreled in the hallway outside her apartment, a fight that sounded to her like a drug deal gone bad. Later she learned one of the men had waved a pistol as he shouted.

The grand old Willoughby was no longer a home. Sheri lived in a fortress under siege.

two

On his deathbed he reached out for my hand

And he said we come from where we get the wound.

JAMES WHITEHEAD

"A Local Man Estimates What He Did for His Brother

Who Became a Poet and What His Brother Did for Him"

My grandfather sat up in bed, felt dizzy and decided to walk anyway. He collapsed a few steps from the bathroom, falling to the floor between the stair railing and the wall where his portrait hung. An artist had made the charcoal sketch when my grandfather was young, when he earned a few extra dollars as a model, his body shiny and hard as glass. He lifted barbells then, in competition with a team from the Hartford YMCA. He had a dimpled chin and dark hair that swept back off his forehead, a face of straight lines, each in proportion. A noble Polish face. That was the face in the portrait. Now Walter Petry lay on the floor, ninety years behind him. The skin on his scalp was spotted from age, his few strands of white hair wild and uncombed after sleep. Without his eyeglasses he looked a bit like a frantic mole. For more than a day, my grandfather had seen the blood he left in the toilet. He didn't know this meant the inside of his stomach was bleeding. He didn't know that pills intended to prevent another stroke had thinned his blood enough to leak through his tissues and that he had lost too much. He only knew that he was

dizzy, that he needed the bathroom, that he was lying in the hall-
way, that his wife, whom he depended on, lay in the bed beside
his, in the room they had shared for nearly forty of their sixty
years together.

Now, in the hallway, my grandmother tried to lift her husband,
to wake him. She tugged at him. He slipped from her hands, and
she jerked into the railing. Her arm scraped against the banis-
ter; her paper-skin broke. Outside on Maple Avenue, streetlights
shined over indifferent sidewalks.

She huddled beside him in that small space on the second floor
of their big, gray house. There was a time when Judy and Barbara
slept in that room there, and Paul slept in that corner bedroom,
the family together on one floor, and if they all stood in the door-
ways of their rooms they could talk without raising their voices.
They could talk even in whispers, they lived so close. Now Arizona,
Florida, and Boston are all too far. Paul slept in that corner bed-
room. Judy and Barbara slept in that room there, with the navy
pillowcases and the glass-topped dresser.

This is what a life amounts to. A dark April night, a too-bright
ceiling light casting silhouette shadows around her fallen hus-
band, blood smeared on her arm. A house made for children. The
children gone. Age alone. Nothing but age.

5

I

Sitting on my grandparents' front porch, I look out into the yellow Hartford night, lit by streetlights and headlights and the city's halo reflected back off the clouds. It's warm, but I've opened the porch windows to let in the breeze and the traffic noise. Sometimes the traffic is a car. Sometimes, an ambulance. Sometimes it is one of dozens of men who ride shopping carts down the street, returning home from the all-hours supermarket where they have redeemed carts full of cans and bottles for the nickel deposit on each. Across the street from my grandparents' house, cloaked by oak trees and maples, Goodwin Park is shadowy. Tomorrow's sunshine will burn off mist to reveal the park's fairways and putting greens and bruised May grass; duffers will wheel golf bags around the flat, nine-hole public course. But at night, the park is a place for anything that requires the absence of light, and we on Maple Avenue must consider it dangerous.

The porch door is shut and locked three times with

chains and bolts. The screen door is heavy steel and locked, too. I sit on an old outdoor chaise longue. Its pillows smell dusty, as if they need a good beating. But I like the smell; it reminds me of a withered paperback with brown-edged pages.

Upstairs my grandmother lies in bed watching David Letterman's show. The volume is loud; the volume is always loud, and I hear clearly Dave's jokes. When my grandmother can't sleep, she watches TV, but it's not her favorite thing to do. The TV serves as a bridge between meals and crossword puzzles and the many chores she insists on still doing.

It's midnight. The phones ring—upstairs and down. I start, but before I can even jump out of my chair, she's answered the phone by her bed. I know who is calling. He calls all the time now.

She yells at him.

No, Walt! You have to stay there. I can't take care of you. I love you, honey, but you have to stop calling me! Don't make yourself unhappy. You're not coming home! All right?

Then it's quiet again except for the TV and the occasional headlong car. It's the year 2000, and my grandfather asks now and then if he has reached one hundred yet, but no, that will take another decade. Let's worry about now, we tell him. You've got to get well to come home.

He isn't so far away. The Mediplex is only a five-minute drive, a twenty-minute walk. He walked farther to his office when he worked as an accountant for the state government. But now my grandfather can't walk. Something happened that night when he fainted, and he has lost strength in his legs. At the Mediplex, in a room with chairs molded from flashy red and blue plastic, men in white tunics and pants spend an hour a day teaching my grandfather to walk again. The rest of the time he lies in a strange bed in a strange place; he shares his room with a man with a broken back who curses and complains from breakfast to lights out. I visit my grandfather every day, bring him clean underwear, speak with him using the little Polish I know, trying to help him grope through his spotty memory to recover a language he once spoke fluently. On his bed stand is a half-pint carton of milk with a straw, a pitcher for him to urinate in, and a telephone. Sometimes I wheel him around the halls of the Mediplex; we sing along with Bobby Vinton on the Mediplex jukebox ("*Moja droga jacie kocham*, means that I love you so!"), and I steer him toward glass doors so he can see that world outside where hydrangeas and dogwoods bloom. The scenery doesn't cheer him. "It's a beautiful green day," I said one afternoon. He said, "It's too bad we have to spend it among such decrepitude."

He telephones the house during *Murder, She Wrote*; he calls after lunch; he calls while my grandmother sits in her chair next to the record player listening as Zero Mostel's Tevye sings "Ya ha deedle deedle, bubba bubba deedle deedle dum." He calls and five minutes later calls again. Sometimes Grandma lets me take care of Grandpa's calls. Other times she wants to talk to him. Sometimes she's gentle; others she's harsh.

Because I know the strokes damaged his memory, I can believe that he forgets he has just called. But sometimes I wonder. Sometimes I suspect Grandpa knows he can't come home, but the wanting is so intense he can't keep himself from picking up the phone. He imagines himself in his recliner waiting for a Red Sox game. He smells roasted chicken wafting from his wife's kitchen. From his porch he tracks chattering squirrels that chase each other through springtime maples. His heart still beats inside those wallpapered rooms on Maple Avenue, but what he sees are chairs the colors of children's toys and disinfected linoleum floors. The contradiction is maddening.

The phone rings. "Get me the hell out of here," he says.

When I visit Grandpa one afternoon, he asks whether my interviews went well. This is a good sign. He remembers that I don't live in Hartford anymore, that I moved away and am only back to work on a book. Days and evenings I study government records and old newspaper clips, tour Hartford Public, chat with Jack LaPlante, search for Butch Braswell. But now I live elsewhere: in Montana, in the Bitterroot River Valley, on a dirt road not too far from a creek. I live there with Sheri, who is now my wife, in a log house we rent that comes with a donkey and a barn and a cat named Larry Bird. Morning sun shines west past the house to the craggy Bitterroot Mountains, so close you can count pine trees on a slope, so massive it would take more than a day to hike to the nearest peak. The neighbors are reserved, polite folk. Their kids ride four-wheel all-terrain ground-churning cycles up and down the road. Sometimes they ride horses. The neighbors don't talk to us much, as if there's no reason to get too friendly with renters who won't stay.

It is a beautiful place. People tell us so, and we know so. We enjoy it, though it is temporary. Maybe we enjoy it more because it is temporary. My wife, in particular, loves to sit outside at night in an Adirondack chair, sip a gin and tonic and watch the quiet sun light up the Sapphire Mountains to the east. We listen to the creek gulp and burble. We eat the apples that come off the trees in the meadow. The deer eat the windfalls, and the donkey, whose name is Annie, eats them, too.

In my grandparents' house, the phone rings.
Ring ring. Ring ring.
The Bells of Maple Avenue.

My grandfather loves company. He's always been a flirt and a ham, and a visitor means an audience, a party, a chance to be impressed by what talents people bring into his house and a chance for him to sing a song about Christopher Columbus or to tell a joke ("When is a woman like a mirror? When she's a good looking lass!"). He hears a knock at the kitchen door, and he rises from his recliner, preparing to make his entrance, stage right, and whooping: "Whodat? Whodat?"

At the Mediplex, he's glad to have guests, but he can't rise to meet them. He's wired with an alarm system that alerts the nurses should he get out of bed. He's tried too many times to wander off, to sneak away.

At Maple Avenue, the phone rings.
Whodat? Whodat?

II

Here is why I left Hartford.

In the Willoughby, in her condominium, Sheri hung near her coat closet a framed poster of a Montana sunset, red and fiery over mountains. In Michigan she had grown up watching weather drive across a great lake. Grand, open nature thrilled her. On vacations in Montana, she had steered a rental car through the alpine country of Glacier National Park and her heart expanded. Mountains. Great plains rolling to the horizon. Rivers wide and slow. She sensed opportunity. The Montana sky, so big, allowed everything.

Yes, we fell in love in Hartford and took advantage of what pastimes could be found there. Good pizza. Movies. Concerts and plays. But we'd also leave: down to the shoreline beaches, to the woods of Vermont, to a cabin on a river in Pennsylvania. Sheri was always most comfortable on those trips somewhere else, and exalted above all the somewhere elses was Montana—the Big Sky Country that threatened to lure her away from the Insurance City.

Sometimes it seemed Hartford wasn't trying to keep her, that the city wanted to drive Sheri—and so many others—away.

A real estate boom, fueled in large part by speculation, had collapsed. At about the same time, the city government revalued all property, leading to sky-high tax increases on land and buildings that were losing their value. Bankrupt landlords abandoned their buildings, adding to the disinvestment so familiar to Hiram Harrington and his father. Worse, in the early nineties, crack had helped fuel a culture of violence that pervaded nearly all corners of the city until Hartford's murder rate flared—from fourteen murders in 1992 to thirty-four the next year.

> A Hartford teenager was killed and his twenty-nine-year-old nephew wounded by gunfire as they argued Monday night with two other young men in a dark corner of a parking lot off Marshall Street and Farmington Avenue.
>
> HARTFORD COURANT, DEC. 31, 1991

I don't know where Sheri was that December 30 when seventeen-year-old Melvin Kardulis had his heart and lungs

138

ripped by bullets from a semiautomatic pistol following an argument a short block from the Willoughby. It was dark then, about seven o'clock. She might still have been in the *Courant* newsroom answering an editor's questions, or maybe she and I were out for dinner.

Melvin Kardulis had been her neighbor, in a manner of speaking. He lived in an apartment at 360 Laurel Avenue, just a few buildings north of the Willoughby. But Sheri didn't know him until she saw his name in the newspaper on that last day of the year.

The final few minutes of Melvin's life began when he and his uncle, not his nephew as the *Courant* had first reported, walked down Farmington Avenue to pick up a few things at a convenience store. Inside were some young men, including sixteen-year-old Ronald Walton, who played at a video game when the Kardulises pushed open the glass doors and stepped inside.

Melvin's uncle got into an argument with someone in the store, a friend of Ronald Walton's. The *Courant* called it a "petty fight," but its momentum carried outside into a dark corner of the parking lot. Loud voices. Shoving. Later, witnesses would say Melvin's uncle pulled out a paring knife. Ronald Walton's response was to draw a semiautomatic handgun given him by a friend that morning, and then to empty the clip.

Someone brought Melvin's body to the hospital, but too late. Ronald Walton spent the night, the newspaper later reported, crying in his mother's arms. He turned himself in the next morning. Months later in court a state prosecutor would paint Walton as a menace who, the newspaper reported the lawyer saying, "had dropped out of school, fathered two children, and been deemed a juvenile delinquent by the courts four times." He was found guilty of Melvin Kardulis's killing and sentenced to thirty-three years, more than twice as many as the sixteen he had lived.

Melvin Kardulis hadn't lived the easiest life, either. His mother was single, and he had been raised mostly by relatives in Tennessee and Massachusetts and Hartford. But he'd turned to art rather than violence. A senior at Weaver High School when he was killed, Kardulis had already received a scholarship to an art school in Georgia. Friends and teachers talked about him the way teachers at Hartford Public would have remembered Eric or Derrick, Harvey, Hiram or Joshua if any of them had suffered the same fate. They called Melvin a good kid, the kind you wouldn't expect to get killed, the kind who walked away from trouble. One of his teachers told the *Courant*: "I would have liked to have seen him grow up as a man, because he would have made a big difference in this world. He stood for right and wrong."

The city celebrated him after his death. His artwork found new homes on banners throughout downtown. His work received a posthumous showing at a gallery near Bushnell Park. He was an unintentional martyr, one of Hartford's many. Kevin Hicks had been another. Aquan Salmon, too. Their names would keep coming. Gary Little, a seventeen-year-old shot while playing chess in his backyard. Takira Gaston, a seven-year-old who survived having her face blown apart by a stray bullet fired during a shootout between rival dealers. James Washington, a seventy-year-old candy shop owner, killed for the dollars in his till. These were people whose suffering or death would inspire marches and protests and angry editorials but little significant change. The latest outrage, a weary reporter friend of mine once called it.

When Melvin Kardulis was killed, his was the second homicide in two weeks in that block of Marshall Street. When Sheri saw Melvin Kardulis's picture in the paper, she saw a good-looking kid who had none of the trappings of a punk, and she felt sad. When she saw *where* he had been killed, she thought, Oh my God.

At home, Sheri lived with the city's daily failures. At work, she confronted the causes. She had switched jobs: from bureau chief to reporter covering Hartford's efforts to invigorate its economy, to make the city livable again. But there were no victories to write about. Instead Sheri uncovered waste and fraud and bickering among those charged with making the city better. New ideas to improve Hartford seemed silly or impotent: Hartford residents discussing a "vision" of what their city could be; red-shirted guides offering directions to what few tourists visited downtown, a futile quest for a convention center years after the convention-center boom had hit other cities. Band-Aids on shark bites.

After a while she could envision nothing better. Not at the Willoughby. Not in Hartford. The city was like an airplane in a death spiral with its passengers busy trying to steal each other's luggage. She needed to get away. Shortly after Melvin Kardulis's murder, we asked the *Courant* to grant us leaves of absence.

We spent the summer in that cabin on the Delaware River in Pennsylvania. In the mornings we let the riffle of water over rock wake us. Over coffee, we might see a heron arise from tall grass along the banks and glide over the river. We trimmed tree branches and raked years of pine needles out of flower beds. We pulled old tires out of the river's silt. Our garden yielded carrots and cilantro and basil. We walked barefoot to favorite swimming holes. Sometimes, if we were only leaving the cabin for a half-hour or so, we left the doors unlocked. Water, light, and air worked their magic.

Our leaves of absence were to end in August. Because I loved the city, Sheri said she would consider living again in Hartford, but she refused to return to the Willoughby. She had escaped; nothing could force her back. We talked about some other place, maybe in West Hartford. She talked about Montana. On a whim she phoned a journalism school at a university there, which it turned out had an opening. One class, one semester, three thousand dollars. That's all the dean could promise. It was enough.

When Sheri told me she was moving to Montana, I didn't think of Harvey Kendall and his friends or what I might have owed Hartford. I didn't even consider my grandparents, and my grandfather, who—only four months before—had suffered his first stroke. Sheri was leaving. I loved her. It was an obvious choice. Heart full and heartless, I looked forward to great adventure and did not give a thought to what or whom I might leave behind. Sheri left on August 28, 1992, flying out of Hartford on a cloudy day. I followed in a rented moving van less than a month later.

In Montana I found a newspaper job. The university hired Sheri for a second semester, then a third. She tried to rent her condo from Montana, but with the collapse of the market, she couldn't charge enough to pay the mortgage. She surrendered the property to the bank in lieu of foreclosure. A decade later, a reporter at the *Courant* would write how a condo in the Willoughby—what Sheri had bought in 1988 for sixty-two thousand dollars—was

tween her work schedule and the expense of travel, her visits were yearly at best. When she and I talked about my grandparents, she was sometimes angry and other times sad. Sometimes she was only resigned. She once suggested to my grandparents that they move to Tucson and buy a condo or take an apartment. But they wanted to stay in Hartford. They refused to give up the paths in the carpet they'd worn over decades at the same address. Besides, there was something in my grandmother that believed someone in her family should have stayed close by and cared for her the way she and her sisters and brother saw her own mother through her final years and days.

When, during our Montana-to-Hartford phone conversation, my grandmother places that burden on her children, I want to defend them. I know I don't need to, but I've moved away, too, and I share the sting of her accusation.

"Great-Grandma left her mother in Poland," I say. It's stupid to bring this up, even cruel, though it is true. My great-grandmother, my grandmother's mother, whose name was Barbara, abandoned her own mother in Poland. I don't mean to say that because my great-grandmother abandoned her mother that it's okay for children to leave parents behind. I only want to remind Grandma of her mother's story because I want her to understand that life presents us with complicated choices—stay or go? past or future?—and unwanted consequences. Nearly two thousand miles from Hartford, I think often about those choices. Inevitably I remember Eric and Derrick, Harvey, Hiram and Joshua and their pledge, and I wonder how they fared. How did they answer the questions: to stay away or go back to Hartford, to return to the past or choose some unexplored future? If they went home, what in Hartford enticed them after their college years when—educated, enlightened—a whole world awaited them? Would a teenage promise suffice?

But my grandmother is still on the phone, and she does not know these young men.

So I say to her, Think of Hartford, Grandma, and what little it offers your children and theirs. Then think of Poland and what it offered your mother. A small village of peasant farmers. No family except her own mother, illiterate, without property, sharing a room with day renters.

"Her mother died young," Grandma says.

I don't know what to make of this. Perhaps Grandma means to say that Barbara Fedor left Poland when her mother was still young enough to need no help, and then her mother, fortuitously, died before old age brought its misery. Or perhaps Grandma means that Barbara's mother died before Barbara left Poland; her death might have even given Barbara a reason to leave. The implication: Barbara would have stayed in her native land had her own mother lived.

If the latter, my grandmother ignores her own family history, an act of which she is capable. She might deny this, but when it comes to passing on family lore, my grandmother is a sentimentalist. The only family stories that concern her are those that reveal nobility and successful struggles. She tells these tales again and again, repeating the easy truths, often ignoring the implicit, aggravating questions, until those easy truths become tombs, the questions buried inside of the certainty. My grandmother relates the facts as they fit her worldview, something we're all guilty of. So, in my grandmother's version of history, her mother made a clean break from her grim life as the poorest of peasants among peasants. She left no one behind.

I'm sorry, Grandma, but on this you are mistaken.

Moreover, Barbara Fedor abandoned her mother twice.

The first parting came in 1903. Barbara Fedor was sixteen when she left Królik Polski, a small village in southeastern Poland. Then, it was part of a region called Galicia that extended into what we now call Ukraine, and Galicia was ruled by the Austro-Hungarian Empire. Family stories say little about Barbara's childhood, though there are suggestions that she was not born in Królik Polski, that her mother arrived one day without a past, without a husband, with only a girl that was her daughter. In family stories, there is never a mention of Barbara's father. Some in the family say Barbara was born out of wedlock.

When Barbara left Królik Polski, it was because her mother, Maria Fedor, could not afford a dowry so that Barbara could marry. Instead Barbara followed the immigrant path, stepping off the S.S. Rotterdam into a line at Ellis Island. She could neither read nor write, and if she spoke English it was a few words, but she had six dollars, and she knew others from Królik Polski who had settled in Connecticut and found work at textile factories. In Willimantic she found those factories and some village neighbors including Jan Urbanik, a teenage boy who enjoyed fancy clothes and fast polkas and who, in America, was called John. They married in St. Joseph's Roman Catholic Church in Willimantic on Sept. 28, 1907.

I have a copy of their wedding picture here as I write this. My great-grandparents sit side-by-side, stiff and rigid in the manner of the day, as the camera slowly remembers them. John Urbanik wears a dark suit with vest and light-colored shirt and tie, and he holds a cigar between the fingers of his right hand. By his expression (unruffled, a little eager), he welcomes the camera. On his right, his bride, my great-grandmother: dark-haired, slim, with a long neck and slight shoulders. She holds a bouquet on her lap; in her other hand, she holds a bit of lace. Her dress is high-collared, and her thick hair is in a bun atop a pillow of hair in the Gibson Girl style, and the hair halos her face. She stares not at the camera, but into the middle distance, seemingly seeing nothing, as if stunned by shock or exhaustion. In the photograph, Barbara Fedor Urbanik is surrounded by acquaintances and in-laws (John's brothers and sister and cousins), but not by any blood relations of her own.

A few months after the wedding, Barbara, fulfilling Roman Catholic expectations, became pregnant. And here is the decision, the shift I cannot understand, the why of which I can do nothing with but speculate. Barbara, family lore tells us, was an exceedingly practical woman of the sort who would buy gray cloth rather than purple if gray were a penny less. Staying and giving birth in the new country would have cost less and been safer than a trip across the Atlantic Ocean and back to Poland, but there the family went. Leaving jobs, leaving friends. John, Barbara, and the little life inside her, barely a pulse. Pushed by something (that pulse?) that compelled Barbara beyond pragmatism and into a need for home.

In Poland, in Królik Polski, in her mother-in-law's cottage (not her own mother's rented room), Barbara gave birth to her daughter, Angela. Family records don't say how long John Urbanik stayed in Poland with his wife and daughter. He was a romantic, though, the cigar-puffing sentimentalist in the couple. It is likely he lingered until the last possible moment, wanting to keep breathing in his daughter's smell, wanting to nuzzle his wife's neck one more time, and then again. But he was only delaying the inevitable. I don't know why he returned to America without his family. Perhaps it was their plan. Or maybe they miscalculated the train fare. Whatever the reason, after his daughter's birth John had only enough money for one traveler's journey back to America. So he crossed the Atlantic once more, one last time—and this time alone. *Bóg dał. Bóg wziął*, the old people used to say. God gives. God takes. In Hartford's factories John would trade sweat for the cash that could bring his wife and child back to him.

Their separation would last nearly four years.

In that time his daughter Angela learned to walk and speak Polish and eat what was on her plate. In the evenings her mother and grandmothers may have entertained her with fairy tales, like the story of wicked King Popiel who was eaten by mice, or of Queen Wanda who drowned herself in the Vistula River rather than marry a German and sacrifice her country and its people. Barbara became stout and firm with a straight back and fingernails clipped short for work in a village of farmers. She and Angela lived in the cottage with John's mother, Apollonia. They lived their village life.

Then one day, the money arrived to send them home, to take them away from home.

I have never visited Królik Polski, but I have seen pictures as it is today. I imagine it hasn't changed much since the time of my great grandmother's young motherhood. There isn't any neon. The roads have no painted lines or curbs; their macadam edges end in dirt or grass or weeds. But it is no drab town. A church that survived the two World Wars is cocoa brown with a white roof. Fences are painted sky blue and the housetops are red. Leafy trees crowd the town's valley. Perhaps in Barbara Fedor Urbanik's time the village lacked electricity and the roads were unpaved. I suppose some of the buildings I see now are new, replacing those destroyed in the wars. But they look intended to replicate the past, as unlike the twenty-first century as oil lamps.

According to local history, Królik Polski from 1908 to 1912 (the years Barbara lived apart from her husband) was a discontented place. Villagers called their town Królik *Polski* to identify it as part of Poland, a nationalistic stance against Austro-Hungarian dominance. A small, secret militia—the Troops of Bartosz—stood ready should there ever be a battle for independence. Barbara Urbanik must have known of these tensions. The town was too small to conceal them. She must have suspected that by leaving she would escape imminent violence. Nationalists around Europe were cleaning and oiling the rifles they would fire in World War I.

Barbara had to choose. The old world and her mother and Apollonia; the new world and her husband. I suspect she wanted both old and new, stuck as she was in that jarring jumble that came from belonging now to two worlds. It was a terrible choice. An obvious choice, really, which made the consequences even more unbearable.

A little over two years after Barbara returned to Connecticut, World War I began, pitting the Germans and Austro-Hungarians against the Russians on the war's Eastern Front. Armies marched across Galicia, and their battles destroyed parts of Królik Polski. It seems likely that Barbara and John suffered the days of the war in helpless ignorance, not knowing whether their mothers in Poland lived or died.

At least Apollonia survived. In the years between the wars, Barbara and John sent her money. Family legend has it that Apollonia always spent her American dollars on a big feast, inviting everyone she knew in Królik Polski for a blow-out party. From her, only one piece of correspondence remains: a photograph. In the picture Apollonia sits in a wood-floored room that is spare except for a few rattan chairs. In her lap she holds a flower and her rosary. She looks nervous and excited to be facing this amazing machine, this camera; her eyes are round and bright. She is small-faced, with tiny nose and mouth, but with fingers twisted and thick like roots. On the photo is a message in Polish. The sentences lack punctuation, the spelling is poor, the grammar shows a lack of education. My family believes that Apollonia wrote it, but perhaps it was a transcription from someone else's hand. Nevertheless it is her message, and in translation her belief in photography's magic, as well as her desire to exist in two places, becomes clear.

"Here is your mother, my children. I am coming to you. Let what will be, be to the praise of Jesus Christ."

As for Maria Fedor, no picture—if there ever was one—remains. I know nothing of her life after Barbara left, nor of her death. Barbara never spoke of her mother.

She lived a long time, Barbara Fedor, my great-grandmother. When I was a boy, she was the oldest person I could imagine. None of my friends had relatives so old. I thrilled to know her, the way I thrilled at the tall ships docked at Mystic Seaport or the Colonial-era millstone in Connecticut's Gay City State Park. She was history, and she was enigmatic without being frightening. She still spoke only a few words of English, with an accent, and she made a sweet bread we ate every Easter. She wore eyeglasses and kept her hair in a loose permanent; she was fond of earrings and detested her girdle. She was fat in a way a great-grandchild would find pleasant: soft and warm and all-encompassing with her hugs. She lived to see her ninetieth birthday but never returned to Poland.

She died in 1978, her children there to hold her hand. It was February; a blizzard covered the ground in snow and froze the earth. Weeks passed before anyone could dig the grave.

It has been years since Helen Petry, my grandmother, visited her parents' burial plots in Mount St. Benedict's Cemetery in Hartford's North End. She doesn't see the point. Mama and Papa aren't there, she says. Their bodies are dust.

Instead she looks at their pictures in frames around her house. She says she dreams of them at night.

IV

In Montana I tried to write my grandparents at least once a month. My grandfather, always the more literary of the pair, usually wrote back, though as he suffered more strokes the letters lost vigor. His handwriting deteriorated and, whereas he used to tell stories, now he resorted to lists of what happened today and what would happen tomorrow, of food they had eaten. Eventually he stopped writing.

We stayed in touch with Hartford friends, mostly reporters, who kept us informed of the city's struggles, and I visited for weddings, anniversaries, business, for any reason, really. I missed Hartford more than I expected. Having regained it in adulthood, after all those years away, I found I regretted giving it up.

On visits back, I'd stay with my grandparents. I washed their car and pulled weed-maples out of the yard. Once I washed the outside windows. Another time I rubbed clean their telephone and reprogrammed its memory with the new numbers of people who had moved, like me, so my grandparents could call family by touching a button. I took them shopping and to the bank, and I planted marigolds in the old tire-pot near the garage. Now and then I'd drive through my old neighborhood, down Curtiss Street where I had once lived above a great aunt. She had since moved out of Hartford, and the house had sold. Now it was wrecked, the front door dislodged from its hinges, the hedges withering, windows broken.

Each time I visited, things seemed worse. My grandmother, who had battled Crohn's disease for decades, kept losing weight. Grandpa lost more of his memory. Though he had worked as an accountant, he could no longer balance a checkbook. She became the brain, he became the body. She was too weak to lift a bag of potatoes, but she could tell him which bag she wanted. He could collect the newspaper from the front stoop each morning, but she had to pay the bill.

VI

When in an art museum I first saw the Burghers of Calais, a sculpture by Auguste Rodin, his figures held me longer than any other exhibit, perhaps for an hour. I didn't know why but later realized that the figures and the story behind them reminded me of Harvey Kendall and his friends. Six-and-a-half centuries separated them, but like Harvey and the others, Calais' burghers had offered their lives to help their broken city survive. Not only that, but

Rodin's sculpture reflected better than youthful idealism the reality such a sacrifice might demand.

In 1347 King Edward III of England and his army surrounded the French port city of Calais and began a siege that lasted more than a year. The people of Calais ate every bite of food they had, then survived by eating rats, then their own feces. Many went mad. Finally the town council decided to surrender. But the siege had exhausted the wisp of good will Edward III might have felt for Calais. Through harsh summer and sloppy cold winter he had been forced to camp with his troops outside the city. Edward wanted to punish Calais and humiliate it. As recalled by the fourteenth-century French historian, Jean Froissart, Edward would accept the surrender only if six of Calais' wealthiest men would "leave their city, stripped, with ropes around their necks and the keys in their hands, and with them I shall do what I please."

In Calais' town hall, Froissart tells us, people wept. How would the city's most affluent burghers respond? None spoke for a long time. Then, Eustache de Saint-Pierre, the wealthiest property owner in the city, stood. According to Froissart, de Saint-Pierre looked around at his neighbors, at the town's priests and blacksmiths, at wives and children. "It would be a terrible pity," he said, "to let such a people as these die." Somehow his words won over the other burghers, or shamed them. So the six walked through Calais' gates, wearing little but the nooses around their necks and bringing Edward the city's keys. Edward ordered the men decapitated.

When latter-day city fathers of Calais commissioned Rodin to recreate the burghers, they expected he would deliver heroic figures, Calais' pride striding toward dark fate with courage, martyrs ennobled by self-sacrifice. But Rodin made something else.

In his sculpture heroism is awful. Look at these men. Barefoot. Stripped to robes. Finding no relief in their fellowship, no courage from sharing a fate. Though they stand together, each man is alone. One cowers, hands slapped against his head, so crippled by fear that someone else must have placed that rope around his neck. And here is another, long-haired and young-faced. His fellow burghers move forward toward Edward's camp, yet he turns to them, his arms spread as if in supplication. Another burgher raises his arm to cover his eyes, unwilling to see what awaits. Even Eustache de Saint Pierre, who offered to be the first stripped because he believed God would reward his sacrifice, even he is flat-footed, head lowered, forsaken.

Only one looks ahead toward Edward and his troops. Jean d'Aire keeps his head upright, his back straight, his mouth a firm frown. The knot of the noose sits on his right shoulder, and his hands hang at his waist; he carries the keys. He is ready to give himself. He knows what he does for the city he loves, for his wife and children left behind. But given his presence of mind—the awareness that comes with acceptance—he alone among the burghers knows that the mathematics of sacrifice can never be calculated. Edward said he would trade six lives for a city, but Jean d'Aire understands that there is no guarantee. The English king might yet kill Calais' hostage burghers and still destroy the city. Jean d'Aire gives his neck with as much dignity as a doomed man can muster. But somewhere, in his most quiet self, is he strangling his soul's lament: Why didn't we flee? Why didn't we run to Paris?

154

Imagine, then, a sculpture of the five friends who promised their lives to Hartford.

Would they walk as one? Or would some turn from the city while others hurried home? It seemed unlikely that Hartford would ask them for their lives as Calais asked its burghers. But it could. The city would require some price. Their children? What confusion would play across Harvey's face as he sent his boys to play in the streets near where he grew up? Would we see Derrick turned away from the city, his attention elsewhere, but always looking back? Whose face would show the satisfaction of an oath fulfilled? Whose silent lamentation would we witness? How would their stories end?

In Calais the story ended this way:

Edward's queen, pregnant at the time, kneeled before her husband to beg mercy for the burghers and Calais. Edward granted it.

Five centuries later, when Rodin presented his finished sculpture to the city, he did so with instructions to install the statue at ground level. Instead the people of Calais placed their six burghers high on a pedestal, demanding once again that they surrender their humanity to become heroes.

VII

I'm sitting on my grandparents' porch, reading e-mails from my wife. She knows that in Montana I miss Hartford. In her e-mail Sheri asks if I would one day like to live in my grandparents' home.

Would I? I would love to.

"I'd have to think long and hard and talk with you long and hard about the wisdom of such a move," I write back. "So yes, I'm thinking about it."

I'm on my grandparents' porch because I love them, and because I have a book to write. The book is about Hartford and about five young men and their pledge, and it's about my grandparents and it's about me. It's about a mystery. How do you solve for x in the insolvable equations of sacrifice? How do you balance hope against regret? "Too long a sacrifice can make a stone of the heart," goes Yeats's famous line. Excess of love, he suggests, can bewilder us so that we sacrifice our fortunes, our futures, our lives, even our capacities to love, for the thing (or person, or place) we love. How do Harvey Kendall and his friends promise themselves to their city, not knowing what it might demand of them? What excess of love led Calais' burghers to tug off their robes and bare their necks? And what if it is also love that compels us to leave our troubled places—as Barbara Urbanik left Poland—never to return? How, then, do you make peace with those you love and nevertheless abandon? Write letters? Send money? Do you ignore them? Do you wait for them to die? When do they stop haunting you?

I visit Hartford. I return to Montana. I visit. I return. Where I am a visitor and where I am home become confused, and when introduced to people at parties I can't answer when they ask where I'm from.

My grandfather's mind slows. My grandmother gets sicker, a little better, then sicker again. Her calves and ankles swell, and the doctor prescribes a diuretic; we know that means congestive heart failure. She can't put on weight no matter how much she eats. At eighty-nine she now has more years than pounds. The decline of her health forces her into the hospital, and she stays for weeks. All her children return to Connecticut in shifts to care for their father. They do not tell him where his wife is. He does not ask. One night, confused and lost, he asks my aunt to sleep next to him in my grandmother's bed. Gently she tells him it's better that he sleep alone.

But my mother, my uncle, and my aunt can't ever stay long, so they hire two Polish immigrant women, one for the day and the other to stay in the house overnight. Neither speaks much English. My grandfather goes about his business as these women—like friendly, quiet ghosts—move through his house, putting things in order, cooking his meals.

My grandmother comes home from the hospital. Now she goes back. There is a hole in her heart. Or her breathing is labored. Blood work. Steroids. She suffers a mild stroke. All she wants is Maple Avenue, her armchair, her crossword puzzles, Goodwin Park across the street, the locks and deadbolts on her doors.

One Montana evening, I come home from work to find the light blinking on our answering machine. We have one message. The machine's voice announces: "Friday, 2:37 p.m."

The first sound is indistinguishable. I'm not sure what he's saying, but it's my grandfather's voice. Then a confused, helpless pause.

"Oh. I don't seem to . . ."

Breathing.

"Michael Downs?"

three

"But what will they do under the artillery when I was told to leave because of the artillery?"

"Did you leave the cage unlocked?" I asked.

"Yes."

"Then they'll fly."

"Yes, certainly they'll fly. But the others. It's better not to think of the others," he said.

ERNEST HEMINGWAY
"Old Man at the Bridge"

6

Harvey Kendall stared at his mother's TV, words coming cold from the evening news, like slaps to his face.

Deputy sheriff . . . arrested . . . drugs . . . Melvin D. Braswell . . .

Melvin D. Braswell? Butch?

Something in Harvey's chest reared at the news—his heart stopping or speeding, who knew which?

Butch? he thought. They're crazy!

It was January 5, 1993. Harvey was halfway through college, but back in Connecticut on a yearlong break to earn some money and to rest his weary legs. The basketball season before, he'd fallen in practice and banged his left knee. Treatment backfired and an infection spread through the joint. Worse, to compensate for the weakness in his left knee he worked the right one harder; that led to tendinitis. By the end of his sophomore year at Blinn, Harvey was tired, worn out, depressed, and in retreat. Not beaten, just recouping his strength, making a cocoon of his mother's new house in Windsor, the town just north of Hartford

161

where she had moved to escape Oakland Terrace ("Every night, you're hearing gunshots," she had told him. "You don't know if something's going to come through the house.").

Man! How can they lie on TV like that?

Harvey's feet led him to his bedroom, to the window, then into the hallway, back to the bedroom. He called Butch's house, but the phone rang and rang.

Craziness. Just craziness. Butch couldn't—

He wanted to cry, but—and this is how messed up things had become—he couldn't even do that. Just turn and move and move and turn and wait for someone to take back the words, explain the mistake, fix the world.

Harvey had aged in his two years away, and the aging depressed him. It wasn't just his legs, old before their time; it was the wisdom he'd gained out there beyond Hartford. He'd always imagined that life was better beyond the city, but now he knew: things were better, things were worse. His mother understood that, of course, she who'd grown up in Georgia in the bad days before *Brown v. Board of Education*, before Martin Luther King Jr., before Malcolm X, when lynching was still a popular Southern response to the black man. When Harvey first left for Texas his mother had warned him to stay away from trouble. "They put people to death down there," she told him. So Harvey kept his head down, stayed in his room at night, concentrated on sports and studies. That first basketball season with the Buccaneers, he scored on a pace that would eventually make him one of Blinn's top ten scorers ever. In the spring he triple-jumped fifty-three feet, nine inches, farther than he'd ever gone before.

But he saw racism in Texas, too. In town. Even in the

athletic department. And the coaches, man, they weren't like Butch at all. They abused their players; he left Blinn believing that. Big-time college athletics was mercenary, and the coaches had used him up. They were like junkies, needing points—need 'em, need 'em, need 'em—doesn't matter how. Doesn't matter if you've blown out a knee so it's big as a grapefruit.

You can still jump, right, Harvey? We'll wrap that knee, you don't need to worry.

So he'd limp onto the field, onto the court. He'd do what he could, and they'd sing him up to the sky. But he knew the cost. He could feel it in the joint, the way his knee complained in the morning as he climbed out of bed. He was hurting himself worse than he'd ever hurt before. The big-time coaches, they didn't want to see it.

Okay, then. Good to get that figured out. When his time at Blinn ended, he accepted a scholarship to St. Augustine's College—a historically black, Division II school in Raleigh, North Carolina—but Harvey opted to defer for a year. He needed to take care of himself. Worm his way inside Mama's new Windsor cocoon, coddle that knee, find that time and space to make sense of all he had learned.

So: to a two-story, white block of a house on a grassy lawn, backed by a small woods. His mother lived in the Wilson section of Windsor, which had become a haven for black people moving the few blocks north out of Hartford. Staying with her, Harvey didn't miss the city. Maybe it was that most of his friends were off at college. Maybe it was the headlines—gang this and gang that, shooting here and shooting there, whole neighborhoods bubbling with crack cocaine. Maybe, with his knees all busted up, he figured he'd sacrificed enough for now. This was to be his time of rest, of ease, and in Hartford, there could be no ease.

He watched TV and he read, worked a little to earn a few bucks, visited with his brothers and sisters and nieces and nephews who kept the house alive with laughter. At night he worked his body the way Butch taught him. Stretching. Easy running. Harvey laced up his shoes at ten o'clock, after the sun set and the earth cooled, after people switched off their lights and settled in around the blue halos of their television sets, and he jogged through his mother's new neighborhood, listening to the quiet.

It wasn't long after the arrest that Butch telephoned Harvey.

We're going to beat this, Butch told him. They don't have anything on me, because I didn't do anything. There's nothing to worry about.

Harvey felt reassured, because Butch never promised anything that didn't one day come true. He had said Harvey would be a champion triple jumper, and he was. He had predicted things about Hartford, about the schools, about the government, about the prisons—things that came to pass. The man's on top of things, Harvey thought. A lot of people supporting him. Nothing to worry about.

And that's what Harvey still believed seven months later when he left town for North Carolina.

II

He wore a beard now, and sunglasses, and it was more than a year since she'd last seen the man with beautiful teeth, but Carma Robinson knew him when he walked into her party, when he joined the crowd of students drinking and playing cards, getting reacquainted in the new school year. Carma, late of Odessa Junior College, a senior now at St. Aug's, saw those beautiful teeth and started to tremble.

Just like that, she couldn't breathe. She ran to the bathroom and splashed water on her face.

Then, back in the living room, she yelled to get everyone's attention, told them all to leave. Party's over! Everybody out, she said, except (and she pointed at Harvey) you.

Once they were alone she told him, I've had a crush on you for two-and-a-half years. And when I've approached you, you've blown me off. (His polite protest and apology follow; she waves them off.) So go look around campus at all the women, but know this: from this point on, it's going to be you and me.

Not long after, she met him on campus and invited him to dinner.

I've got basketball practice, he said.

After practice, she said.

It'll be late. I have to take a shower and everything.

Don't worry about the shower, she said. I like a sweaty man.

Harvey showed up for that dinner.

She turned him inside out, Carma did. That's what he would say, years later. Everything about her: her class, her self-respect, her intelligence, her understanding of the life of an athlete, her feistiness. All of it. He'd shake his head and chuckle.

"Just messed me up, man."

A few months of courting—only a few months—and now Harvey found himself in Fort Worth, Texas, at the Robinsons' home, asking Mr. and Mrs. for their daughter's hand in marriage. The Robinsons said yes. Then Harvey and Carma made their plan: they'd wait until after Harvey graduated—more than a year. Then they'd have a big wedding there in Fort Worth.

But Harvey, he was messed up, getting all soft around the edges. He couldn't wait. His junior year wasn't even over when he said to Carma:

My tax refund came in the mail. Four hundred dollars. Let's go this weekend and get married.

And the two were off to Myrtle Beach. In the chapel Carma wore an evening gown she'd bought at Dillard's: yellow and trimmed with lace. She and Harvey stood before each other, repeating the vows the pastor uttered, and Harvey, intent and focused, said to the man, "I do."

Carma punched him, playfully. "Harv," she said, "you're supposed to say 'I do' to me."

"Oh, baby," he said. "I do. I do."

They ate that night at a Chinese restaurant, then took a beachside room and listened to the Atlantic Ocean tumble against the shore.

That was April 8, 1994. Four days earlier, in Hartford, jury selection for Butch's trial had begun.

III

Butch's attorney didn't like the jury. He wanted one that was less white. He complained to the judge that of the thirty people from which he could choose, only one was black. The judge had noticed, but unless Butch's attorney could show that there was some flaw in how the pool had been selected, the jury, the judge said, would stand. So here was a six-member jury of Butch's peers: three white men and two white women who all lived outside Hartford, and one man, a father of six who had lived in Hartford since 1957, who was African-American. Their professions: an accountant, a nurse, a roofer, a saleswoman, a toolmaker. The man from Hartford held two jobs: a truck dispatcher and part-time nurse's aide.

They took their seats in a courtroom at 101 Lafayette Street, headquarters of the Superior Court for the Judicial District of Hartford/New Britain. It was also the building, prosecutors said, where Butch had passed drugs to an inmate. In this same courthouse Butch had been arrested and taken away in handcuffs.

He was charged with four crimes: a criminal attempt to sell narcotics on December 11, 1992; a criminal attempt to smuggle narcotics to an inmate the same day; a criminal attempt to sell narcotics on December 15, 1992; and a criminal attempt to smuggle narcotics to an inmate the same day. The charges were felonies, some with mandatory sentences of at least five years. He pled not guilty to all of them.

The allegations stemmed from meetings between Butch and an undercover state trooper who, the state argued, had given Butch green balloons, telling him they were filled with cocaine. Butch, the prosecution said, agreed to pass the balloons to a prison informant in the courthouse lockup. The state's prosecutor would try to prove that at least one of the balloons had reached the informant.

The trial judge—Joseph Q. Koletsky—owned a reputation for running a by-the-book court. He was a former naval officer who liked to joke about his paunch (once telling the jurors that he "hadn't missed many lunches"). He had an entertaining habit of excusing the jury for odd amounts of time ("Ninety-seven seconds, plus or minus") but his playfulness ended there; during the trial, he once chastised Butch's attorney for leaving the courtroom without permission.

The prosecutor, Paul Murray, was a senior state's attorney, a big man at six foot three who had started his law career as a Hartford cop in the 1970s. As an attorney he had worked on a special state law-enforcement team called the "public integrity unit," and later as a special prosecutor for drug cases. In that role he would one day win convictions against a city cop and a state trooper for taking cash, cars, and drugs from drug dealers at gunpoint. In 1999 a Connecticut judge described Murray to the *Hartford Courant* as "a former police officer who has little tolerance for rogue cops."

M. Donald Cardwell—Butch's attorney—was a longtime Hartford lawyer who had once been the head of Hartford's Republican party and who had made a career out of criminal cases in the city. Butch's case, he told the judge, he had agreed to take pro bono.

Butch, whom Harvey Kendall had taken for some homeless dude when they first met, wore a suit to the trial.

Murray first called as witnesses the three state troopers who ran the undercover operation that had targeted Butch (an operation Cardwell consistently called a "set-up"). Led by Murray's questions, the troopers told a story of corruption. They had heard rumors of deputy sheriffs using balloons to pass drugs to prisoners, of deputy sheriffs letting prisoners have sex with visitors in private rooms. Deputies had even "lost" an inmate, who walked out of the courthouse while in their custody.

Names got attached to the rumors. Butch's name got attached to the rumor about drugs.

Where the names came from was never clear; some witnesses testified that police themselves came up with the names, others said it was prosecutors from the state's attorneys office, others said it was the prison informant.

Ultimately, the sources didn't matter to the state police, nor did investigating the rumors. State officials decided to run stings inside the courthouse. If a deputy took the bait, the rumors—when it came to that deputy—must be true. If a deputy declined whatever temptation the state troopers lay before him, the rumors were false.

For their prison informant, police chose Gary Ortega, a convicted heroin dealer and thief who had records of multiple escape attempts. He told police to use a balloon in their sting and to send to the courthouse a young, pretty woman—Hispanic or black—who might seem believable as the girlfriend of a drug dealer.

For the girlfriend role, state police chose Regina Rush, a soft-spoken trooper who had served in the field for nearly five years and had taught at the State Police Academy for about two more. She was a staff sergeant in the Army Reserve, and her military manners came through during the trial; she often answered questions with "Sir, no sir," or "Sir, I am sure, sir." Still, for all her experience, Rush had never worked undercover.

The plan was this:

Rush was to sneak a transmitter made to look like a beeper through courthouse security. She would approach Butch to offer him the balloons. The transmitter would broadcast her conversations to a car outside where her fellow officers could listen in and tape them.

She was to ask Butch to deliver a package to Gary Ortega; state police had arranged for Ortega to be in the courthouse that day. If Butch agreed, Rush would give him a green balloon, knotted at the end and filled with a harmless powder. She was to tell him, "It's a little coke." This last was important, because if Murray could prove that Butch believed the balloon held drugs and agreed to deliver the balloon, Butch could be found guilty of selling narcotics. He didn't have to actually sell, and the powder didn't actually have to be a drug. This was Connecticut law.

But the transmitter that Rush carried didn't work. Outside, the other two officers drove around and around, vainly trying to find some spot that would allow their equipment to pick up Rush and Butch's voices. So it was Rush's word alone that the jury would have to consider regarding her meeting that day with Butch.

Rush found Butch on the second floor lobby and watched him work for nearly twenty minutes. Then:

"I went over and spoke to him," she told the court, "and said, 'Are you Butch?' And he hesitated and then said, 'Yes' . . . And I asked him, could I speak to him in private."

Butch led Rush into an attorneys' lounge where she told him that she had a package for a prisoner. The prisoner had told her to ask specifically for Butch. But Butch seemed confused. Rush told the court that Butch asked her more than once to repeat the prisoner's name and once asked whether she was certain Gary Ortega knew him.

"[A]nd I said, 'I guess so,' and he said, 'And I know Gary?' I said, 'I guess so. He told me to ask for you.'"

Butch left, saying he was going to search the building for Ortega. When he returned he said he couldn't find anyone with that name. Together he and Rush looked at the court docket. Still nothing. Rush glanced at her watch, then asked again to speak with Butch in private, and he led her once more to the lawyers' lounge.

According to her testimony, she then told Butch: "'Well, I could give it to you and you can hold onto it until he shows up' . . . And he said that he couldn't—he didn't want to risk something like that because of his job. He made a similar statement to that, and that he couldn't do anything like that, that wasn't his style, and he opened the door to exit the room."

But Rush called to him.

Butch's attorney, Cardwell, wanted to know why. The man had said "no." Why not let him go?

"Because I had one more question for him, sir," she answered. Rush asked Butch, "Is there any way that I could get this to my friend?"

Here, Rush told the court, Butch asked her whether she would risk her job for such a thing. Who would support his family if he got fired?

Rush said, "He told me to take care of you."

She reached into her jeans for the cash.

It was then, Rush testified, that Butch's demeanor changed. His voice fell. He stepped toward her and asked whether she had an envelope. She didn't, so he pulled a sheet of paper from his pocket and held it out, and she lay the money on the paper. He folded the paper around the money, put it in a pocket, and took the balloon. Just after she handed Butch the balloon, Rush said, "It's a little coke." That's what she testified.

"I said, 'You'll get that to him today?'" And Butch, according to Rush, said, "Yeah, I always do."

But Ortega, who had in fact been in the courthouse, returned that afternoon to the Hartford Correctional Center without any balloon. The sting hadn't worked. So the state police decided to send Rush back to try again.

Rush's December 15 meeting with Butch followed much the same pattern as the first, except this time the troopers had arranged to park in a state lot near the building. Reception improved. They were getting a sentence here and there, but much of the transmission was inaudible. For example, they did not pick up Rush repeating her line, "It's a little coke," though that's what she told the court she had said upon handing Butch the second balloon.

During that second encounter with Rush, Butch again left her to search for Ortega. He came back saying, "I found him." The two retreated to the foyer, and again she passed Butch money and a balloon. This, according to her testimony, is when she said, "It's a little coke." Butch, on tape, can be heard saying, "I'll get it to him."

Later that day, according to the testimony of Sergeant Jeff Hotsky, corrections officers received a balloon from Ortega. It wasn't the balloon Rush had given Butch that day, Hotsky said, but the one from December 11. He could tell because he had prepared the balloons, and he had tied two knots into the December 11 balloon. The other had only one knot. That second balloon, he said, police had never recovered.

Gary Ortega, bound with leg irons, seemed to enjoy being in the witness box. He seemed happy to thrill the jurors or to shock them or disgust them ("A guy took my TV while I was in jail, because I am a small inmate," Ortega said. "I stabbed him in the eye with a pencil and put his eye out. He got lead poisoning. I came to court and said he tried to rape me."). One juror, following a break, switched seats to put more distance between herself and Ortega.

Ortega said that yes, he had received a green balloon from a deputy sheriff on December 15. He smuggled the balloon into the Hartford Correctional Center by sticking it up his ass. He clarified: between the cheeks, "not in the anal cavity."

Murray showed him a green balloon, one officers had

testified was the one they'd collected from Ortega. Is this the balloon? Murray asked.

No, said Ortega.

The balloon he'd smuggled had a burned spot on it, he said, and there was no such blemish on the one Murray showed him. Murray's balloon had pen marks that weren't on the one Ortega smuggled. And the knots on Murray's balloon weren't the same. "There wasn't a big bulge," Ortega said. "This wasn't on it. This wasn't on it because this would have been very uncomfortable in my ass."

Ortega challenged the state's case in other ways. The state police, he said, didn't know how to run a sting; they had suggested he do things that would have blown his cover. "The state troopers," he told the court, "are very unprofessional." Moreover, he had never told police to target a person named "Butch," he said. He had never met a deputy named "Butch." The balloon was given to him by a small man, someone he had been told was named "Butch," but who didn't look in the least like Butch Braswell.

"He looked like a troll," Ortega said. "He was gruff. He was a rough man. He had a broad nose, he was stocky, he had big forearms and—he looked like an alcoholic."

Cardwell asked Butch to stand up for a moment.

"This is Melvin Braswell," Cardwell said to Ortega. "I want you to look at him very carefully, and I want you to tell the ladies and gentlemen of the jury and the court whether or not this person ever gave you a green balloon in December of 1992 or any other time."

Ortega asked to see Butch's profile, and the judge ordered Butch to step nearer Ortega, then to move side to side.

"No," Ortega said.

"This is not the man?" asked Cardwell.

"That ain't him."

Now the state had to debunk Ortega's testimony. Murray tried to paint Ortega as a liar who would do anything to get what he wanted. Under Murray's questioning, Ortega told the court that in prison he had been an executive director for the Los Solidos gang, but a bloody power struggle was afoot. He wanted protection. Murray noted that Ortega had asked—in exchange for his work as an informant—for a TV set and for a transfer to a prison in Montville, Connecticut, that had lighter security and fewer violent inmates. Ortega had received the TV, but not the transfer. Now, Murray suggested, Ortega was angry with the state.

"What are you afraid of?" asked Murray.

"What am I afraid of?"

"Yeah."

"Afraid of ending up in ICU with tubes in my nose, sitting in a coma; I'm afraid of not seeing my children again; I'm afraid of not seeing my mother again; I'm afraid of not making it out of this state, out of the Department of Corrections again; I'm afraid of getting seventy-two stitches across my throat, inside and out, again; I'm afraid of some of the people that were youngsters when I—when I met them who are now Solidos, who I have trained, who I have sent to stab other people I know."

Murray pressed him harder.

"And what do you think you can do at this point in time to guarantee your safety?"

"Realistically, there's basically nothing I can do," Ortega said. "I'm in too deep now. . . . You understand that

I've already been labeled as associating with the wrong side by inmates within the Department of Corrections, by staff, for that matter."

"Are you trying to redeem yourself today?"

"No. There is no redemption. There's—once you step over the line, there is no turning back. It's like jumping in the water. Once you're wet, you're wet."

"Okay," Murray said, a few minutes later. "And is it fair to say that you have decided to deal with those security concerns yourself by changing what you've told people in the past and testifying as you have here today?"

"No, that's not fair or safe to say."

"Is it fair to say . . . that you did tell people that you knew Butch Braswell and that you knew him socially from outside of jail?"

"Yes," Ortega said, admitting to a lie.

"Do you know what's truth and what's not?"

"Yes," Ortega said. "I do."

The defense began its case with witnesses to Butch's good works. Called to testify was a teacher from the Hartford school district; Butch's supervisor among the sheriffs; Hartford Public's principal, Amado Cruz; a seventeen-year-old honors student from Hartford Public; high-ranking officials with the Hartford Police Department; and a fellow deputy sheriff who testified that he and Butch worried about the corruption in the courthouse and believed that higher-ups were doing nothing about it. Many witnesses wanted to offer not just testimony but testimonials, until the judge curtailed them. Koletsky told one witness to stick to answering the questions. "We've done it this way for the last couple hundred years," Koletsky said, "and I'd appreciate it if we didn't change the rules."

All of the witnesses testified to Butch's aversion to, and his outright hatred of, drugs. They told how Butch insisted that kids who worked with him keep themselves free of any kind of drug. Principal Cruz told how he'd even asked Butch to work with his own daughter who had gone on to captain the track team at Harvard. "I attribute a lot of that to his coaching and advice," Cruz told the court. He concluded, "I do feel that his integrity is impeccable."

But the bulk of the defense argument was yet to come. And it would be a complicated argument. It involved union politics, corruption, and Butch's assertion that he recognized the sting for what it was. Yes, Butch took the balloons from the undercover officer. But he knew she was a cop. And he never delivered the balloons to anyone. Given that the courthouse was rotten throughout and that Butch could trust so few people in uniform, Cardwell would argue, Butch had decided to reverse the sting and ensnare those setting the trap.

Why they set a trap for him, Butch could only guess. But he believed it might have to do with his support of a union for deputy sheriffs, an idea his bosses at the highest level didn't like. That connection led a *Hartford Courant* city beat columnist to wonder in print whether "Braswell, a tough and well-respected deputy who is pro-union, [was] arrested to send a message." Tom Condon defended Braswell as one of the few honest deputies in a statewide system that he deemed "a sewer."

"I do know Braswell," Condon wrote, "and I find his arrest very hard to swallow. If Braswell told me he took drugs, I wouldn't believe him."

The defense case also depended on two friends of Butch who testified that they were witnesses to the reverse sting. Paul Coogan was a personal athletic trainer who often worked out with Butch. Robert "Monte" Jones was Butch's assistant coach with the Hartford Public track team and a cofounder with Butch of the Inner City Striders track club.

According to their testimony, Butch asked them to sit in a room in the courthouse from where they could look into a courtroom's foyer and spy on Butch and Rush.

The story the two men told followed this basic thread:

Butch talked to each of them the weekend after he first encountered Rush, and he told them his suspicions. Butch believed the woman was a cop, and he worried that she was part of the corruption he knew infested the courthouse. Either that or it was a setup. Whichever, the woman would return, because Butch had never delivered the first balloon. He asked his friends to visit the courthouse every day until she came back. They were there, they testified, when she returned.

When on December 15 the friends first saw Rush through a window into the foyer, they agreed that she was a cop, not the girlfriend of a drug dealer.

"Anyone that's dealing drugs is going to look and check," said Coogan. He described Rush as nervous, but without drug-dealer smarts. "She didn't go up and check inside the courtroom . . . She didn't look inside the room where we were. She don't know if anyone was there or not. She didn't look any place."

After Rush and Butch talked, Coogan testified, Butch returned to his friends and said, "See, I told you something was up and you guys weren't just wasting your time. I'm not paranoid. These people are, you know, trying to set me up."

But Jones's and Coogan's testimonies were filled with discrepancies: they didn't agree, for example, on the amount of light in the foyer or how to operate the lights; they disagreed about how many times Rush and Butch met. Robert Jones even suggested that the reverse sting happened in late December.

Cardwell tried to help his witnesses. The cops, he pointed out, had all taken notes they could refer to during the trial to refresh their memories. Cardwell asked Coogan:

"Mr. Coogan, at any time have you ever made any notes regarding this incident . . . ?"

"No," Coogan said. "That's why I'm real—a year and a half is a long time."

Murray acted incredulous. Why not take notes? Didn't all this seem important enough that you write something down? Or maybe, he suggested, there were no notes because the testimony was a charade concocted after Butch's arrest. He pushed the question: Why didn't Braswell just say no? Why was he afraid of a cop? What was a cop, Murray asked Coogan, going to find out about Braswell that could hurt him?

"Find out?" said Coogan. "Nothing. Setup. That's why it's called a setup."

When I covered Butch's teams as a sports reporter at the *Courant*, I always had a difficult time understanding him and, therefore, using him as a source. He spoke quickly, faster than I could hear, let alone record with pen and paper. He sometimes mumbled, and his answers to my questions were often discursive, ranging from a sixteen-year-old time in the 100 meters to a perceived wrongdoing by the administration at Hartford Public to a pronouncement based on a Gospel passage. He was fascinating—and maddeningly impossible to quote. I didn't often trust his facts or myself to record them accurately, but yes, I trusted him. I believed in the honesty of his passions.

His courtroom testimony—two hundred and forty-seven pages—reads much the same way. It is filled with discursions and malapropisms and odd syntax. He called the foyer a "fornier." He admitted, "I talk quick sometimes." Imagine the jurors trying to keep up with Butch, trying to make sense of what he is saying and trying to find logic in the midst of what might seem to them an outlandish paranoia. As I page through Butch's words, I find myself worrying about the jurors, concerned for them as they prepare to judge. I want them not to make a mistake. I imagine them considering a story told by police that is appealing in its simplicity and lucidity against a story that is confounding in its complexity, one that defies common sense, a story that requires we believe a man would try to set up a clumsy reverse sting that even his defense attorney called "unwise."

But it was a story, Butch insisted from the witness box, that was true as daylight.

Yes, Butch broke rules as a deputy sheriff. Yes, he told the court, he sometimes let family members visit prisoners, and though he or another deputy would sit with them, it was—yes—in violation of courthouse rules. And yes, he'd bring a hamburger or some Kentucky Fried Chicken to hungry prisoners if they asked, but he'd never take any money for the service, and he'd buy the food himself. He wouldn't pass food that others asked him to deliver; still, drumsticks and French fries broke the rules, too. And yes, he'd work through lunch, then leave early during the winter and spring, so he could be on time for track practice at Hartford Public. His supervisors gave him permission, he said, but he didn't always work a full shift—another broken rule.

He had left the courthouse early that December 11 after his first encounter with Rush. He still carried the cash and the green balloon she'd given him. The more he thought about what he believed was a setup, the angrier he got. A man puts his life on the line as a deputy sheriff, helps cops with gang fights—because the gangbangers know him, respect him, so he steps between them, wedges himself between kids armed with frustration and despair and knives and baseball bats, maybe even guns. And now this clumsy setup, accusing him of dealing poison. At the school, he told the court, he threw the green balloon in a garbage dumpster.

But what about the balloon in evidence? asked Cardwell. Isn't this the December 11 balloon you took from Officer Rush?

Nope, Butch said. I threw it away. This is not the balloon she gave me that day. The knots are not the same.

In truth there was no perfect proof that the balloon in the courtroom was the same balloon Butch had received. That winter the police had used a variety of different colored balloons in courthouse stings, including one sting that led to a different arrest and a deputy who pleaded guilty. The officer who prepared the balloons for all the stings testified that he had made identifying marks so he could tell one balloon from another—basing identification on color and a pen stroke or a knot. But he also admitted that he'd never written those details into reports. Nor had he ever shared them with his fellow officers. It was his word against Butch's.

Now, said Cardwell, what about that second green balloon?

"Right here in my pocket," Butch said. He reached into his jacket, then held a clear plastic baggie at arm's length for all to see. Inside the baggie was a green balloon.

"You kept it?" asked Cardwell.

"I most certainly did," said Butch. "I wasn't going to throw this one away."

Cardwell offered the balloon as evidence.

Now it was the prosecutor's turn to question Butch. Murray began by trying to show a motive: money. He asked Butch about income from his three jobs, about child support. He wondered whether money was ever tight for Butch and Butch's mother.

"At times it was, but we managed to make it with the grace of God," Butch said.

And how much did Butch spend a year on the Inner City Striders? Murray wanted to know.

About six thousand dollars, Butch told him. But there was no record of that because Butch had never claimed the money as a deduction on his taxes.

But Murray's main attack was directed toward Butch's decision to run the reverse sting. Why do that, he asked, rather than tell the undercover cop to go away, to leave him alone? Why not arrest her or call other police? "She was already a cop," Butch said. "I knew this. And why would I go back to the people who were causing the problem to get a result?"

But how could you tell she was a cop? Murray asked.

"You could smell it," Butch said. "You could smell it in her style."

Again Murray asked, "Why would you be concerned about a police officer if you were not doing anything wrong?"

"A lot of people don't do anything wrong that police pick up."

The news of the day proved Butch right. During his trial, the *Hartford Courant* revealed that police in a wealthy suburb to the west of Hartford, had made a habit of stopping—for no legal reason—black and Hispanic people driving through town on the way to the Barkhamsted Reservoir. The reservoir was a favorite public swimming beach of Hartford's residents. Intimidation and harassment was a favorite strategy of police in Avon. The scandal over the "Barkhamsted Express" lasted more than a year.

Nevertheless Murray's questions seemed designed as if there were no such thing as a bad cop. To help the jury see illogic in Butch's approach, he asked: If you suspected someone in the courthouse of smuggling drugs, what would you do?

"If you hear a name," said Butch, "I think they should bring them down and talk to them, in my opinion."

"Who is 'they'?" asked Murray.

"Whoever is in charge."

"So you expect that if you suspect a particular sheriff of bringing drugs in, and you call him in and say, Are you bringing drugs in, he's going to say, Yeah, sure I am, I am going to stop?"

"I would pull him aside and say, I've heard some rumors, and is there any truth in these? You're going to be under observation. If it's true, you're going to be out. But I'd give him the respect of calling him to the side and let him know what I heard first."

One can almost hear the jurors groaning. Butch is making it difficult for them to find him innocent. Where is his common sense? This is a courtroom, a place of law and reason and rules, and sitting in the witness box is an admitted rule breaker whose actions defy common sense. But Butch is speaking from another world. Imagine, for a moment, that Butch has heard rumors: one of the Inner City Striders hangs out after practice on Marshall Street. Word is he's dealing. What does Butch do? Send someone over to Marshall Street under the guise of buying drugs to see if the kid is there, to see if the kid will sell a vial of crack? No. Does he call the police and say, One of my kids might be a dealer? No way. *No way.* What son or daughter of Hartford would ever trust Butch again? What Butch *does* makes perfect sense: he takes the kid aside and says, I hear you're mixed up in some things. Then he warns him of consequences, explains that a dealer has no place with the Striders. It's your choice, Butch says. This, to Butch, shows the kid respect.

This is common sense in Butch's world. At the end of each day of the trial, Butch heads home to Martin Street where drugs and the war on drugs ravage neighborhoods, lead sons to betray mothers and mothers to betray sons, where rain falls on a ruined bicycle left to rust on the sidewalk, where a teenage boy plays Nintendo, then in bed sleeps with a handgun under his pillow. Here, Butch must follow other rules.

"You had your own suspicions about people taking drugs into prisoners, didn't you?" Murray asked.

"Yes, I did," Butch told the court. "I had my own suspicions."

"Why didn't you tell this person you thought was a cop, I don't do that, but why don't you go see Joe or Sam or somebody?"

"I wouldn't want to jeopardize someone else if I'm not sure, I haven't seen with my own eyes what they're doing.

. . . People will start believing things they hear without any evidence, and I don't do that."

So, fatefully, Butch went along with Rush. "I just wanted to see how far this so-called wicked plan would go," Butch said. He took the balloon. He took the money. He told her he would search for Ortega.

"I said I couldn't find him," Butch told the court, "which was a lie, because I didn't look for him. I had no intention of looking for him."

"So you lied to her?" asked Murray.

"Of course I lied to her. Just because you're a police officer doesn't mean I have to tell you the truth when something is going on with me. I'll tell you anything you want to hear, but I'm not going to do what you want me to do, and you'll believe that."

"So you'll tell us anything we want to hear?"

"I didn't say you. I said I'll tell her. I didn't say you. I'm not that stupid, sir."

Murray returned to the subject of lying again and again. Butch grew angrier until what had started as testimony escalated into argument.

"So," Murray said, "it's okay to lie to a policeman under those circumstances, is that correct?"

"Who says policemen are honest?"

"I'm just asking about whether you were lying, Mr. Braswell."

"Oh, I lied to her extensively."

"Who is okay to lie to and who is not okay to lie to?"

"It's okay to lie to people trying to set you up. But it's very important that you tell the truth to the jury and right here and now, because your life is at stake. Mine."

"That's a pretty strong motivator, is it not, Mr. Braswell?"

"Truth is always a strong motivator."

"That's not what I'm talking about Mr. Braswell."

Butch replied, "That's my answer."

Murray, in his closing arguments, repeated Butch's defense with a tone that showed disdain for the story, saying that "the only thing that makes sense is that the defendant did commit the crimes charged and is guilty beyond a reasonable doubt."

What is "beyond reasonable doubt?" The fairly standard definition Koletsky gave the jury was that a reasonable doubt is "a doubt based on reason." It was "a real doubt, an honest doubt," a doubt to which a reasonable person would pay heed. It does not, he said, require absolute certainty.

In the transcript of Butch's trial, there is nothing—no fingerprints, no video of him passing a balloon—that proves he ever smuggled drugs; the trial proved only that he twice took from an undercover cop a green balloon filled with harmless powder. There are opposing stories about why Butch took the balloons, and there are reasons to doubt elements of both.

But, says the prosecutor, who would set up a reverse sting? He asks the jurors: Which of you would do this? He expects each will answer, Not I, and find that Butch's defense is too outlandish, too unreasonable, to be true.

But what if the prosecutor also asked: Which of you would stay in one of Hartford's worst neighborhoods when you could live elsewhere? Who among you would fund a nonprofit track club without taking the deduction on your taxes? Who among you would spend so much time and money to help kids when many of them will still be lost to the streets?

The prosecutor is right. Butch's defense is outrageous, unreasonable. As is his life. What makes sense is not always what is. How then can reason help us know which unreasonable thing is true and which is false?

Wendy Hurlbert was, she would say years after Butch's trial, a bit of a Pollyanna then, a bit of an idealist. She was excited to sit as a juror, something she had never done before. But by the time she entered the deliberation room, that excitement had become a dull sorrow, one she sensed among all the jurors.

"We liked him," she said of Butch. "We thought: 'What were you thinking?'"

The jurors deliberated for nearly two days. Peter J. Brighenty, the foreman, wanted to make sure they did things right. "There were some people who were, as soon as we got back in the jury room, who were like, 'It's over,'" he said, years later. Brighenty wanted to take his time. Though his initial impression was that Butch was guilty, he didn't want to learn someday that he'd made an irrevocable mistake. "This is somebody's life," he said. "I don't take that lightly."

So the jurors talked. They discussed the phrase, "It's a little coke," and decided that whether Rush said the words or not, Butch had to know that no one would give him a balloon to pass to an inmate unless it contained contraband; he must have assumed the balloons contained drugs. They decided that Ortega was such a liar they needed to discount everything he said. They agreed that Butch probably hadn't passed the balloon to Ortega, but having someone else do it was his attempt to distance himself from the crime. They talked about the job of the two attorneys, agreeing that Murray better argued the case than did Cardwell. As for Butch's reverse-sting theory? Outlandish.

Eventually they found no reason to doubt the prosecution's case. As Hurlbert said, "The majority of us came to the conclusion that he was justifying what he was doing in order to do something really great for his community. What he was doing for his community was terrific. We were sad that he chose to sell drugs to inmates."

Because the December 11 balloon was the only one apparently passed to Ortega, the jurors decided that Butch was guilty of only the December 11 charges and not those associated with Rush's second visit. Brighenty surmised that Butch had suspected the sting, so kept the second balloon as a way to start building his reverse-sting defense.

When the jurors entered the courtroom to announce the verdict, they found the place wall-to-wall with Butch's supporters. Adults. High school kids. It was a scene Hurlbert would remember clearly years later. She would remember the reaction to the verdict. It wasn't unruly. It wasn't outrage. It was the sound of hope defeated. "When they announced what our judgment was," Hurlbert said, "they all audibly went, 'Oh no.' That's what I remember."

The trial had lasted until April 28. Judge Koletsky raised Butch's bail from $35,000 to $70,000 and set Butch's sentencing for June.

Harvey Kendall wrote a letter to the judge. It was all he could do, newly wedded and in school and building a life for himself and Carma among the magnolia trees and crepe myrtle. It was track season, and he was busy out at the field, at the jumping pit that ran north to south so that Harvey's back was always to Hartford as he practiced. He sprinted and leapt southward, always southward. Farther and further away. But he did the one thing he could for Butch. He wrote a letter.

Koletsky received a stack of letters. He brought them to the courtroom on the day of sentencing. They were, he told Butch's attorney, "very moving."

Nevertheless, the prosecution argued for more than the mandatory sentence. A guilty plea would have meant at least five years. Butch needed a longer sentence, Murray argued, because he had violated the trust the public placed in its deputy sheriffs. Worse, Butch had disappointed teenagers all over Hartford.

"It's unfortunate," Murray said, "when someone who holds a position of respect of almost hero worship, particularly of the young . . . commits an act such as this and jades perhaps forever the view of those people."

The defense, in turn, faced Koletsky from an awkward tactical position. Courts, in general, go easier on those found guilty if they admit their guilt. Butch was not going to do that. "Mr. Braswell maintains his innocence," Cardwell said. "There will be no apology, no mea culpa, simply because there is no admission of guilt. . . . If that causes added time, well, then that's simply a risk that Mr. Braswell has to run." So Cardwell returned to the old defenses. Butch's community service should mitigate any sentence, he said. And, he added, the verdict was flawed given the makeup of the mostly white jury. Cardwell, a white man, stood before Koletsky, a white man, and said:

"People who have never seen the inner city in Hartford cannot understand the conduct that goes on on a day-by-day basis. They haven't seen the police kick down doors in the execution of search warrants. They haven't seen people waving twenty-dollar bags of drugs out on the street corners. . . . They sit over there in the jury box, and they now decide whether or not the defendant is going to be judged guilty or not guilty."

Finally he turned to Murray's charge that Butch had betrayed Hartford's youth. "Happily, he is wrong," Cardwell said. "These kids have not lost faith in Melvin Braswell, nor have so many of the other persons who came here and testified on his behalf lost faith in Mr. Braswell. . . . The community's perception is going to be that this jury didn't understand."

Then Butch spoke. He seemed particularly offended by what Murray said about the community's trust, as if he sensed that behind it lay cynicism and cruelty. After all, people had written letters! There was the evidence right there that the community still believed in Butch. Murray knew that but used the trust issue to argue for a stiffer sentence; it was an attempt to turn Butch's good works into longer prison time.

So Butch, angry now, addressed Murray directly, his fury twisting his words and his syntax into something at times unrecognizable.

"What man is this?" he said. "And I'm not saying this in turn to disrespect you. I'm saying this in terms of what the community thinks." What the community thought, Butch said, was that the system had once again struck a blow against it. An innocent black man sent away, and the people diminished by one, as they had been diminished man by man by man and would be again. It was wrong, but the people would persevere even through prison walls. "If I go to jail, they'll still come and see me," he said. "I love the black community. I love every youth in there."

And Butch offered one last, defiant claim of innocence, speaking again to Murray. Maybe, in the same situation, Murray might have done things differently. But, Butch said, "I can sit here and tell you honestly, I stand here, brother, and tell you honestly, I passed no drugs to no one. I gave nothing to anyone to give to anyone at any time."

When it came time for sentencing, Koletsky gave Butch the option of sitting or standing. Butch stood.

Koletsky stammered as he talked, as if the difficulty of his job made him hesitate. The verdict, he said, was not a bad verdict. The balloon was powerful evidence. That noted, he wanted Butch to know he was sentencing both a defendant and a crime. Sentencing the crime was easy. Sentencing the defendant, "a defendant with a truly spectacular record of service to the community," was hard. Moreover, Koletsky said, though it seemed that more and more defendants in his courtroom maintained their innocence even after conviction, such a stance was a "significant hit against rehabilitative potential."

Then Koletsky took a few minutes to lecture Butch about breaking rules. He seemed to believe he was talking across cultures, a "middle-aged, traditional, educated white guy" talking to somebody from a community too far separated from the rest of mainstream society. He wouldn't use Butch's testimony about breaking courthouse rules as an aggravating factor to add to the sentence, but the rule-breaking—deciding, as he said, "when people should visit with their families and . . . when people should get a cheeseburger"—clearly aggravated him.

"[It] makes me crazy that you take the law into your own hands and decide what regulations are good and what regulations are bad," he said. "I'm here to tell you that that approach can get you into big trouble. The process is here; the laws are here. They may not even make a whole lot of sense, but if we—if we don't respect them, if we take the law into each other's own hands whenever we think it's appropriate, then society as a whole has a real bad long-term prospect."

The mandatory five years was required on the charge of selling narcotics. On the charge of smuggling, Koletsky sentenced Butch to one year. Six years total.

"Six years to serve," Koletsky said, "is a right sentence for this."

Wendy Hurlbert and Peter Brighenty believe they did the right thing in convicting Butch. They never heard during the trial Cardwell's argument about the suburban-ness of the jury, but they have now; it does not change their minds. They believe they were fair.

Brighenty himself grew up in public housing projects in New Britain, a tough town just southwest of Hartford. He understands, to some extent, life in the city. "To this day, I think I could, and did, give him a fair shake," he said. "It might have made a difference had there been three or four black people on the panel. I can't tell you.

"We dealt with it the way we could."

IV

Harvey and Carma married in April, the school year ended near the start of summer, and the time came for Harvey to introduce his wife to his family and his city.

They drove north in an aqua-colored Chevy Cavalier. Carma—polite, well-mannered, Southern—had never been "north" before. She was asleep in the passenger seat as

Harvey slowed to pay his toll at a booth on the New Jersey Turnpike. She jolted awake. Loud voice. Shouting. Not her husband's voice.

"THAT SON OF A . . ."

Harvey handed over his money. The voice came from the booth. Why was this man shouting at her husband?

"AND I'LL GO AFTER THAT GUY, AND I'LL TAKE A BASEBALL BAT AND BUST HIS FREAKING—!"

"What is *wrong* with him?" she asked as they drove away.

"He's just mad about the guy in front of us," Harvey said.

"Is he crazy?"

Harvey laughed. "Don't worry about it, that's just a Northeast attitude."

In Hartford Carma met Harvey's family, those related by blood and those related by love. Butch had found help to appeal his case: a program run through the University of Connecticut Law School. Law students intended to make a complicated argument about double-jeopardy on Butch's behalf. He was out of prison while that continued, though he didn't talk much about the case when Harvey and Carma visited. What was there to say? They knew each other's minds. They ate sweet potato pie.

"You make sure you take care of this young man," Butch's mother told Carma. "He's like a son to me."

But even amidst all this love, Carma felt nervous and vulnerable in Hartford. She drove with Harvey and saw a landscape she recognized only from television or the movies. People dressed like gangsters. The streets seemed dark even in full sunlight, with hopelessness dusting every wall, smearing every window. A junkie here. A dead washing machine there. Potholes in the pavement as if

Hartford had been bombed. And, one afternoon outside a credit union, a man appearing on the sidewalk and holding a shotgun.

"Drive!" she ordered Harvey.

But the worst of it came when they steered along Albany Avenue, turned left onto Oakland Terrace, and Harvey parked in front of his old house.

"You used to live here?" Carma asked.

She saw the spot where police had beaten Bo Kendall. She saw where the man in red suede Converse sneakers had collapsed, his body full of bullets. She imagined Harvey, her sweet laughing man (then a sweet laughing boy), walking these sidewalks.

Harvey could have told her that things weren't so bad then. His parents did what they could to make life comfortable. The house was the haven. There was love and family.

But in the passenger seat of their aqua Cavalier, Carma saw only a grim vision of all her husband's boyhood suffering and fear, a lifetime's collection of griefs and pains collapsing into this one moment and overwhelming her. She could not stop her tears.

In May of the following year, in Wake Medical Center in Raleigh, Carma gave birth to their first child.

The baby was a week late, but the labor lasted only twelve minutes. Harvey stayed with his wife the whole time; he welcomed his son, cradled him in his big arms. He held the boy, breathed in his scent, touched the creases in his wrinkled skin. Everything changed, and Harvey was overcome by the sense that this little creature—Harvey Marshey Kendall—must be kept safe, his life made easy. The boy was the world.

In the weeks that followed Marshey's birth, as Harvey changed another diaper or ran another load of laundry, he understood without thinking too much about it that he would never again live in Hartford. The desire had disappeared, the way a bruise fades without announcing its passing. Harvey hardly noticed.

7

Derrick Walker had come home. It wasn't the homecoming he had promised, with college diploma in hand. He hadn't wanted to trade textbooks for a blue uniform and a walkie-talkie, or Virginia State's lawns for the concrete caverns of the Hartford Civic Center and its shopping mall. Now when he stayed up late it was not to cram for a test on electrical schematics, but because he worked second-shift security until midnight. Endlessly, it seemed, he walked past stores, looked over merchandise, and chatted with clerks: the twins who worked in the peanut shop; John, an Italian guy, who ran the tobacco shop; Velda from the drugstore on the mall's second level; and Charlie, who had cerebral palsy and used a wheelchair, who owned the candy wagon and sometimes accepted Derrick's help to close up. Jose and Maria had the liquor store, which was where Derrick broke from his security rounds now and then to buy his lottery numbers. A dollar here, a dollar there. Just like flirting with the peanut-shop twins—no big winners, but no harm either. And just like flirting with the twins, it was a way Derrick disguised the dull reality of the hours.

The stores closed early was the problem. Six p.m., except for Jose and Maria's, which stayed open until eight for stragglers needing a pint of Wild Turkey. On those nights the empty Civic Center left Derrick with time to wander and watch and think. To let thoughts run through and run out. This problem or that. A sadness. A solution. A phrase. A joke. A reminder of Joshua or Hiram or Harvey or Eric. A regret. Each night he clocked out, caught a bus to Vineland Terrace, and then walked to his mother's house, and to his old room in his mother's house.

He'd started work in October 1993, not long after he left Virginia and his classes for the last time. It was football season then. If he had been back in Virginia, he'd be spending Saturdays watching college games on television, looking for Boston College just as he had the year before. He'd point at the screen, at Eric Shorter dashing across the field, slamming a shoulder into some sucker halfback from Miami or Notre Dame, and Derrick would shout, "THAT'S MY BOY RIGHT THERE!"

When he walked through the mall, he did so bolstered by the belief that he would return to school. Not Virginia State, no. Too much money. But maybe he could go to Central Connecticut over in New Britain. Take classes in the day, work at night. He wanted to study something so he could work with kids; he could still live up to his promise.

But for now: check the cookie shop, the shoe store, stop by the place that sold sweatshirts and hockey pucks of the Hartford Whalers. Derrick's job was to be visible, a watchdog more than a guard dog. He was to bark into the walkie-talkie at any sign of trouble. But he worked for more than two and a half years at the mall, and the worst he would have to deal with—besides the boredom—was a shoplifter at the drugstore. Derrick and some other security guards had him surrounded when the thief brandished a hypodermic needle, stabbing toward them. None of the guards had to mention AIDS. They let the man go. He escaped with a few little items; the most expensive was a can of Similac, a kind of baby formula.

II

Think back now to Eric Shorter's first semester at Boston College when he volunteered for the team, then quit to concentrate on his classes. That was the story for public consumption, for coaches and teammates and family. Sometimes he himself might have believed it; most of the time he knew better.

He quit to pout. He quit because the coaches dissed him. He quit because they demeaned him by his locker assignment and his jersey number.

Here's what the assistant coach had promised, back in the summer before Eric's freshman year, when the coach delivered the bad news that Eric wouldn't get a scholarship: Come to BC anyway; we'll treat you like everyone else if you join us as a walk-on. We'll give you the same opportunities as a scholarship player.

That's how it worked, too, those pre-semester weeks in the summer of 1990. The older players had yet to report, so the nineteen freshmen had the weight room and the field and the coaches to themselves. Eric practiced with the defensive backs coach and the quarterbacks coach, and maybe they would have preferred that he become a defensive back, but in practice he studied the freshman who *had* received a scholarship to play quarterback and Eric believed he was as good. Then one afternoon while the players lifted weights, that freshman quarterback, the one on scholarship, interrupted with the news that the coaches had assigned lockers and jerseys. Sweat-slick, the players rushed from the weight room, eager as kids on Christmas morning. *Jerseys, yo! Lockers!* Each player might have imagined himself in BC's maroon and gold, darting on a green field lined with chalk, recognizable by a number that over four years would become more a part of him than his name. The jersey number was magic, a kind of voodoo, like Batman's logo or the Lone Ranger's mask. Players took their numbers so seriously that some guys had them tattooed on their skin. Others decorated their cars with them, ordering vanity license plates. Some wore jewelry with the number. That number was a trademark, a brand name. It made you recognizable to the fans in the stadium and the ones watching on TV. Linebackers wore jerseys numbering in the fifties and sixties; running backs in the thirties. Because he was a quarterback, Eric's number should have been no higher than the teens.

Most of the freshmen found their lockers easily, opening them and yanking their jerseys from inside, learning quickly who they would be. Eric kept looking. His locker was not near the other freshman quarterback's. His was not alongside the defensive backs, either. Name by name he searched, until finally he found his in a lonely part of the room where lockers came in triple digits: 105, 106, 107 . . . a ghetto for walk-ons. Separate, he knew, meant unequal.

Disappointed, he looked at his jersey. Number 39. No college quarterback in America wore 39. Eric knew what it meant. Thirty-nine was a duplicate number, one that belonged to someone else, a senior probably, maybe a defensive back, but someone who played a lot. Players couldn't share numbers, not on game day. Only one 39 would play. Which meant Eric wouldn't.

In pregame warmups, he took the field with the quarterbacks, threw pass patterns, stretched—all a fraud. Everyone knew it. Even fans in the nosebleed section, looking through binoculars, could see by his number how little the coaches thought of him.

Two objectives had drawn Eric early that summer to BC. One, preseason workouts. Two, to get his tuition paid the first year by completing an academic program called "Opportunities Through Education." Indeed he found opportunities—and not all were academic.

She had light-colored skin and straight black hair and a toughness Eric liked. Yes, he still had a girlfriend in Hartford, but this young lady demanded investigation. He introduced himself, made chitchat, and pretended to know what she was talking about when she said her family originally came to the States from Cape Verde. Her name was Taren, Taren from Rhode Island, and there, contained in her smile and her voice, was all the solid earth Eric would ever need.

Do what you think is best, Taren told him. So he lied to himself, said quitting would help his grades, and, in the early fall when the leaves had just started their slow sensational death, he did that thing he'd never done before. Four games into the season, Boston College had only one player wearing 39.

But his grades didn't improve. He had free time now, less structure, and he put off assignments, let the books stay closed. Much of that free time he dedicated to worry. His tuition was covered for the spring, but what about room and board? Asking his mother for fifteen hundred dollars was like asking her for twenty-five thousand. And even if she paid once, she couldn't pay every semester for four years. So he needled his pride a little more and let his football buddies buy him food (they could fill their meal cards whenever they needed, and Eric wanted to conserve the money on his).

He'd still sit with freshmen players in the school cafeteria; they'd sometimes make jokes he didn't get, jokes about practices he no longer attended. After lunch they'd head for a team meeting, and he'd say, "I'll hook with Taren, go to the library." There he and Taren toiled on homework, and when he got frustrated because he still struggled in the classroom, she'd say, Keep your head up; you can get this done. And in the dirty gray of November, when he complained that he'd robbed himself of a chance to prove what he could do on the football field, she said, I know you can compete with them. And when in winter the head coach got fired after a 4–7 season, and an assistant coach on the new staff said Eric had an open invitation to come back, Taren said, Do what you think is best.

The new head coach called a team meeting early that spring semester of 1991. Everybody associated with the program—players, assistant coaches, secretaries, equipment managers, physical trainers—crowded into the big football meeting room. Decorating the white walls were plaques from bowl games the Eagles had played, football helmets from each school in the conference, "BC Football" painted in maroon and gold, and dwarfing it all: an attacking eagle, all wings and talons and ferocity. Eric had not yet seen Coach Tom Coughlin, but he knew he'd worked at the Super Bowl just a few weeks before, handling wide receivers for the New York Giants. Eric had a mental picture of an NFL coach, and he expected a hulk, someone with the size to intimidate an all-pro linebacker, but in walked this small, skinny Irish fellow, pink-cheeked with a pointed nose.

His eyes, though. Even from where Eric sat, he could pick up the emanations from Coughlin's blue eyes. Those eyes shone with a need to win.

Listen, Coughlin said, and when he spoke, he did so without using the microphone at the front of the room. Listen. I don't care if you're a walk-on or a freshman or a sophomore or a junior or a senior. We're going to put the best eleven players on the field. Trust me when I say this: everyone is going to get an opportunity to compete. I don't care who you are.

Eric had heard it before, but this time, somehow, sounded different. The way Coughlin talked, his attitude—the man was genuine. He spoke and Eric believed.

Once more a walk-on, Eric gave up trying to play quarterback and concentrated instead on strong safety, a defensive position that required the mentality of a human missile. Unlike most defensive backs, the strong safety cares less about intercepting passes and more about slamming into whoever happens to have the football. To win the position required work: bench-pressing piles of iron, struggling up the stadium's bleachers as if running for heaven, and those brutal end-of-practice sprints called gassers. Eric attacked them all as if—again—he had something to prove, as if only playing time would earn back the respect he had lost when he quit. Swiftly he made his mark. By

201

the start of that following season—the 1991 season—he had earned a place on the team's traveling squad and special teams, meaning he'd go along for road games and he'd play during kickoffs and punts. Then, during the season's first game, when the Eagles' defense was letting Rutgers score too often, the coach of the defensive backs lost patience, benched his starters, and turned to Eric and the other young guys. They must have done all right because each game those youngsters played more and more, and Eric must have impressed the coach, too, because when the Eagles headed onto the field for their final game that season and the school bands played and the announcer over the public address speakers revealed who won the coin toss, Eric—a walk-on, a volunteer—was the starting strong safety.

The 1991 season ended, and Eric returned to his mom's apartment on Sigourney Avenue for the holiday break. Hartford had pulled out its Christmas traditions: lights strung into the shapes of reindeer and angels glittered on downtown's Constitution Plaza; Christmas carols played on WJMJ-FM, ecumenical radio from nearby Bloomfield. Derrick and the rest had come home from school, too, so when the telephone rang about two o'clock on Christmas Day, Eric expected it would be one of the fellas. His mother fussed about the kitchen, getting ready for the day's big meal, leaving Eric to answer.

"This is Coach Coughlin," said whoever was on the other line, and then Eric knew for sure it was Derrick. That was one of Derrick's regular jokes, calling and pretending to be someone else. "Merry Christmas," said Derrick, sounding a lot like Coach Coughlin. "Congratulations on your scholarship."

And it was then Eric realized this was not Derrick, that the voice did indeed belong to Coach Coughlin, and that he, Eric—

He didn't have to play football for free anymore.

Even better, he didn't have to pay for school anymore. His mother didn't have to scrape to help him with room and board. He didn't need to take gifts from aunts and uncles. Grades had never been the hurdle; he could handle those. Always it had been the money. Always the money. Now everything he dreamed was going to happen. Law school. His return to Hartford, degrees in hand. The promise would come true.

"Thank you," he said into the telephone. He didn't know what else to say. When he tucked the receiver back in its cradle, he looked over to his mother in the kitchen. She asked who it was, and he told her. Eric said, "I'm going to graduate, Ma."

Boston College had become a show; Eric had become a star. For every game, BC's players received four complimentary tickets to give family or friends. For home games, Eric needed ten at least. There was his mother and his Uncle Lenworth and his Aunt Betty. There was Taren and her family. And there were friends, like Jonah Cohen, the Upward Bound counselor, and fellas from Hartford Public. Eric begged teammates for tickets they wouldn't use.

Oh, it was a ticket-frenzy in Florida that season—Eric's first on scholarship—when the Eagles traveled to play in the Hall of Fame Bowl in Tampa. Eric's father came down from St. Petersburg to the team's hotel, leading a troupe of uncles and aunts and cousins. Eric made the rounds of the Eagle freshmen to see who among them hadn't used all of his tickets; eventually he scrounged eighteen. The work was worth it. When he came out of the tunnel into the stadium, man, that was the dream! Right there! His family—off to the left, starting three rows from the bottom. They stood and shouted, all wearing maroon and gold. Eric's mother, and Taren's, too. Cousins. Aunts. And of course, his father. Robert and Eric had sat together in this very stadium on two of Eric's summer visits, watching the NFL's Tampa Bay Buccaneers. Eric had sat in those seats, looking down on the players. Now he looked up and saw his father in the crowd, the first time he'd ever been able to look into the stands of a football stadium and see that man looking back. And somewhere in the group, with a voice that carried, his Uncle James chanted: "Shorter! Shorter! Shorter!"

Eric tried to send tickets to Derrick, too. When he heard Derrick was home from Virginia State, he telephoned. Always his offer was rebuffed. Eric asked his mother: If you see Derrick, invite him to a home game; tell him he can drive up with you. And she did, but Derrick turned that down as well. Eric left messages. Derrick wouldn't return his calls.

Eric was not alone in trying to reach his old friend. Hiram tried, too. He and Derrick had been friends since seventh grade, nearly ten years. When Eric, Harvey, Hiram, and Joshua returned to Hartford for holidays, they'd often get together. Only Derrick stayed away. "He was lost," Hiram said, years later.

"There was a common denominator we shared that he no longer shared with us," Eric said. "We would reach out, but he would push back."

They worried about him, and in their concern considered the worst: maybe he was drinking too much or maybe he was starting to "affiliate," as Hiram called it, with the wrong people. They worried, but they were in North Carolina or Virginia or in Boston, living their own lives. They didn't know and couldn't find out. After a while they stopped trying.

In the football office at Hartford Public High School, behind Jack LaPlante's desk, at the highest spot on a wall full of pictures of Hartford Public Owls and of news clippings, is a cover from *Sports Illustrated*. The magazine is dated Nov. 29, 1993, and its headline reads, "Down Goes No. 1." Notre Dame had been the top team in the country that week, but had lost, 41–39, on a field goal kicked as the game clock ran to zeros. It was Eric Shorter's Boston College team that beat the Fighting Irish, and on the cover of *Sports Illustrated* are three Boston College Eagles tackling a player from Notre Dame. The Irish player hugs the football as players hit him high and low. The player hitting high, ready to fall hard on an Irish back, wears No. 6: Eric Shorter.

Three seasons he played on scholarship, and in three bowl games. Twenty-four victories against ten defeats. More than two hundred tackles, including eighty-three—the second highest on the team—in his last season.

"The first 30 minutes of this game?" wrote a *Boston Globe* reporter of a season-opening victory over the Temple Owls in Eric's final year. "A BC display of athletic brilliance. Sacks, tackles for losses, forced fumbles, interceptions—in general, athletic terrorism . . . BC defensive back Eric Shorter ended the Owls' fun by returning an interception 35 yards for a touchdown."

On Christmas Day 1994, Eric played his last game. His

football career ended with a 12–7 victory over Kansas State in the Aloha Bowl. Eric finished the game with three tackles, crowing to reporters in the locker room that Kansas State had shown Boston College disrespect and paid for it. Wrote Michael Vega of the *Boston Globe*: "He wanted to have the last say . . . senior strong safety Eric Shorter blew up in a volcanic eruption of words.

"'All week they had been talking about how we didn't deserve to be here, but we dominated 'em. We dominated 'em,' Shorter barked. . . . 'These guys? They couldn't mess with us and they couldn't touch us.'"

His playing career ended, too, with success in the classroom. Because he'd started football as a sophomore, he finished his coursework for a degree in political science before he finished with his four years of football. He'd used his extra year of scholarship money to start graduate school in social work. The coaches rewarded his example by naming him winner of the Thomas S. Scanlan Award, given to the team's Outstanding Senior Scholar Athlete.

Finally he ended his football career engaged to be married. He had proposed to Taren on Valentine's Day as they ate Chinese food in her dorm room. But he wanted to hold off on marriage until he'd completed two tasks, and when Taren heard them she agreed. First he wanted to take her to Florida to join him in a hunt through records at the Pinellas County Courthouse in St. Petersburg, to search newspaper clippings, to talk with family about what happened the night his father and James Cooper fought over that shotgun. He wanted her to know who he was, where he had come from, to face with her what violence had formed him. He wanted to understand it all himself.

The other goal was to finish graduate school, and that he did in spring of 1996.

The July day of the wedding was clear and bright and warm and Eric knew it was the best day of his life. They married in a Catholic church—he had converted for her sake—and the pews were crowded with family and friends. So many familiar faces, like Hiram Harrington's, and some unexpected ones, too. Joshua Hall showed, who had not received an invitation because Eric had misplaced his address. But Joshua had heard about the wedding and browbeat one of his older brothers, who had a car, to drive him to East Providence. And Jonah Cohen, Eric's counselor in Upward Bound. And Eric's brother, Gerald, and his sister, Candy. And Michael Reed—the fellow Eagle who had loaned Eric his car years before when Eric needed to drive from Boston to Hartford—Michael Reed served as best man.

Derrick Walker did not attend.

III

Jack LaPlante gave me Eric's phone number when, in May 1998, I decided to find the five friends. I hadn't talked with any of them since I left Hartford, and I had no idea how their lives had gone, but I wanted to know. I still longed for Hartford, still felt I owed it and my grandparents more than I'd given, but what did that mean? How much did I owe, and what was I to do with that debt? How could I square it with the realities of my life? It seemed necessary to compare my Hartford story with others. The five seemed the best choice. They, too, had believed they owed the city, but they had made a promise that clarified and sanctified their belief. Perhaps by studying their stories I could find my own answers.

Now, by phone, I told Jack about the promise they made and how I thought they might have a tough time keeping that promise.

Yeah, it's getting worse, Jack told me, meaning Hartford. A fellow football coach from Bulkeley High School had recently sold his house in the city and moved to the suburbs. The guy had been dedicated; his wife also taught at the school. But their Hartford home had been burgled too many times. They still worked at Bulkeley, but living in the city wasn't worth it anymore.

Jack gave me Eric's number. It didn't include a Connecticut area code.

I reached Eric at his home in the Boston suburb where he and Taren lived. They had a baby now, a girl, and Eric had taken a job with the Metropolitan Boston Housing Partnership, an organization that helped build places where poor people could afford to live, places cleaner and safer than slums or public housing. He remembered me and was glad to recall old times. We talked about the others: where they lived, how they were doing to the extent that he knew, phone numbers if he had them. He sounded as if he still meant to return to Hartford.

"It's a goal of ours," he said. "A goal is long term . . . Eventually we'll do something collaborative. We'll all give back in our own way. When I speak to Hiram and I speak to Harvey, constantly it's on my mind."

But the timing for a return to Hartford wasn't right. He needed more skills, more resources, and those he could get in Boston. He imagined one day bringing those skills and resources home. But already he had begun to question the wisdom of such a move. Shalyn Shorter, not yet a year old, gave him pause. "I want my daughter to have the things I wasn't able to have," he said. "I want my daughter to have an excellent education."

He liked my idea for a book, of having the stories told. He still believed in the pledge and in the notion that Hartford needed its lawyers and teachers and business owners to make homes in the city's neighborhoods. "It's imperative they live there, for the kids coming up, that they see you are part of the community," he said. "I just think it's crucial. Unfortunately, if you're successful, you tend to want the finer things in life. Those things aren't in Hartford."

We agreed to stay in touch.

One by one I reached the rest. Derrick and Hiram and Joshua in Connecticut. Harvey in North Carolina. In the spring of 2000, I arranged to visit Hartford, to reconnect with those who lived there or nearby, to learn about their lives, and to discover how the pledge had fared.

When I first became reacquainted with Derrick, by telephone in February 2000, he worked third shift in an expensive hotel in downtown Hartford but had moved out of the city. He lived across the river in an East Hartford duplex with a new girlfriend and her children. "You can count me in," he said, voicing his hope that the book might "get our core and us back on track to what we decided back then." He had been thinking about his old friends because their ten-year high school reunion loomed. He and another alum wanted to organize it. "I'm in the process of getting things on the ball," he said, "getting in contact with fellow pupils."

By May when I visited, Derrick's life had changed. Now he worked days for a company that installed security systems. The electrical work satisfied him, he said, because he could put to use the engineering he had studied in college; he hoped his job might lead to work with the phone company. Also, he had moved out of the duplex and back in with his mother who now owned a house in Hartford's

South End. Derrick's mother's house was typical of those in the neighborhood, two-storied and angular, with a postage-stamp front yard guarded by a waist-high cyclone fence. When I went to visit, Derrick greeted me from the doorstep. He'd grown into a good-looking man. His smile was pleasant, though uncertain and guarded. His body was trim and well-muscled—testament to the hours he still spent "massaging the anchor." His beard and mustache he wore as short as his hair, barely a whisper across his face and over his head. We shook hands, and then he introduced me to his mother, who was as soft-spoken as Derrick.

He and I ate at a nearby pizza parlor. When Derrick spoke, he interrupted his sentences with many "ums," but he was unfailingly polite. When he paused in mid-sentence to sip from his soda, he said "excuse me" before drinking. He talked about Upward Bound and the football team, and about the time he broke his ankle and missed so much of his junior season. He talked about his return to Hartford after Virginia State.

"I knew that I wasn't going back," he said. "My intention was to go to Central. But I got a job and started working. More and more I put my education on the back burner." Then he moved out of his mother's house into an apartment. "Bills needed to be paid," he said. "I just started getting jobs. That's where I am now."

Yes, he felt frustrated, not being in school. But he told himself he could still make a difference, be a positive role model. "I helped a lot of kids that went the wrong way," he said between bites of pizza. "I helped a lot of them get out of gangs."

Later we visited neighborhoods where he had lived. We cruised lonely Mather Street—all sidewalks and ominous bare buildings, the only sign of life a dreadlocked teenager in baggy jeans who vanished as soon as he saw our car—and the SAND public housing project, and Collins Street where the building in which Derrick's family had lived was now abandoned, and Vineland Terrace, with mature oak trees and large, sloping lawns, the nicest of his neighborhoods. But he had no affection for Vineland Terrace; he was in high school then and more concerned with life at Hartford Public, the place that harbored him. When we parked on Forest Street, at the curb outside the high school, he surrendered to a powerful nostalgia. His voice softened to a whisper, and he stared at the building, seeing more than its ugly façade and trampled lawn. Here, he had been part of student government. He had been homecoming king. He had played football and basketball. He had left here atop his world. The last best time.

"I knew the teachers cared," he said. "That's what made my four years. I wouldn't change it for anything in the world. I wouldn't change coming to Hartford Public for anything in the world. I had a wonderful four years here. A wonderful four years. Mmm hmm. . . . I knew I could just come to school and everything was all right."

From Hartford Public, we drove by Trinity College where he and Eric and Joshua had spent summers in Upward Bound, and he told me how he came up with the meaning of B-Side.

"So when did you start losing touch with Eric?" I asked.

"I'm not sure," he said. "When I came back home. We pretty much—after that."

"Why did that happen?"

"I'm not sure. I think about it. I think about it all the time. I miss him. For so many years we were so close and so tight." He said, "I'm not really sure why it happened," and perhaps that was true. But a clue to his separation from Eric and the others might be found in their yearbook. Under Derrick's photo reads the caption, "We are the dreamers. School has taught us history now we must create the future." Perhaps, once he'd come home from Virginia State, the intensity of his disappointment matched that of his hope. With Eric and the others he had dreamed a different future than the one he had made. Perhaps it was too hard to watch from the bench, as it had been too hard when he broke his ankle. He could not watch the future come true without him.

He looked forward to the reunion. He hoped it would succeed. For the brief time that he'd considered organizing it, he'd not had much response. "A lot of people we ran into said, 'I probably wouldn't go anyway.'" Now Joshua Hall had taken up the yoke; he had scheduled the reunion for October.

"Hiram and them," Derrick said, "for our fifth year put on something, and it wasn't really that good of a turnout. So I'm not sure, I'm not sure what the tenth year is going to be like."

But he would go. True to the blue. He'd be there.

IV

Just outside Providence, it was raining. Earlier the sky was clear as I drove out of Hartford, only sandals and socks on my feet. Foolishly, I'd brought no shoes, so now I hurried as I splashed from the hotel lobby through puddles into Eric's car, a little Volkswagen, the interior of which was a garden of clutter with two empty child seats strapped into the back. My socks got wet.

Greetings exchanged, Eric turned onto a highway that

took us into Providence. The rain reflected the streetlights and headlights, and in the dark I couldn't tell where streets turned or ended and where curbs began. I was glad Eric drove.

He parked outside Lincoln School, an expensive and old private school on the city's east side, and we hurried through the rain into the school's gymnasium. Inside, some players already shot around on a three-quarters-length basketball court. Eric stripped out of his sweatpants to shorts and a T-shirt. The game began as a little easy three-on-three as I watched, but eventually a seventh person arrived, and, invited now, I made the game four-on-four. I hadn't expected this, hadn't dressed for it, and I played awkwardly, running in sandals and blue jeans, but no one seemed to mind. This was middle-class basketball, slow and civilized.

I played with Eric's team, and I could see why football fit him so well. He played basketball like a strong safety, charging straight to the basket as if it were a running back in need of tackling. He played guard on the court but without a guard's smooth moves: no pretty jump shot, no shimmy or shake, no glide. His game was strength and determination, and the first basket scored that night was his when he powered through the lane, caught the rebound of his own miss and put it back. His strength simplified the game: there's the basket; I'm putting the ball in the basket.

The gymnasium glowed with the luminescence of money. Clean backboards, shiny nets, and overhead lights that replicated clear sun. The floor was without dust. High windows surrounded us. The men who played had money, too. From their conversation I gathered they were lawyers, accountants, executives, land developers. They had so much money they could joke about it (one said of another: "He's got to rent an apartment in Central to store all his unused paychecks").

At the end of the game, everyone contributed six dollars for the use of the court. I noticed that not only did we play in a gym named for someone, but the court itself was named: the Amy Beth Leeds Basketball Court at McLoughlin Gymnasium.

Just a few days earlier, I had sat in Hartford Public's unnamed gym, watching kids dribble and drive. The floor there was yellowed with old wax, the lights dim, the bleachers scraped. There were no windows, and the dirty walls echoed with the garbled profanities of teenage boys challenging each other's games. A wobbly student desk sat in the corner where gym teachers could sit and monitor their charges while finishing paperwork.

I mentioned this to Eric, noting the contrast between where he used to play and where he played now.

"It's the haves against the have-nots," he said, and I was reminded that Eric often sounds like a coach, framing the world with aphorisms, with adages. "That's the way it works until folks do something about it."

The next morning, the child-safety seats held Eric's two daughters, the two reasons he and Taren moved to East Providence where her side of the family lived and could help raise the girls. Sydnee on the right squirmed against her buckled straps. Her older sister, Shalyn, sat calmly behind her daddy. Sydnee wouldn't look at me and covered her eyes with the backs of her hands. Eric wore a Phillies baseball cap, not because he liked the Phillies, but because he liked the color red. He told me what awaited him at work that day: "Half a million dollar deal with a church," he said. This was his job, acting as the lubricant that smoothed the way for developers, local governments, nonprofit groups to use federal tax credits and build inexpensive, safe, clean housing all over Rhode Island, the kind of housing he helped build in Boston—apartments poorer people could afford.

We stopped in an orderly, working-class neighborhood to leave Shalyn and Sydnee at day care. Sydnee frowned. Eric cooed, coaxing the girls out of their seats and into his arms. Back in the car, he rubbed his knees. All the rain, that humid air, made them sore. The pain was a holdover from his football days; Boston College's field was artificial turf, little more than a carpet thrown over concrete. Four or five times during those seasons, Eric's knees would swell. With hypodermic needles, the team's athletic trainers drained his knees on Thursday so he could rest Friday, then play Saturday. "I know I'm going to have arthritis," Eric said.

He worked in a beautiful office, the walls exposed brick with vast, factory-sized windows that looked out on city hall. It was dress-down Friday, and Eric wore tan linen slacks, a tan vest to match, and a dark sapphire silk shirt that shimmered. The project on his neat desk read "Lawnsdale Village Revitalization." When he explained it to me he glided over phrases like "flat interim financing" and "market-to-market programs." At lunch, his boss, Laurel L. Bowerman, told me how glad she was to have hired Eric, who marketed himself when he applied for the job, talking nonstop and proving that he could do the same for affordable housing. "My only thought was," she said, "Will I ever get a word in edgewise?" But, she added, "He's made an impact. He is what he says he is. He truly is a team player. It really is a give and take."

On a drive later that afternoon, she and Eric showed

me projects they made happen. Their company was private but worked with public money to implement public programs. Rhode Island law required each town to make 10 percent of its housing "affordable." So the company helped build affordable housing throughout the state, even in old-money Newport. In the south side of Providence, the housing they built was automatically some of the nicest in that neighborhood. As we drove through the Olneyville section, Laurel recalled that she once toured nearby buildings that needed renovation, and the tour party found a baby alone on a bed, its arms flailing, mother nowhere to be found. The group even happened upon a drug deal—an unscheduled part of the visit—and the dealers didn't bother to hide the transaction. The block would have fit nicely into some of Hartford's more blighted neighborhoods; Marshall Street was its cousin. Laurel looked around as we drove, said, "Huge disinvestment here."

Meanwhile, in Connecticut, Gov. John G. Rowland had looked around Hartford and said, Huge disinvestment here.

This was a problem. Rowland, a Republican from the western part of the state, believed that a flagging Hartford damaged Connecticut's business reputation. He wanted a capital city that could serve as the state's showpiece, that would convince business leaders from around the world that downtown Hartford (and, by association, Connecticut) was dynamic, active, thriving.

To that end, he gathered a group of Hartford's leaders (but not its political leaders; what had they done, after all, but drive Hartford to despair?) to devise a plan for downtown's revitalization. The group arrived at six goals, what Rowland's office called "Six Pillars of Progress." The pillars ranged from increasing parking to bringing a college campus into the downtown. But the group's most ambitious goal neatly dovetailed with the plans of some downtown business leaders who wanted to start an eruption of brick-and-mortar such as Hartford hadn't seen in decades. The project was called Adriaen's Landing, named for Adriaen Block, a Dutch mariner who in 1614 was the first European to step onto the banks of the Connecticut River at the spot where Hartford would one day arise.

The business leaders who dreamed of Adriaen's Landing envisioned a monolithic new section of downtown spread over some thirty acres of what was at the time parking lots and abandoned buildings and polluted fields where factories once stood. In their place would rise a convention center to attract business tourists from throughout the country, a grand hotel to house them, a shopping district where they could spend money, apartments for upper middle class professionals who would add to downtown's new energy, promenades and bridges to connect downtown to new parks along the riverfront, and a sports "megaplex" where fans could gather for—if all plans came to fruition—professional football games.

The plans changed, of course.

Altered by economics and politics and the decision of the NFL's New England Patriots to spurn Hartford and stay near Boston, Adriaen's Landing's shape proved amoebic. The sports megaplex idea gave way to one for a smaller stadium in East Hartford where the University of Connecticut's team would play. The number of apartments fell by half. Rowland proposed a science center to further attract tourists (another proponent argued that hundreds of other American cities had successful science centers, why not Hartford? apparently unaware of the definition of *glut*). But the project's guts remained the convention center and the hotel.

It would only cost the public half a billion dollars.

The numbers, as first estimated in a year 2000 financial report from the Office of the State Comptroller: $771.1 million for the project, of which $528.7 million would come from the state. Private investors wanting to build the hotel or the rental apartments or the shops would pay the rest. Four years later the state revised the numbers: a growing Adriaen's Landing would reach a billion dollar price tag, the higher cost to be paid almost solely by public funds.

What would Hartford get for this investment? About 1,100 permanent jobs and 3,400 temporary jobs during construction.

"Given the substantial investment," argued the comptroller's report, "Connecticut's state government will not realize a positive return on its investment and local municipal governments may only see a negligible return. However, state policy makers believe the resulting infrastructure of Adriaen's Landing is essential to ensuring the long-term economic competitiveness of the Hartford region."

Others weren't so sure. Weren't there already two highly successful tribal casinos drawing scores of conventions elsewhere in the state? How could Hartford compete with gambling and Vegas-style shows? Critics noted that so much public investment leveraged against so little private money showed that the business world still wasn't willing to take a risk in Hartford; why, therefore, should taxpayers? Early in the debate, some neighborhood activists accused Rowland of paying too much attention to downtown while ignoring the rest of the city. Adriaen's Landing, they argued, was a façade, a gaudy state-funded curtain meant to mask, but not solve, Hartford's real problems, a boon only to the business elite and construction industry. A better name for the thing? Potemkin's Landing.

The ceremonial first shovel broke ground in May 2000, the same month I met Eric Shorter in Rhode Island.

Eric considered himself a developer, too, but one with a conscience. When he oversaw projects, he worked to make sure builders used quality materials, not stuff that would fall apart in a few years. He remembered Woodland Drive, and he didn't want people who lived in his apartments to face the daily degradation of their homes. He believed in building attractive homes for the poor, rather than the kinds of Gulag-style projects he'd seen at Hartford's Rice Heights or Stowe Village where people lived in lumpy brick buildings without trees, without porches, without sunlight because their windows were too small.

Many of his ideas for how to build came from a philosophy that originated in the early 1990s called New Urbanism. The first New Urbanists—architects, land-use planners, academics—had gathered in 1993 to figure out where America's cities had gone wrong and what could be done to fix them. They saw connections between bleak urban landscapes and sprawling suburbs and disappearing farmland. Racial and economic segregation, they argued, resulted from years of government policies that subsidized highway construction and made it less expensive to build in rural areas than to repair dilapidated cities. Cheap land and highways nearby encouraged white middle-class Americans to head for suburbia in pursuit of a two-car garage, a big backyard, a grill on every patio.

New Urbanists believed that the success of that American Dream meant the end of the cities.

As a solution, New Urbanists encouraged government leaders to change how they built—and rebuilt—cities, regions, and neighborhoods. They recommended regionalism, so that a city like Hartford might share in the tax base of its neighboring suburbs. They recommended improved public transportation, so that Hartford's bus system might run more regularly, with cleaner and safer buses. They recommended that postwar public housing be replaced by new buildings adorned with front porches and courtyards so that neighbors might spend time outside rather than behind bolted doors at the ends of long, dark corridors. Improve police patrols and street lighting, the New Urbanists argued, and people might live in a place like Hartford again. And if people live in Hartford, rather than its suburbs, they won't clog the interstates at rush hour trying to speed the dull hour home. If the city repaves the sidewalks so they are not buckled and treacherous in winter, more residents will walk. In a sense New Urbanism pursued nostalgic visions. In looking to improve itself, a New Urbanist Hartford might use as a model old Hartford, my grandparents' city, a place of good pay, healthy industries, and safe streets.

A New Urbanist looking at Adriaen's Landing might have appreciated some of its elements. By putting high-quality housing in downtown, the project encouraged less reliance on the automobile. It was, in its way, a form of regionalism, using state tax dollars to remake a central city. It was an effort to improve an inner-city economy. Placing apartments above shops and restaurants was also a good idea, harking back to a time when people didn't expect to live on a street that after five p.m. went quiet except for birdcalls and the tch-tch-tch of lawn sprinklers.

But other elements would trouble the New Urbanist. Planning for Adriaen's Landing included few considerations for regional transportation; no rail line would zip people from the suburbs in and out of downtown. Developers imagined national chains (an ESPN restaurant, a Starbucks coffee shop), but not a grocery store—a must for a New Urbanist neighborhood. The project worked against the New Urbanist ideal of bottom-up development, of making small investments and recycling old buildings. Such a model protects heritage and revitalizes cities in more permanent ways than does demolition followed by mega-projects that appear as if dropped from Mars. "We must think incrementally—street by street, block by block, neighborhood by neighborhood," wrote Harvey Gantt, a New Urbanist and former mayor of Charlotte, North Carolina. "Sometimes it may be a simple improvement, like a mini-park, a reformed slum lord making improvements of his property, or an adaptive reuse of an abandoned shopping center." What good is it, a New Urbanist might say, to bolster Hartford's downtown with such spending when city roads still suffer from disrepair, when crime still keeps people out of downtown after dark, when prostitutes still lie helpless in public parks less than a mile from the state capitol building, working off their latest crack high? Who would live in such a city? How could an Adriaen's Landing draw people away from the suburbs and into a place such as this?

Or would small victories work instead? Take the success of Park Street, what had been a thriving Hispanic market area in the midst of a blighted war zone; in the late 1990s and into the new millennium, Park Street cleaned up, drawing visitors from throughout Hartford and its suburbs. Hartford had other neighborhood-level triumphs, usually created by some combination of grass-roots groups working with established institutions. Trinity College worked with its neighbors to demolish a deteriorating city block, replacing it with a "Learning Corridor" of new magnet schools. The city recruited a private children's hospital from its home in Newington and helped it rebuild next to Hartford Hospital where I was born. A private nonprofit group had won millions of dollars in state and federal highway dollars to rebuild Hartford's waterfront and construct a pedestrian bridge from downtown, over the interstate, to a riverside park. The city began to tear down and rebuild its postwar public housing projects, replacing them with houses poor people could buy. And by early in the twenty-first century, the city would begin an $800 million campaign to rebuild the Hartford schools.

All of these were moves a New Urbanist might praise. All contributed to Hartford's "livability," the abracadabra word among New Urbanists.

It wasn't enough, of course. Hartford, once so far down as to be damned, showed flickers of resurrection. But few American cities had known depths of degradation to match Hartford's. Its problems were systemic and corrosive, and it remained one of the most unappealing cities in America. In the decade since Eric and his friends had graduated high school, the city's population had dropped from about 140,000 to just over 124,000. The percentage of its citizens living below the poverty level climbed from about 28 percent to just over 30 percent, the second-highest poverty rate among American cities, behind only Brownsville, Texas. And the amount of vacant housing, as a percentage, broke into double figures.

We're taking steps forward, said the optimists and boosters.

Quixotic quests, mumbled the doomsayers.

This much was true: it would be years, perhaps decades, before the New Urbanist-style changes or Rowland's great, glamorous gamble could be deemed triumphs or failures.

In Providence the rain had abated as Eric drove into the five o'clock rush, but it remained a dreary Friday with gray clouds folded over and around each other, horizon to horizon. Eric liked working in Providence, he told me, which was well-muscled in a way Hartford was not; people lived in Providence and liked living there. We crossed a wide finger of Narragansett Bay into East Providence, and Eric took an exit into the town. He and Taren had bought a white raised-ranch with blue shutters in a well-groomed, working-class neighborhood called Riverside. East Providence, he said, was maybe like what East Hartford used to be when Jack LaPlante was young: working class, mostly white. "I love it here," he said.

Suddenly we were in a different East Providence neighborhood, a kind I'd not yet seen with Eric. The houses were stately, with porches and columns that held roofs over the porches, shaded by thick-trunked maples that formed a canopy over the road. The roads narrowed and became nearly rural, lacking curbs or sidewalks, indicating a neighborhood built before the town cared about such standards. This was old New England. Yards bloomed with azaleas and tidy lilacs. We crept down the streets, and I half expected to see someone jog by with a golden retriever on a leash. The neighborhood, Eric said, was called Rumford, and it was where he wanted to build his dream house. "Occasionally I just drive by," he said, "so I know it's important. If you don't have a plan, how you gonna do something?"

His plan? To buy a lot and start building by the time he turned thirty. With a thirty-year mortgage, that meant he'd pay off the debt around the time he turned sixty, five years before his retirement. I realized, then, that he was not moving back to Hartford. Not ever. This was the first time I'd heard him admit that. He hadn't spoken the words, but the truth hung there, and as if he saw Asylum Hill floating between us, he said, "I love Hartford, but I'm bitter."

He craned his neck over the steering wheel so that he could look up at this neighborhood, watch it unfold before him. The Phillies cap sat tight on his head.

"I have a cousin in jail," he said. "He's got fifteen years for attempted murder. But I emphasize, without fear of contradiction: he did not do the crime. I read the transcripts. I've never read a case where I've seen anything like this. You have the victim testifying on behalf of the man on trial. The prosecutor said my cousin's brother scared the victim into saying that he didn't do it. The attorney didn't do crap."

The story came in bits and pieces. The cousin's name was Greg. One night, around two a.m., Greg was hanging with the wrong crowd on Asylum Hill, not far from where Eric's mother lived, and, Eric said, not far from where two white guys in a Datsun got lost. They stopped at a stop sign, and two black guys approached their car, demanding money. When a white guy said no, one of the black guys shot him. Or at least, that's the story. Eric guessed it was a drug deal gone bad, that or the guys in the Datsun were hunting for prostitutes. What else would two white guys want in Asylum Hill at two a.m.?

Whatever. The cops picked up Greg. Yeah, he was hanging out with homeboys who were doing him no good. But, Eric said, Greg didn't shoot anybody.

"Now a young man is sitting up in jail for a crime he did not commit." His voice quieted. His eyes filled up. "For a long time," he said, "for a long time, I felt a sense of failure in my life. I was the strength of my family. I had said to myself, I'm going to become an attorney." He turned right, drove twenty or so feet, then realized he had taken the wrong turn even though he had been to this neighborhood dozens of times. He backed up, retraced his path.

"If I would have done it, we wouldn't have hired some piece of shit attorney. My aunt busted her tail to pay for that attorney, and now my cousin's sitting there for fifteen years. Fifteen years!"

Tears marked nickel-wide paths down each cheek. His cheeks flushed, and I could see that his mouth had become gummy. He found the correct turn, took it, and drove us into a neighborhood of mostly empty lots. This wasn't quite like the rest of Rumford: we'd gone from an old neighborhood to a place not yet born. The only trees stood at a distance at the edges of the subdivision. In the grassy lots, wild daisies outnumbered surveying stakes. Eric pulled to the curb, put the car in park but left the engine running. He waved his hands, then slapped the back of one into the palm of the other.

"I would've been of assistance," he said. "It's crazy! Everything happens for a reason. That's Hartford for you, though. 'Let's throw these niggers in jail!' I don't think I'll go back there. Because of that."

He gripped the steering wheel with his big hands at

ten and two, squeezing, then letting go, then squeezing again. He apologized for crying. This place, he said, always made him emotional. "This is my place," he said. He squeezed the wheel, and Greg was gone, out of the car for the moment, and instead Eric saw his little girls grown into grade school, pedaling bicycles on this street with streamers fluttering from the handlebars. He saw himself outside his house grilling steaks on a wooden deck, then dancing with his wife in a spacious kitchen.

"This is my place. I'm going to move my wife and two girls over here. We gonna have us a nice little cul-de-sac. A nice environment. Not too big a house. Just a nice house. A Jacuzzi. Look at this. Look at this," he whispered. "I drive here because I know this is within my grasp. These new lots. Look at this. Look at that porch right there. I'll get one over here and have the lake behind the house. Go out there and fish and get a peace of mind."

He put the car in drive, steered through the lots, into a cul-de-sac. "I think you need to do this sometimes. This is what I do with my free time. I dream. I dream about stuff like this. Even if it ain't here, it'll be something similar. A cul-de-sac. You leave your door unlocked. You know all your neighbors and everyone looks out for everyone else's kids. This is what it's about, I think. And it's not selling out—as long as you have your commitment. Some people think you got to be living in the city, but lots of folks who live there don't do crap. They just do *that*. It takes guts to live out here, you know? It's easy to live among folks who are like you, who look like you. But you live amongst folks who are a little different? It takes guts."

He paused close to the entrance of the development, not yet ready to leave. "I dream about stuff like this. I'm twenty-eight years old. I've owned two houses. I've been a homeowner since I was twenty-five years old. I want to buy a lot here and sit down with my wife and design our house, talk about everything I want."

He glanced at the house near where we had parked, one of the few houses already built in this subdivision. He grinned, the city kid once again. "I'm sure they're taking my license plate down right now. Maybe not. Maybe they've seen me here before. I've come here so many times."

We drifted back into old Rumford, and like that the spell broke. Eric talked again about cousin Greg, about the week after Greg's arrest. There was a party for Eric, who had just graduated from college. He sat in a stairway, enjoying the fun, when Greg stepped up to see him. "I'm so proud of you, man," Greg told him.

Then they talked about the arrest. "It's the best thing that ever happened to me that they locked me up for a week," Greg said. "I'm going to turn it around." So that was it, then. No more hanging at odd hours with the corner crowd. Greg even started going to church. But he hadn't committed the crime, see, so he refused a plea bargain; he wanted to make his case to the state.

"That's the man right there!" Eric said. "He was faced with his freedom. He had to make a decision, and he stood up for principle. You know how many of my people are in jail because they wouldn't plead out?"

I asked if he had visited the prison to see his cousin. He shook his head.

"Can't. Can't go see him. I wrote him a letter that I couldn't even send."

Then he was shouting. "Ain't nothing promised to you out here! I experienced it as a two-year-old kid and as a twenty-three-year-old man. Life isn't fair, so you live life to the fullest. Nothing is promised to you. My father can attest to that. My cousin can attest to that." We drove away, saying little else, and a few minutes later he dropped me off at my hotel, then continued on to his home with blue shutters.

The first time Eric lived in a nice house with two parents in a good neighborhood is a time beyond his memory. His father, his mother always said, was a good provider who loved his children. But hard work and love proved insufficient, and on a night poisoned by jealousy and drink the nice house in the good neighborhood vanished with the blast of a shotgun. See how it is? You never know. Eric has driven past that house in Florida. He uses it, not to remind himself of what might have been—that would be a foolish regret, after all, given his life, this good life—but because he wants to remember how frail is the future, how the contract offers no guarantees. It is a lesson proved to him over and over because Butch Braswell is in prison, and his cousin, Greg, is in prison, too; and Aaron Fisher sells ball caps from the back of a van; and Wendell is dead and Kamala is dead and Block is dead and Kevin Hicks is dead. So much potential lost, and yes, potential fails everywhere, but there are places where it fails less often, with charitable consequence. There are places where—with discipline and passion—a man can believe that his future will match his promise. Hartford is no such place. In Hartford it's broken promises all the time.

8

Jeremy is mouthing off to Hiram, refusing to sit at his desk, though Jeremy is a flyweight as second-graders go and Hiram brings to their contest about 270 pounds.

"Have a seat," Hiram says.

"Man, take a hike."

Though the day's class won't begin until all eleven students are sitting, Hiram says nothing more. He doesn't move, either. He towers over Jeremy, and he towers, and none of the other students dare speak, and Hiram stares at Jeremy who looks everywhere but at Hiram's belly looming only inches from Jeremy's head. Hiram keeps silent; the students keep silent. Jeremy twists and rolls his head, but with each twist and roll he edges closer to his seat. Now he's leaning on the desk. Now he buckles and falls into its chair.

"Thank you," Hiram says. As he steps away, Jeremy mumbles.

" . . . ragging my butt . . . "

Hiram glowers and Jeremy stops mumbling. Now all the children are seated and quiet. Mrs. Heyman, who has watched performances like this a hundred times or more, begins the lesson.

Here is a promise kept. Hiram Harrington, whose home is an apartment in what used to be a tool factory in Hartford, is living the terms of his pledge. If he does not actually work within the city, that is a technicality hardly worth noting. Hiram works with the city's children. Moreover he works with some of its most troubled.

We are at Woodland School in East Hartford, a sturdy two-story building of brick and concrete and high windows, with a coat of arms wedged near the roof between two turrets—factory architecture made scholarly by a hint of Cambridge. It was once an elementary school, but now is for children of all ages and grades who suffer severe behavioral problems. These are children who break things and steal. Some spew the word "fuck" as naturally as they breathe. Some are suicidal. In Hiram's class only two of his eleven students have fathers at home, which is why Hiram calls each of the boys "son." These kids suffer from ADD and ADHD, and, as Hiram says, "every initial you can imagine." They come to Woodland from throughout Greater Hartford. Some, in fact, live near Hiram's apartment. Here at Woodland, they're part of a TEP—a Transitional Education Program. It's a bureaucrat's way of saying these kids wreak havoc at regular schools.

Each Woodland classroom includes a teacher and a behavioral manager. Hiram is the behavioral manager in Mrs. Heyman's second-grade room. He's worked this job for four years now—at different grade levels—learning how to talk with children and teenagers, how to discipline them quietly, how to remain firm, when to rest a palm of his big hand atop their wee heads, and—because they sometimes get violent—how to pin their arms behind their backs without hurting them.

This happens mostly with older kids, but the second-graders now and then need "restraints" if, in the midst of a tantrum, a child will hurt himself or others.

In Mrs. Heyman's room, sunlight rushes through large paned windows. Donald Duck and friends prance around the walls. A piano bench sits near the front of the room, hidden in its own cubicle. On Mrs. Heyman's desk lies a book: *Teaching Conflict Resolution Through Literature*. This is a special week in her class. There is a new girl, shy, who grips her desk as if a thunderstorm might blow her away. Today she wears a pink dress embossed with Barbie, and her hair is decorated with ribbons. Around her neck she wears a token of recent victory: a red, white, and blue band with a gold-colored medal hanging from it. Her eyes are large; she has never seen a classroom like this. Undoubtedly she has never seen someone like Hiram standing beside a teacher.

The next half hour passes with only one incident: Jeremy again. He back talks the nurse who has come with his pills, and he resists swallowing them. Eventually the nurse wins, but Jeremy's concession comes too late. Hiram exiles him to the piano bench, behind the cubicle's walls. From there, Jeremy glares at Hiram with as much insult as he can muster. Hiram ignores him. The punishment lasts until it is time for gym class, and the children all line up like proper little second-graders and march down wood-trimmed hallways. As we walk, Mario, a boy whose head barely reaches my knee, takes my hand. His touch is soft and cool. No one else holds hands—this is not a requirement—but Mario clasps mine, and he doesn't let go until we're at the gymnasium.

As the students play, Hiram keeps careful watch. He has to. "They watch wwf," he explains. "Imagine Benjamin running over there to clothesline Mario." Benjamin is the class's mini-Hiram, round and solid, and I wince at the idea of him raking a forearm across sweet, elfin Mario.

We sit at the front of the gym on an auditorium stage while the kids horse around. There's a gym teacher, and he's organizing the students into team sports so they might learn to work together. The children laugh and smile and jump in place, glad to be free of their desks. They appear perfectly perfect, everything children should be.

Hiram shakes his head. George, he tells me, knows no ABCs and can't count to ten. When George first arrived at the school this year, Hiram had to teach him to unroll toilet paper. "Sometimes kids even go backwards," Hiram says. "Odell could tell time last year. Now he can't." And Mario, who held my hand, can put together a string of profanity, says Hiram, "so he sounds like a sailor." Hiram has learned that he can stop Mario's rants by whispering in his ear.

Back in the classroom, when Greg slams his chair against the floor because Hiram won't let him trade snacks, Hiram says, "You tell me why it's not appropriate for you to drop the chair."

Greg turns his back.

"I don't like your tone," Hiram says. "Because I tell you you can't trade with Cliff doesn't mean you can hurt the chair."

Outside Woodland these children live through tantrums and shouting. Left on their own, they will repeat the habits of their outside world, mimicking teenagers at a bus stop or angry neighbors in apartment building hallways, or siblings or parents, all shouting as if the loudest voice wins, as if voices are weapons or tools of punishment. Hiram doesn't shout, yet the children listen. They seem to think his voice a curiosity, as if they aren't used to one so steady and patient. When he talks to the kids, Hiram asks questions, or gives directions. By example, he teaches them that language and voice are for communication.

Punishment is something else. Hiram will discipline the students when necessary. The piano bench, the corner, withholding a treat, or—if a student is very bad—the detention room. Tatiana earns her time when she throws a tantrum after a boy in class breaks her pencil. Hiram orders her into the hallway, giving her a chance to choose communication; when that doesn't work, he walks her to the detention room. The room is thickly padded in blue and empty of anything but walls and floor and ceiling. Two men—both behavioral managers—sit outside the room to watch the students, to guard against them injuring themselves, and to talk them through their trouble.

The message they give Tatiana is that it's okay to be angry, but she must learn to control herself when she's mad, and she must learn what's worth a storm of anger and what's only an annoyance. The pencil is a small thing, yet she won't surrender her rage. When Hiram chastises her, she yells, "Tell him not to call me a bitch!" Hiram tells her to sit down.

"Now," he says, "let's talk about the pencil stuff. If someone broke my pencil, I'd be kind of upset. But what you're supposed to do is come over here and be quiet."

It is 9:25 a.m. In little less than two hours, Hiram has

sent one student to detention, another to the piano bench, and given a talking to three others. After that, the kids find a rhythm in the work of the day. They concentrate on Mrs. Heyman's instruction in math. Lesson by lesson, they learn. But then, that rhythm is broken. Lunchtime requires a walk to the cafeteria to collect a box of food, then a walk back. It's a daily test of freedom, to see how the students behave away from their desks. On this day, when the students return to the classroom, Hiram keeps them from eating. Almost everyone in class behaved badly in line. Hiram makes the students stand facing the walls of the classroom, their lunch trays left on their desks, waiting. He tells them to stand still. He wants them to show self-discipline.

Hiram presses a button on the CD player. There is music now, Samuel Barber's *Adagio for Strings*. Hiram prefers the lunchtime accompaniment be classical music; the kids get too much rap at home. "I love rap," he says. "I was raised on it. But rap is different today. It has the n-word in it. The b-word in it."

The children remain standing. One by one Hiram asks them why they must face the classroom walls. Each answers. He reminds them: all you are to do is face the wall. No leaning, no chewing fingernails, no sighing. He waits. He pops his knuckles. He notices. Lateshia, the shy new girl, is standing properly. "Lateshia can sit down and eat," Hiram says.

Tatiana, the girl with the broken pencil, kicks the wall.

"I just warned you four times," Hiram says. "Four times." Her punishment, he declares, will be no recess in the afternoon. "You don't want to go because you don't want to control yourself." Tatiana pouts. She calls Hiram a liar. "I don't care," she says. And she repeats it. *I don't care I don't care I don't care I don't care.*

When recess comes, Tatiana stays behind. She's the biggest girl in the classroom, a giant as seven-year-olds go, and it's clear she depends on the chance to play games and get physical. As the other children leave she sits at her desk, tears sliding down her cheeks. She stares at Hiram and makes no noise.

Outside under a bleached-blue spring sky, Hiram and I sit on swings, and some of the children push me, little hands in the small of my back, so that I sway back and forth and sometimes side to side. Across the stubbled lawn, Lateshia sprints against all comers, finishing first by a few yards each time and earning her place in the class as the fastest runner. Around Hiram and me, Mario and Clarice are smiling and dancing, little herky-jerky attempts to perform. I can't help smiling back at them, but that's because I don't have Hiram's discipline. He doesn't smile. He is as much a Puritan as Rev. Thomas Hooker, Hartford's seventeenth-century founder. Hiram doesn't care if the children love him. Their salvation matters more to him than their love. "Everybody in here for six hours is my child," he had said to me earlier in the day. And now, on the swing set, I remember when Jeremy stared from the piano bench, hurling with his eyes every outrage and wound at Hiram's big back. That was no more effective than Mario's charm. Anger will not make Hiram flinch and charm will not make him grin. Only one thing makes Hiram happy.

The children must behave.

Hiram's workday at Woodland ends, but no rest awaits him. His second job is even more trying than the first, with longer hours. The commute takes him on Interstate 84 west through the center of Hartford where he passes the old Billings Forge tool factory that now houses his apartment and his bed. But if he is tempted to stop, to nap, he gives no sign. He speeds past . . .

Hiram lives in a neighborhood where residents rely on the spiritual and the physical to protect them from the hazards of city life. Neighboring storefront businesses include a karate self-defense school and a Baptist church. A gray, dented Dodge Omni parked streetside sports a club lock across its steering wheel; from the rearview mirror hangs a crystal angel. Hiram's apartment waits behind a metal gate, part of a ten foot tall fence with ribs of black steel every few inches. A note on the gate reads: "This area is under 24 hour TV surveillance." A foot or two behind that fence is a second in case the first fails. But that one—a cyclone fence—is bent as if heavy people have scrambled over it, getting in or out.

When I visited Hiram at his apartment a few days before our trip to Woodland, I had to telephone in advance; his girlfriend met me at the gate to let me in.

Hiram's decor reflected his Puritan sensibilities. The necessary furniture, but few knickknacks. Some art on the walls, including a print of a Diego Rivera painting: a Mexican peasant bent beneath a massive basket of flowers on his back. Hiram's parents had kept a copy of that painting in their basement when Hiram was a boy. "I'm the laborer," he said, pointing at the man and his burden.

Why two jobs? I asked.

He doesn't like having money problems, he told me. He remembered his family's financial struggles from childhood. Also he wanted to build his savings and buy a house. Renting, that's like throwing away money. His fa-

236

ther had taught him that. But he wanted to be careful. He saw what happened to his family's efforts at 22 Sanford. He worried about Hartford and its property values. He'd lived on half a dozen different Hartford streets and some of those weren't worth a dime of his investment. On days off he drove through the city seeking "For Sale" signs, trying to imagine in what neighborhoods a wife, should he ever marry, could be happy. He wanted neighbors who would share his values so that if he ever had children the neighbors would reinforce his teachings. Keney Park near Canterbury Street where Joshua grew up, that might work. Or the deep South End, with Italians as neighbors, because it was quiet there. He liked houses with polished wood floors and tall windows.

I also liked those houses. Hiram and I talked about Hartford's good neighborhoods, gesturing south and west and north in their directions. We talked about what was affordable and what was safe.

It was the spring of the new millennium, and my grandfather lay in a bed at the Mediplex. I had been gone from Hartford eight years, and though I was only on a visit, I hoped the trip might lead to something else, to a change of address, a house in Hartford to call my own. Every day, via e-mail and telephone, Sheri and I talked of leaving Montana for Connecticut. It was possible. It was frightening. In Hartford, between interviews for this book, over lunch or a cup of coffee at Mozzicato's, I tried to read optimism into newspaper ads for housing. A story in the *Courant* claimed Hartford's real estate market was rebounding (a little, at least), and I took heart and was scared. I tried to imagine my money, my wife, our lives, tangled with the city once more. I understood the care with which Hiram searched.

Missoula, Montana, is a kind of Shangri-La. Its mountain valley beauty—especially early summer's green and early autumn's alpenglow—makes visitors yearn to uproot their lives and resettle. It is a small city of 60,000 or so people—the second largest in Montana. In winter people ski the mountains and in summer they kayak rivers. Families enjoy late afternoon bicycle rides past the blooming flower and vegetable plots that lead Missoula to call itself "The Garden City." To let customers know it is open, a bread store lights a neon sign in its window that reads "Yep!" Missoula is a town excited to be open.

In May 2000 I had been gone from Hartford for eight years, off to Montana, then to Arkansas while I attended graduate school, then back to Montana to temporary work teaching at the university there. Sheri and I both worked at the school, but we had no guarantee we'd be hired for a second year. Moreover, like many Missoulians, we were paid too little to afford a home in the area's seller's market.

So that spring, before I flew to Hartford to meet with Eric and Hiram and the others, I called editors at the *Courant* to let them know I was visiting. Would they be willing to consider me for a job?

I brought a desperate hope to my interviews at the *Courant*. I wanted so badly to reclaim Hartford. My adventure away had succeeded; I was happily married, and I had finished graduate school. It was time to start a new phase of life, one with more stability. Perhaps it was time to return to Hartford, to work at the *Courant* and live again in the city or maybe in a suburb so as not to repeat my wife's Willoughby ordeal. In truth, she wanted to stay in Montana. At that year's university graduation, she cried as the assembled students and faculty sang *Montana, My Montana*. She observed the Bitterroot Valley with the attention of a lover about to leave, reveling in a mid-May cold snap. "It snowed again today," she wrote to me in Connecticut. "Big sloppy wet kisses." She held a fatalistic and grief-tainted confidence that the *Courant* would offer us money and jobs we could not refuse. She wrote, "I am already planning our move."

For my part, career and money seemed less important than a reunion with the place. As I drove from the airport into Hartford, I smiled to see the downtown skyline, Traveler's Tower, and the boat-shaped headquarters of the Phoenix Insurance Company. I read street signs and heard music in the names: Wethersfield, Campfield, Zion, Salem, Nepaquash, Pulaski, Brainard, Huyshope. The city enveloped me. Salsa and rap played out the open windows of apartments and from the trunks of cars. Block to block, I smelled garbage or baked goods or garlic. The humidity was a caress in contrast to the West's dry indifferent air. But my need for Hartford was too great, almost unreasonable. I didn't trust it. After all, wasn't Missoula a kind of paradise?

Yes. But through all my years in western Montana, I had never learned to love it. Most Missoulians possess a deep satisfaction with their little town on the river; I felt rootless there. The culture of "The Last Best Place"—as Montana's literary establishment likes to call the state—was rich enough, but it was not my culture. I didn't fly-fish; my ancestors hadn't homesteaded the land or migrated with the buffalo. Montana was a rural state; I was raised in the suburbs, with a family history in a city. Montana's beauty seemed cold; Missoula's college town quaintness a Disney-like falsification. This wasn't the attitude to bring to gatherings with neighbors or to share with colleagues. Those who live in western Montana are supposed to adore the valley and the state. But I didn't, a dirty little secret that magnified my alienation.

I lost patience with the town and particularly with its great, though mostly harmless, myth: that it is a tolerant and diverse community. No, I silently argued, not diverse, not when the population is more than 95 percent white and fairly well educated. Tolerant? Perhaps. Tolerance is easy for a tribe self-segregated from the world, many of whom had fled (as did I) rough places (such as Hartford) where tolerance is tested every minute of every day. Missoula gives much but requires little.

In places like Hartford, with more people and more differences, our better natures face the challenges of an insolent car horn, a snooty customer, an indifferent neighbor's screaming infant. In such places the triumphs of civilization and civility (a whisper in Mario's ear, a lunchtime adagio) are less frequent, overcome greater odds, and are therefore more precious. Yes, in Hartford there is corruption and racism and cavernous gaps between the poor and the rich, but there is no illusion about it. Hartford, even with Adriaen's Landing, cannot hide itself from itself. Living in Missoula seemed to me a dishonest act, an escape into a comfortable lie about life and about America.

So when Eric and Hiram and the others told me their reasons for returning to Hartford and their reasons for staying away, I looked for clues. Like a wayfarer lost beyond the horizon, I searched for a sign to lead me home.

Hiram exits the interstate into the town of Farmington and onto quaint New England roads. He passes colonials and capes built more than a century past and some that are a decade new. Roses. Dogwoods. Azaleas. As he drives, he scouts for the magic words: "For Sale." Hartford is his first choice, but he's practical enough to look elsewhere. If he finds something affordable on the outskirts of Harwinton or Burlington or anywhere beyond Hartford (what he calls "out here"), he'll buy it. There was a foreclosure in Torrington, a four-bedroom cape he considered bidding on. "It had a yard. Little sun porch," he says. "I wouldn't have found that in Hartford. It's my kind of neighborhood. There's not much out here but peace and quiet."

Two teenage girls stand on a sloping, grassy Litchfield lawn that is bordered by high, wild hedges and songbirds and the chirp of crickets. The low sun throws evening shadows and infuses this world with golds. Tina, who is chubby with dark thick eyebrows, says she wants to be a mortician because then she can work with makeup and help people, too. Kay, faerie-faced with straightened black hair, is already a poet. "Sometimes I feel like I live a diseased life," she writes, "like a pregnant virgin." Kay once smashed a boom box over the head of someone who made her angry.

Other teenage girls crowd the area, and though we are surrounded by more than sixty acres of warm, comforting nature, most of the girls—true city kids—keep to the asphalt driveway.

They are far, far from home.

Among their griefs?

Sexual assault. Drug addiction. Abusive parents. Absent parents. Failure in school. Failure at jobs.

Among their crimes?

Theft. Possession. Sale. Assault. One girl knifed her mother.

The state gave each of them a choice: jail time or nine months at Touchstone, a private rehabilitation program run with state money. Twenty girls live on this New England estate straight out of a tourist brochure, with its three stories and dormer windows and wraparound porch and flower beds, and its horse barn that is empty now of horses. During the day the girls attend classes in one of the outbuildings. They learn math and English and science, but also habits and patterns designed to help them survive their return to the cities they call home. Sometimes it doesn't work. Sometimes girls end up back at Touchstone for a second round. Sometimes they end up in jail. But many do make it. Some earn a GED. Some still call Hiram once a month for guidance and support.

"Girls that are here get a different perspective," Hiram tells me. "This is a great place to be, though they don't think it is. It's safe. There are deer. Varmints. They get to see all of that. It's picturesque."

Hiram supervises the night shift, a bevy of young counselors who oversee the girls during quiet time, during their outdoors play time, as they do homework, then as they make dinner, clean the kitchen, and prepare for sleep. The counselors start their shifts at the third-floor office, reviewing the day's reports and the standing policies (all incident reports must be faxed to a girl's parole officer, a sign reminds them). A wallboard shows each girl's name in dry-erase ink, along with important instructions such as "must not accept calls from mother, per DFS." Another sign translates a passage attributed to the German poet Goethe: "If you treat an individual as she ought to be and could be, she will become what she ought to be and could be."

The counselors receive training before they start, but much of what they learn is on the job. Hiram had no special training when he was hired at Touchstone, though he believes his undergraduate degree in human resources management helped prepare him for both his jobs, which are, essentially, about managing people, albeit young ones. In that sense, these teenage girls have been promoted. Back home, few people see them as resources.

The first word any Touchstone employee or resident must learn is *support*. At Touchstone, hundreds of times a night, the girls and counselors answer each other with *support*. Girls *support* each other when they need to confront the staff about an issue—say rude treatment from a counselor-in-training—or when they confront a new girl who hasn't yet learned to be polite or who may have stolen something from a roommate. The staff *supports* the girls when they make good decisions and when they acknowledge bad ones. *Support* is a catchall term that means "I agree with what you're saying. I *support* what you're saying. We are together on this. You are not alone." It is an affirmation and a password that says, "we are linked, and this is our language." *Support* is to the girls at Touchstone as *Amen* is to a church crowd. Hiram is the high priest of support.

Outside he walks with slow steps across the lawn. He's in no hurry. Tina, who wants to be a mortician, likes Hiram. "He's nice," she says. "Funny. He's strict sometimes. He seems confident in things. He has faith in us and helps us with what we need to do. He's strong-minded. He speaks well."

Kay, the poet, calls Hiram her champion.

"He's like a philosophy speaker," she says. "He talked with me about hypocrisy. He was my advocate."

She remembers sitting with him outside one clear night. Out there in the country, they could see the stars. They were talking about something important, an issue of hers. She pretended to pay attention but wasn't. He could tell, so he changed the subject. Without changing the modulation of his voice, without warning her, he started to talk about the stars. When she noticed that she was no longer the topic of conversation, he explained: "You're not paying attention to our process. So let's talk about the Little Dipper."

And they did. They talked about the Little Dipper and the Big Dipper, about the spoon and the handle, about beauty and distance and time and mystery.

"I like to speak all that philosophy stuff," Kay says. "He just challenged me to be on his level."

A few girls—Kay among them—move down to the pond that sits a couple of hundred feet from the house. They want to fish. Hiram sits on a nearby picnic table watching and munching on graham crackers he takes from a bag in his shirt pocket. Even with the girls' hooks and lures splashing in the water, the pond remains still enough to reflect the trees that surround it. It reflects, too, the occasional puff of cloud that slides overhead. Hiram knows how to fish. He guides the girls, and when Kay comes to him with a fish on her hook, squealing, he knows what to do.

The fish—six-inches long and gray—yanked so fiercely on the line it pulled the hook through its eye socket. Slick blood runs over its scales, and most of the girls shriek again and again, hands in the air near their heads, turning away. But one calm girl—Dollie—picks up Kay's fish and holds it with both hands while Hiram works loose the hook, trying to save the eye. Once that's done and the fish returned to the pond, Kay casts again, hurling with so much follow-through that the line's path describes a perfect circle and the hook lands at her feet, and she laughs.

Angela, younger than most of the other girls, comes to sit beside Hiram. He's atop the picnic table, she settles on the bench. She wears her long hair pulled back from her face, and her hair is kinky and thick, and her head leans forward on her long neck so her chin and nose seem beak-like, making an impression of a goose. She's new, which is why she isn't fishing or joking with the others. Hiram hasn't had much of a chance to talk with her.

He asks why she is at Touchstone. "Fighting?" he says. "With whom?" His questions are almost whispers. Angela mumbles her replies, mouths them in the fewest possible words. Hiram finds a new question after each answer.

"Were you big and bad? You can say it. *I was big and bad.*"

"What are you going to be when you grow up?"

"Where do you live?"

"How do you spell that?"

"Who do you live with?"

Angela lives in Hartford, in the South End, a block or two—it turns out—from my grandparents' house. She lives with her mother and her sister.

"How old is she?"

The sister is twenty-three. The sister has a baby. The baby is a year old.

"She getting married?"

Yes.

"Do you have a boyfriend?"

Yes.

"What's his name?"

Manuel.

"What does he do? He goes to school? Where?"

Bulkeley.

"Bulkeley High School? What grade is he in?"

Ten.

"Wait." Hiram starts counting with his fingers, as if he plans to ask about tenth grade, but really he's buying himself time. He's figuring where he wants to go with this.

"Do you love him?"

No.

"Do you know what love is?"

No.

"Me neither."

He pauses. Looks out over the pond. The voices of laughing girls rise from the brush and brambles along the pond's edge.

"If you were home right now, what would you be doing?"

Talking on the phone.

"Me too."

He pauses again.

"You ever go to the public library?"

She shakes her head.

"It's a good place to be."

Another girl—Chastity—runs up to the table eager to tell Hiram some news or a funny story, but she stops short. She can tell something is happening here, even if all that is happening is the construction of a trust that will be necessary through months of confrontations and support. Chastity looks from Hiram to Angela, then stares at Angela. It's a startled look, as if Chastity has just come upon something sad and sacred on the fringes of a party and doesn't know whether to go back to the revelry or show sympathy.

"It's okay, Chastity," Hiram says.

"What's okay?"

"Everything."

Later that night Hiram takes a call in the office. It's a real estate agent. Hiram asks the number of square feet on a house he'd seen advertised.

"That's small," he says. "It's okay. It's a good starter."

II

> Do not wish to be anything but what you are and to be that perfectly.
>
> A GREETING from Joshua Hall's telephone answering machine

Joshua Hall called Canterbury Street home, and he loved it, the sap that stuck on his palms when he climbed the pines, the evening parade of cars bringing parents home from work, his father's backyard garden—loves it still, though it hurt him once. Not a crippling wound, but one that changed him.

His parents, Sonja and Edrick Hall, closed on their Canterbury house on September 15, 1973. Edrick had found the squarish, two-story home at the south end of the street. He deemed it spacious enough to hold his growing family (the Halls had five children with a sixth on the way), and he prized its three fireplaces. He particularly liked the high basement ceilings that allowed him to stand to his full six feet four inches.

Sonja thought Canterbury a wonderful and interesting street. It was first integrated in 1958 when Catherine and Boce Barlow (she a teacher; he a state judge) bought the gray colonial revival house at No. 31. The Barlows had first telephoned the realtor listing the home, but he turned them down. No black family lived on Canterbury then; nor would one, not by his sale. But the woman who owned the house did not share her agent's misgivings, and when the Barlows called her directly, she showed them the house. It was while living on Canterbury that Judge Barlow became Senator Barlow, the first black man elected to the Connecticut state senate. People like the Barlows gave Sonja Hall reasons to enjoy living on Canterbury. Her neighbors included a state treasurer, a fire chief, a city councilman, two doctors, a lawyer, a priest, and a stockbroker. Edrick was a computer engineer, and Sonja worked for the Hartford school district as a teacher's aide. She felt comfortable in the integrated neighborhood where there were, at that time, more white households than black. The neighbors were friendly. The children got along, hers often playing with the Sullivan children from a white family living next door. Sonja remembers that, sometimes, as she and Mrs. Sullivan—Gerri—stood outside talking, Gerri would imagine aloud that they would all—together—grow old on Canterbury Street. Maybe Sonja nodded her head in agreement, or muttered a quiet yes, but she didn't believe that.

"When a black family moves in, whites start moving out," she said years later. "I knew that eventually the street would become all black."

What was happening on Canterbury was happening throughout Hartford's North End. Black families moved north out of neighborhoods closer to downtown that had been leveled as part of urban renewal, finding homes nearer to Keney Park. By 1965, in the area north of Albany Avenue, the black population had soared as the white population plummeted. A few years before, nearly all the residents had been white. Now only a quarter were. The Sullivans stayed longer than most. But there would be no growing old together. In 1984, the Sullivans bought a house in another part of Hartford, near Elizabeth Park. The new house wasn't far—only a drive of about two miles, no more than seven minutes. As Sonja remembers it, Gerri Sullivan said another street would be better for her children. They would feel more comfortable with children like themselves.

"And that was okay," Sonja said years later. "We understood it." It would have bothered her more, she said, if Gerri had made up a lie.

Nor did Sonja lie to Joshua when he came to her one afternoon as she washed dishes in the kitchen and asked, Why did the Sullivans leave?

Why do you think? she answered.

"It was the hardest decision we ever made as a family," Gerri said, some two decades after. "I cried from the time we put the house on the market until we moved."

Tim and Gerri Sullivan bought on Canterbury in 1972 full of hope for the civil rights movement and for integration. Relatives told them not to go, pressured them to stay in Hartford's Irish and Italian neighborhoods. "Friends and family went crazy," Gerri said. "It was the Shot Heard 'Round the South End." But Tim and Gerri wanted their children to grow up in a mixed-race neighborhood.

For many years Canterbury worked for them. "It was just the most wonderful experience of our lives," she said. "And the Hall kids were a big part of that. Wonderful, wonderful kids. We couldn't have been any closer. That's exactly what we envisioned."

But what they hadn't envisioned was their own growing rarity as a white household in the North End. As other white families moved away, the Sullivans worried about the isolation their youngest, a daughter named Bethany, would face at school. She was the only white child in her class, which didn't matter in elementary school but might well as she grew older. "Canterbury was like an island," Gerri said. "But when you left the street, there were issues about being white. There was some anger." So the Sullivans moved. They chose a neighborhood with an integrated school. Thinking back on that time, Gerri said, the family might have stayed on Canterbury. The move that was meant to help Bethany devastated one of the Sullivans' boys. "As a parent, you don't know. You just call it as you see it," Gerri said. "In retrospect we still could have been successful. We loved our neighbors. But it was almost like a false world."

The Sullivans—all of them—went on to live Hartford lives. Gerri served on the city council, and her brother was a Hartford mayor. Bethany teaches in Hartford, and another Sullivan boy grew up to teach, coach, and work as an acting principal in Hartford schools. "We're very much a Hartford family," Gerri said.

The boyhood Joshua had known on Canterbury Street seemed to have been Martin Luther King Jr.'s dream fulfilled. Its block parties had been a table of brotherhood, its backyards had been playgrounds for all of God's children, its peaceful nights a sign of hope that the crooked places could be made straight. Once the Sullivans left, for better or for worse, Joshua began to see life in terms of skin color. He learned to question people's motives, to treat with skepticism everything white people said or did. He wondered what constituted friendship, and what truly lay in the hearts of others. He began to notice how much of TV was for white people, and the movies, and books, and school. He became angry. His parents had given him a middle name—Malik—that honored Malcolm X's Muslim name, El-Hajj Malik El-Shabazz. Now Joshua woke each morning to a portrait of Malcolm X his parents had hung on his bedroom wall, and he thought, Maybe Malcolm X was right. Maybe whites and blacks should live separately. Why build bonds that are torn apart?

Canterbury remained a friendly and stable street. "We deeply regretted the white flight," said Catherine Barlow. "But we felt good that the street remained a very solid neighborhood. And we were grateful for that."

But the Barlows eventually moved, too, in August 2000, forced by Judge Barlow's poor health. He had damaged his spine in an accident, and he and Catherine needed to be closer to family. They decided to move to Maryland where their son lived. "My husband did not want to leave," Catherine said. "Hartford's meant so much to him. He did not want to leave. Funny thing. He got so sick that morning. It was just a case of nerves."

The house still bears the Barlow name. In 1994, 31 Canterbury Street was added to the National Register of Historic Places in recognition of Judge Barlow's status as a pioneer.

In the summer of 1967, the race riots that burned city-by-city across America reached Hartford. That summer and in the two that followed, anger over unemployment and slum housing and police brutality and white racism enflamed the city—particularly its North End. In melees that would last days at a time, people tossed firebombs and bricks as police fought back with tear gas and gunfire. The city imposed a two-day curfew in the summer of 1969 as rioters looted stores and set buildings afire. That summer alone, police arrested more than eight hundred people during riots.

Things had calmed by 1974 when the school district opened a new school building on Granby Street in the North End. But the new Weaver High, with its massive, windowless walls and hidden entrances, seemed designed to withstand the summers of the late 1960s rather than shelter a pre-calculus class. As Hartford historian Andrew Walsh has noted, the building's fortress exterior suggests that Hartford's leaders lacked confidence in their city. Perhaps, after the riots, they did. An urban legend rooted in that idea has grown up around the new Weaver, supposing that its design was influenced by mob control strategies: a flat roof could double as a helicopter landing pad; the nearby railroad tracks would make for easy transport of National Guard troops; the lack of windows would prevent militant students from tossing a desk or a brick or a teacher through the glass. More likely, says Walsh, the building is a reflection of the Brutalist architecture that defined so much urban construction in the 1960s and 1970s. Given its era, Walsh argues, Weaver was typical.

Urban legend or not, the building's design is frightening. Weaver's interior suggests some dystopian nightmare: a warren of steel doors along fluorescent-lit halls, the only air machine-breathed through vents. Behind the doors, students face four windowless walls. Those who stay inside through the day can suffer a school week without sunlight. On winter's short days, they arrive in darkness and might, after band or basketball practice, leave in darkness.

The Halls lived in Weaver's neighborhood. Sonja Hall

worked her connections within the district and sent her children to window-filled Hartford Public instead.

At the Pub, Joshua was known as a radical who preferred to be called Malik. His fiery, clumsy attempts to argue his politics led white students to accuse him of racism. It wasn't that. Only a teen, he had yet to learn how to clearly and precisely speak about his passions. They tumbled out of him: his disputes with the justice system and white capitalism and even with his school's faculty. A few HPHS teachers were black, and an assistant principal as well, but if Joshua could go all those years without instruction from a black teacher, then—in his mind—Hartford Public needed more. So when he made the pledge with his friends, he did so with a vision of himself one day added to Hartford Public's roster of black faculty. He would instruct Owls in history: history of the world and of the country but especially their own.

Even after he left for college in Virginia he was like a comet in far-flung orbit, circling back each summer to Hartford. He worked with Hartford's Project Care, a program that taught kids to improve their city. Once, they collected trash at Keney Park. Another time they fixed up a churchyard. As they worked, Joshua instructed them:

You really have to come back. You really have to help out because if not you, who?

He graduated, then listened as older siblings who had left Connecticut whispered to him those mystical incantations, "Atlanta" and "DC", and Joshua recognized the lure: good nightclubs, quality restaurants, a professional circle of young African-Americans helping each other toward ever-larger slices of money and comfort. He listened and was tempted, but all he had to do was remember the summer faces of those Project Care children who—being city kids—had already heard too many broken promises and too many lies.

If not me . . . ?

He moved back in the summer of 1996, and he began looking for a teaching job. There were no openings at Hartford Public, but he applied at middle schools and at Weaver. Later, he would say it seemed he'd been brought to Weaver by design, as if some power intended him to arrive there—at the school meant for Canterbury kids—one way or another, as if his Hartford Public years had been only a detour. The moment Joshua finished his interview with Weaver's principal, he had a job and (yes, he sensed it) a home. He felt a greater communion at Weaver where nearly every student was black than he had in the multiracial hallways of Hartford Public. Weaver's kids came from his neighborhood and the neighborhoods nearby. Weaver fit his identity, as if in that swirl of students he *knew* who he was and what he was supposed to do. He attended football games and other after-school events, chaperoned at the prom, even wore Weaver-green jackets when the Beavers played sports against his alma mater. In that windowless, stuffy palace, Joshua had rediscovered his world.

But it was a world in the midst of collapse. District-wide, the Hartford schools had hit bottom. Worst in the state, among the worst in the country, they suffered from racial and economic segregation and record dropout rates. Children were promoted to seventh grade despite their third-grade reading levels. The district's financial mismanagement teetered on the edge of criminality. Hartford Public couldn't even keep its boys bathrooms supplied with toilet paper and soap.

In 1996, the summer Joshua came home, there were

no riots over the condition of the Hartford schools. There should have been.

Gayl S. Westerman wanted her students to be witnesses in the hope they might some day become warriors. It was 1993, and Westerman was a law professor teaching a civil rights seminar at Pace University in White Plains, New York. Her students had attended suburban high schools and were too young to remember the heyday of the American Civil Rights movement in the 1950s and 60s, so she required them to visit an urban school and to write a paper comparing it with a suburban school. Westerman hoped to show them that—nearly forty years after *Brown v. Board of Education*—there remained reasons to fight.

During this seminar, Westerman and her students also visited Hartford to observe a trial about school desegregation. For days, they sat in court while witnesses testified to how Hartford's children suffered in the classroom and how suburban children succeeded. But the testimony, though horrific, came secondhand. Westerman and the students decided to see for themselves, to take a field trip that would fulfill her class requirement and bring the trial to life. So, one morning, they toured elementary schools that sat a couple of miles apart: one in wealthy West Hartford, the other in Hartford.

"We spent several hours in each," Westerman recalled years later. "We interviewed students, sat in classes, spoke to principals, spoke to teachers, and pretty much had our antennae up." Of the difference between the two schools, she said, "It was a textbook distinction."

They started in Hartford. The schoolyard, Westerman remembers, was littered with broken glass. The chain link fence that surrounded it stood high, and the Pace students felt as if they were stepping into a prison yard. Inside, they walked across cracked linoleum floors and watched children read from textbooks that had been repaired with tape. There were hardly any computers. In a kindergarten class, children learning to read dates followed the teacher as she pointed to the wall near her desk at a calendar taped where the pages had been torn.

In West Hartford the school's floors were clean and polished, and in the window-filled lobby, inside glass atriums, papier-mâché statues of jungle animals, positioned as if alive, munched on living plants. It was, Westerman said, "a kid paradise." In the hallways sat boxes of computers awaiting hookup. In a fourth grade class, the children practiced measurements, and each used his or her own rulers and scales. And in a West Hartford kindergarten class, where children also were learning to read dates, each boy and girl studied from his or her own laminated calendar.

But the greatest distinction between Hartford and West Hartford lay in how the children reacted to the grownups from Pace. In the fifth grade in West Hartford, a child asked: I'm interested in becoming a lawyer. How do you do it?

In the fifth grade in Hartford, a student asked: Is your school hard? Do you have homework at your school?

The tours proved quick, superficial, and shocking, but they illustrated the arguments the Pace students had heard while attending the trial. The case was called *Sheff v. O'Neill*, and it would become a landmark case—not only in Connecticut but in the nation—because it was the first to challenge school segregation based on a state's constitution rather than on that of the United States. Seventeen children from Hartford and West Hartford—including

Milo Sheff, a ten-year-old—were named as plaintiffs in the suit, brought in 1989 against the state and its then-governor, William A. O'Neill. The suit challenged the state's cherished tradition of "home rule," a doctrine that meant each town—one hundred sixty-nine of them—was responsible for itself and no other. Connecticut had no regional governments, no counties to reapportion wealth and services. Each town ran its own police force, its own public works department, its own schools. With a few exceptions, the boundaries of most school districts were the boundaries of a town—and it had been that way since the state legislature made it so in 1909. But Connecticut's towns were also segregated; the Latino and African-American populations lived mostly in the core cities of Waterbury, Bridgeport, New Haven, and Hartford. Whites lived in suburban enclaves like Greenwich and Avon and Litchfield and Old Saybrook. So the schools were segregated, too.

The Sheff lawyers argued that the system violated the state constitution. Article 8 mandated free public schools; other articles guaranteed that Connecticut's citizens would not face racial discrimination or segregation in pursuit of their constitutional rights. If free public schools are a right, the Sheff lawyers argued, then students pursuing that right must not be hampered by segregation. But nine out of ten Hartford schoolchildren come from minority families, and most students in the suburbs are white—isn't that segregation? And if the education is better in the suburbs, doesn't that imply that segregated minority students in Hartford receive an unequal and unconstitutional education?

The trial began in December 1992. Through testimony and documents, the Sheff lawyers revealed the inadequacies of education for Hartford's twenty-five thousand students, the most of any state school district. News reports from the trial included testimony about an elementary school at which nine of ten students came from families who lived in poverty. A health concern was chronic depression: three students had attempted suicide in the last year; two were third graders. At another school, a ceiling gave way, dumping the corpses of dead pigeons into a classroom. The district's dropout rate of 17 percent was the highest in the state, even though Hartford spent more in state, local, and federal money per student than any other school district in Connecticut. Its test scores were awful. In 1991–92 only 6 percent of Hartford sixth graders passed the state's math test.

The state denied none of this bad news. What its lawyers argued was that Connecticut didn't cause the problem and so should not be held liable for the solution. There is no state-sponsored segregation, the lawyers said. People live where they choose.

The implication? If minorities and the poor want better schools, they should improve their own or move.

From the governor's office to the homes of PTA members, people paid careful attention to the trial. Its outcome had the potential to force busing—sending suburban children into Hartford and vice versa—or to create giant school districts that grouped poor towns with wealthy ones. If the state lost, home rule might even collapse, making a change in the Land of Steady Habits as monumental as the American South's surrender of Jim Crow laws.

But Judge Harry Hammer found for the state, agreeing that no government actions had led to segregation. In praising Hammer's decision, the new governor, John

Rowland, told the *Hartford Courant* that "the state did not force whatever racial balance or imbalance exists . . . It's a result of human nature, people's decision to live where they want to live."

Rowland's assertion ignored the fact that poor people seldom live where they want to; they live where they can or must. Avon and Simsbury had no equivalent to Hartford's Rice Heights, Dutch Point, Stowe Village, Bellevue Square, and Nelton Court housing projects. Most poor people—and in Connecticut that often meant Latinos and African-Americans—could not afford the suburbs. Moreover, most services for the poor—health care, state welfare services—could be found only in Hartford. Imagine a poor, single mother who somehow found an affordable rent in Simsbury as she tried to reach the city without a car—bicycling? hitchhiking? walking?—and dodging all the Lexus sedans that zoomed by her. Poor people didn't choose Hartford because they liked the crime and vacant buildings; Hartford was often the only option. It remained so because Hartford was where government had decided to place its services for the poor. Perhaps those decisions were made without the intent to segregate. Perhaps the poor lived in Hartford first and governments chose to place services so as to be more convenient for those who needed them. But the result of those decisions was a cycle of segregation.

The Sheff lawyers appealed to the state Supreme Court. In July 1996, the court announced its decision, overruling Hammer by a 4–3 vote.

"We hold today that the needy schoolchildren of Hartford have waited long enough," wrote Chief Justice Elizabeth Peters for the majority. "Racial and ethnic segregation has a pervasive and invidious impact on schools, whether the segregation results from intentional conduct or from unorchestrated demographic factors."

The cause of the segregation, the court decided, was immaterial. Given the phrasing of the constitution, what mattered was that the legislature knew of the problem. Knowledge carried with it an obligation. Awareness required action.

The court ordered the state legislature to ensure that all Connecticut children have access to an equal education—and to do it soon, "to make a difference before another generation of children suffers the consequences of a segregated public school education."

But another generation *was* suffering the consequences. It had been almost a decade since *Sheff* was first filed. Milo Sheff was now seventeen. In the three-and-a-half years since the trial, the schools had grown even worse.

The death spiral of the Hartford public schools accelerated in 1996, the year the Supreme Court overruled Hammer in *Sheff* and the same year that Joshua Hall returned home. Kindergarten students learning to read a calendar could trace the district's descent torn page by torn page.

January 1996: the school board ended a failed year-and-a-half experiment with privatization by firing the Minnesota company it had hired to run the district. Private company or public administration, Hartford was still spending more money per student than any other Connecticut school district and getting fewer results. "It's like buying a Cadillac and not putting any gas in it," Mayor Mike Peters told *Education Week on the Web*.

May: the city council passed a resolution asking Peters to declare the school district in a "state of emergency" as if a flood or earthquake had struck the schools.

July: the state Supreme Court issued its opinion in *Sheff*.

October: a team from the New England Association of Schools and Colleges visited to decide whether Hartford Public met the minimum qualifications of schools deemed fit to educate students. It didn't. Dropout rates were too high, teacher morale too low, the library underfunded, the school lacking necessary computer equipment, and the dilapidated building "the most serious problem."

November: the state's Commissioner of Education released forty-eight recommendations for improving the Hartford schools.

December: the city council considered a resolution asking the elected members of the Board of Education to resign. At a board meeting a week later, Stephen Fournier accused his fellow board members of corruption, nepotism, and unethical behavior. Fournier was a white Hartford lawyer who had sent all his children to Hartford schools—his oldest boy Jake had played football at Hartford Public with Eric and Derrick, Harvey, Hiram, and Joshua, finished as valedictorian, then attended Yale. Now the elder Fournier caused a row with his charges. An angry parent stormed the stage and knocked over a pitcher of water that spilled on Fournier. He resigned before the new year. Later the weekly newspaper in Hartford, the *Advocate*, gave credence to Fournier's accusations when it reported that five of the seven school board members had relatives who worked for the district.

January 1997: the staff of the New England Association of Schools and Colleges sent a letter to Hartford Public principal Amado Cruz announcing its recommendation that the school's accreditation be revoked. The letter cited fifty-seven failures or inadequacies based on its team's October visit. Classes were too large, its building housed rodents and insects, it offered too few courses, and its library lacked sufficient books. (A later news report in the *Courant* noted that Glastonbury High School's library had a 1996–97 budget of between $30,000 and $40,000. Hartford Public's library budget had actually shrunk over the previous two years by one thousand dollars, leaving it only $7,469). The Board of Education too often meddled in the affairs of the school, the letter alleged, and the school had no enforceable attendance policy. The visiting committee had found "substantive evidence that Hartford Public High School fails to meet the teaching and learning needs of its students," the letter read.

March: a thousand Hartford Public students walked out of classes to protest the crisis.

April: the state legislature intervened. It approved Special Act 97–4, which declared the Hartford school district to be in a state of crisis. The act also dissolved the board of education elected by Hartford's citizens, and it gave the governor and others power to appoint a new board of trustees to run Hartford's schools. The act passed 135–7 in the House and 27–9 in the Senate. Governor Rowland signed it into law. The state had, in essence, declared Hartford unfit to run its own schools. It had taken the children away from their parents.

June: Joshua Hall ended his first year as a social studies teacher in the Hartford school district.

Behind the door of Room 4056 at Weaver High School, Joshua Hall sharpens yellow pencils. He wears a dark suit, white shirt, and tie. It's May 17, 2000. A Wednesday.

On the lapel of Joshua's coat is a button that reads "I ♥ teaching social studies." He tries to wear a suit every day. "Teaching is a profession," he explains, "and you should dress professionally. Our kids, they don't get to see black male professionals in suits unless there is a problem. And, of course, my dad always wore a suit to work." Joshua wears eyeglasses, too, and though his face is still round and full and smooth as a toddler's, his sobriety is such that he sharpens pencils with the gravity of a mortician.

The ceiling—maybe eight feet high—intrudes on the stuffy room. Computers sport mouse pads from the Travelers Insurance Company, and chairs in front of them are marked with graffiti'd names: "Bridget" and "Juan" among them. A tapestry made in Ghanaian style—a kente cloth—is tacked to a bulletin board. On the chalkboard are questions about the Fourth Amendment to the U.S. Constitution.

Joshua teaches government and history to tenth graders, but he also teaches standardized testing. The state-appointed board recently hired a new superintendent who, upon learning of Hartford's failure at standardized tests, famously promised, "We will never be last again." So Joshua's marching orders—like those of many district teachers—demand that he follow a curriculum that allocates much of the school week to teaching students the skills they need to pass the Connecticut Academic Performance Test or CAPT. On Joshua's chalkboard is this admonition:

"Think CAPT."

This morning, his homeroom will take a CAPT practice test. Hence, the pencils.

Hartford's schools have improved since the state takeover. In the year 2000, test scores are up. Administrative practices—everything from ordering supplies to negotiating with labor unions—are more efficient. An investigation by the state attorney general's office has found god-awful bookkeeping, but nothing provably criminal. Hartford Public alumni have started a fund for the school's library. The changes made now will in two years lead the state's commissioner of education to declare that the people educating Hartford's children have moved "away from the (pre-1997) climate of accepting failure." But that will happen in two years, and now work remains. Hartford Public languishes on probation. The school's juniors, who numbered six hundred as freshmen, will muster only one hundred seventy at their graduation. A state study has declared that the state's worst elementary school (they call it "lowest performing") is in Hartford. The schools remain segregated. In fact, Hartford's schools—at 96 percent nonwhite—are more segregated than five years before.

In Room 4056 the only white people are a student teacher and me.

The students take their practice test in silence. Joshua walks among them, his back straight, his gait careful, watching them work. He's military. He maintains this march for ten minutes, then turns on the computer at his desk and sits. Then he walks again.

When the test ends, Joshua hands out a snack: crackers and cartons of orange juice. Social time begins because this is homeroom and homeroom has no real lesson plan. The kids hop up and stroll. Some head for the hallway. They come, they go. Voices rise as if the students are on the street shouting above the boom of a car's bass speakers or the din of a construction site. Another teacher—white, gray-haired—stops by. His name is Frank. Suddenly Frank and Joshua are in a tag-team confrontation with a short, chubby boy named Jimmy King. Jimmy wears glasses and a stud in his earlobe, and his mouth is filled with silver caps. It's a fashion statement. The statement makes him look twelve, though he's probably sixteen. His attitude smacks of something even older. Two days earlier one of Jimmy's street gang was stabbed in the hand during a fight outside Weaver where the school buses drop off students. Now Jimmy refuses to leave Joshua's room for his next class until his boys come by to accompany him. Since the stabbing, he says, the school hallways aren't safe. Joshua and Frank argue that he should quit his street gang. That, they say, would be the safest thing. No, Jimmy says, everybody's got to have his own backup. Even Frank, who wears his protection to school.

"Take off your bulletproof vest," Jimmy says to Frank.

"I'm not crazy," says Frank.

"That's why I've got my boys. Without my boys, my friend would be dead. Without my boys, they get rolled."

Students bustle about the room. Some girls crowd near to show Joshua pictures from the prom the night before. Joshua attended as a chaperone. Now and then a student calls out, "Mister! Mister!" Most of the students call Joshua "Mister" rather than "Mr. Hall." Joshua thumbs through the prom photos, but he's not finished with Jimmy.

"So what are you going to do?" Joshua says. He's still flipping through the snapshots. "Disassociate yourself with your boys?"

"I can't do that, Mr. Hall. I was in with them. I stay in it. Can't get out of it, Hall."

Joshua shakes his head. "That's not Jimmy King. Jimmy King doesn't have to be that way."

"I have to protect myself, Hall."

"No one else in our homeroom has to hang around for

protection except you. Why? Because you hang around that group."

That's the Catch-22. Don't expect Jimmy to figure it out. Instead, he allows himself to be distracted elsewhere; he disappears with his boys into the hallway crowds. Over the loudspeaker, a voice from the main office talks about asthma. Joshua sits down with a girl in a pink sweater who holds a pink pen. "So are you saying that the Fourth Amendment should be extended?" he asks the girl.

"I think it should be extended."

"So talk to me about that."

Nearby, a girl brushes a boy's hair with the care of a surgeon.

Through the day Joshua will rush to the aid of a star pupil who has a ten thousand dollar scholarship to Providence College and also—apparently—bleeding ulcers. He will work with another teacher on a slide presentation about the Civil Rights movement, and he will give a quiz. He will lead exuberant students through discussions of their constitutional rights, focusing on the right to privacy and whether it implies a right to life—or to death. Their arguments will be loud and spirited, a passionate call and response peppered with teasing insults and sincere support. ("You're like a role model for the male race!" "You shut your mouth!" "Johnny! High Five! Go ahead, Johnny!") He will vote in a faculty election for a seat on the teachers' union school committee, vote for himself because he's on the ballot, though he thinks unions aren't for teachers, that teachers should have a professional association as do doctors and lawyers. He will admit to concern about the curriculum, wonder whether he is teaching students to think or to take tests, but acknowledge that it seems necessary, that Hartford's schools and its students must improve. Lives are at stake.

And this is just the workday. This isn't all of Joshua's life.

He's making plans. Some involve graduate-level classes in the fall at Central Connecticut State University. He wants a master's degree, and he wants to learn more about Hartford and Connecticut's African-American history. So there's paperwork and scheduling for that.

He also wants to revive more recent history with the ten-year reunion for Hartford Public's Class of 1990. Some former classmates will help, but mostly the reunion is his to arrange and promote. He foresees an evening that renews acquaintances and friendships while celebrating achievements, a reminder of where the Owls of '90 began so they can see that they are alive and vital, that they have, after everything, progressed. Who knows? Maybe that reunion will create energy that pushes them further, makes them better still. He wants everyone to come. Not just E 'n' D and Harvey and Hiram, though certainly them (how long since they've all been together?), but also all those Hispanic classmates he never knew so well. The greater the turnout, the greater the proof of their success. So he's spreading the word. October 21, a Saturday. The downtown Elks Lodge. Buffet dinner and dancing to a disc jockey. Balloons and streamers.

One other plan. It's time to change addresses. For nearly four years, Joshua's drive home from work has taken him across the Connecticut River into Glastonbury, south of the town center, south of the restaurants that serve shrimp pizza and gourmet bagels, and the new bookstore and the new clothing stores and the new shops that sell kitchen gadgets to people with lots of new money.

Drive *home*? No, that's not right. It's never felt like home, living in Glastonbury in a big white house. He had a good reason to move there, having taken a second job as residence director for a group of young men from New York City. The teens are bright; college material. They live in Connecticut because federal money pays for them to escape failing Big Apple high schools and enroll at better ones. Joshua's crew attends Glastonbury High. As residence director, he acts as their parent. When Joshua took the job, he imagined after-dinner discussions about affirmative action or the Nation of Islam or the social questions raised by Spike Lee films. But they are teenage boys, after all. If they talk about anything after school it's more likely to be about East Coast rap versus West Coast rap, Biggie Smalls versus Tupac Shakur, or about whether the Knicks will take the Celtics, or about girls. Moreover, Joshua finds Glastonbury dull. In truth he hasn't given the town much of a chance. He hasn't explored beyond Main Street, the route he takes to and from Weaver. Nothing about the town entices him; it has no vibration to match his. A fine experiment, living in the suburbs. Worth a try. But this school year will be his last in Glastonbury. It's time to go home for real. In Hartford he knows his past and can imagine his future. There he can be himself. Perfectly.

9

I chose Montana.

I chose chattering magpies over shrieking blue jays, and arid valleys over mosquito-filled woods. I chose summer over autumn, the Rockies rather than the beach; bicycle rides to work instead of bumper-to-bumper rush-hour grinds; sirloin over pizza; an unlocked garage door over a car alarm; time, not money.

The *Courant* had offered us work. We were prepared to accept—until our boss at the university said he could improve our lot there. Not as much money as the *Courant*, but enough.

How to choose? This was, after all, our move toward stability. We intended to commit to one place or the other for years, perhaps for our lives.

As I thought through my half of our decision, I considered Eric and Derrick, Harvey and Hiram and Joshua. It seemed to me no coincidence that Harvey and Eric, both married with kids, had been the ones who broke the pledge to Hartford. Their self-imposed exiles arose from complicated reasons and could not be charged solely to family concerns, but there was no denying the power love brought to bear. Sheri and I had no children, but I knew her first choice was Missoula.

I also considered the five friends from another angle: I was still writing their stories, still writing this book. Choosing Hartford meant proximity. Reporting and research would be easier. No more flying across the country to check facts and study documents or to spend a day at Weaver High School.

Yet what about energy? Would I, at the end of a workday reporting in some Greater Hartford suburb, want to go home and report some more? Would I be like the accountant who can't keep his own checkbook balanced or the cobbler whose children go shoeless? In Montana I would teach, an activity separate from writing and reporting. Moreover the academic schedule offered me months when I could return to Hartford, see my grandparents, visit Hartford's public library or City Hall. Working for the *Courant*, I might chronicle day-by-day the life of some small Connecticut town, but what I wanted to write—needed to write—was something else. The story about Hartford, I was coming to understand, meant more to me than Hartford itself.

What fueled the writing, what compelled me to tackle that story, was absence. In Montana I needed Hartford, so I would write about it. In Montana I could keep the story and hold fast to a kind of Hartford. Not all of the city all of the time, but something. When I was unable to travel by airplane, I could still sit in my office, and return through memory and imagination, writing my way home. As prompts I could surround myself with talismans of the place: framed pictures of the state capitol and of Mark Twain's house, a Connecticut artist's abstract watercolor that had hung in my aunt's home, a yardstick from the old *Hartford Times* afternoon paper, a Hartford phone book, pictorial histories, my grandfather's penknife, and the bookends from a shelf in my grandparents' home. In Montana I could still surround myself with my grandparents.

Perhaps if I lived in Hartford, having the city, I would let the story go. I couldn't risk that.

No Hartford then, except one I might haunt from time to time, and another I might create for myself. My own Hartford. It seemed in one sense perverse—like a sports fan who would rather count his inventory of pennants, posters, ball caps, and jerseys than go to a game. But in another it seemed pure: this book was a love letter to Hartford, and I could write it better here than there.

Except, as a result, I also chose to embrace my grandparents in memory rather than in fact; I chose to hold them in imagination rather than in body. There was no way to convince myself that such a thing was right. My choice seemed harsh, perhaps unforgivable, and it seemed also irrevocable. Though all logic said nothing was permanent, said I could return to Hartford in five years or ten, it seemed foolish to think so. If Hartford could not lure me back now, when could it ever? No, if I chose Montana, I was as a consequence renouncing my claim to Hartford as home, turning in my membership card, surrendering my keys to the gate.

So I no longer belonged to Hartford. I no longer belonged in Hartford. In Montana I still felt like some stranger in a strange wilderness. I belonged nowhere. I called no place home.

I never told my grandparents that the *Courant* offered us jobs. I never told them that when given the choice to love them as neighbors or to love them as living memories, I chose the latter. I suppose, even so, that my distance made it obvious.

II

Connecticut's Willard-Cybulski Correctional Institute is a Security Level 2 state prison. That means a lot less razor wire and fewer guards. The prison sits in a field that slopes slightly and can be green as late as October. Follow the Shaker Road out of Enfield into what passes for rural Connecticut, past the sign that reads "Turkey Crossing: Please drive carefully," and you'll see it as you near the Somers town line. Parking is easy and close. Walking into the lobby is like walking into a high school, much like walking into Hartford Public. The two share colors, blue and white. In Willard-Cybulski's lobby, the floor is white, except for the blue tiles that spell "WCI." On the walls are lockers. Through glass doors to the right, you can see the visiting room, which looks a bit like a high school cafeteria—long white tables—and which has on its walls posters straight out of English class. One says "READ." By appearances, WCI is even more welcoming than Hartford Public. Cleaner and shinier, it is in a strange way more affable. Prison trusties polish the floors with buffing machines and wipe the door windows with spray bottles and cloths. The grounds—hills and oak-filled woods—are prettier than the grounds that surround Hartford Public. As at Hartford Public, there's a security officer in a blue uniform waiting to meet all visitors, though at HPHS, the officer sits behind a table. At WCI, he sits in a compartment behind some kind of glass, probably bullet proof. WCI could, in fact, be a high school if only it echoed with the laughter of teenagers, and that absence is what tells you WCI is a prison. It is silent here, except for the shrieks of circling sea gulls and crows.

Here, Butch Braswell served much of his sentence.

Though he was found guilty in April 1994 of two of the four counts brought against him, he didn't enter prison right away. His appeal to the state Supreme Court, handled by students from the University of Connecticut's law school, lasted nearly three years. But once the Supreme Court decided against him, he had to surrender himself. He began serving his six-year sentence on December 15, 1997, five years to the day the state made its second attempt to capture his voice on tape as he accepted a green balloon.

At WCI the dorms were broken into cubes with six inmates to a cube. Butch passed the time counting his sit-ups: 455,000 by the time he got out, he would later say, nearly five hundred a day. Serving that time was, for Butch, like serving time in a day-care center. There were counselors and activities. Butch became a gym worker, leading classes in flexibility and refereeing inmates' basketball games. When he had quiet time, he mentally revisited his case, looking for flaws in it, probing and poking it, haunted by what he believed to be inconsistencies and errors, proofs that his prosecution was a persecution—and unjust.

He would eventually tell me all this, but not on the day I'd stepped into the lobby at WCI. It was a Friday morning, the day before Hartford Public's class of 1990 planned to gather for its reunion. Though, months earlier, I'd arranged with Butch through a prison counselor to meet that morning, he refused me at the door. He sent a note to the lobby. The envelope was addressed to my attention in Butch's handwriting, with an official stamp that read "THIS CORRESPONDENCE ORIGINATED FROM AN INMATE AT A CONNECTICUT CORRECTIONAL FACILITY."

Dear Mike,
I would very much like to do the interview but considering where I am at it would be much wiser and safer to do it when I am out. Everyone here is so nosy about my case and they might even hold me longer if information gets out about my law suit. I'm sure you will understand! Call my home and set up another date through my family . . . and leave your number so I can contact you. Most people only think of me as a track coach, they don't realize I worked as a sheriff, please understand . . .

In High Regards,
Melvin Braswell

His release date was December 14, less than two months away. I imagined, as I drove back to Hartford along the Connecticut River valley (car windows down, admiring the eastern sunlight tangled in New England's autumn leaves) that with freedom so close Butch couldn't and wouldn't take a risk. December 14. He would serve only three years of his six—out early, making room for someone else.

Harvey Kendall told Joshua he couldn't come to the reunion. He'd only recently moved from North Carolina to Missouri, and he'd already used up his time off with another trip to Hartford. That previous June had marked fifteen years since his father's death, and his mother had called her children home for a family gathering and home-cooked banquet.

The Hartford he visited that June had changed little from the one he remembered. But one thing heartened him: no more games at Dillon Stadium. Hartford Public had resodded its football field and replaced its worn-out running track with a new one.

"You can't rock the Pub, say you can't rock the Pub!"

A decade since and cheerleaders still called out that chant on this Saturday afternoon, the day of the reunion, as the Owls' football team charged across its home field. I arrived during halftime. A small crowd sat scattered through the bleachers, maybe fifty people, nearly as many to cheer on the visitors as the home team. In a cloudless sky, the sun hung low; its glare interfered with the view of the field, but the scoreboard was plain. The Owls led, 22–0.

Derrick sat alone in the front row. I hadn't seen him in months, and we shook hands, and he invited me to join him. He wore Hartford Public colors. From his sneakers to his blue jeans to his plaid short-sleeved shirt, he was white and navy and sky blue. "I am true to the Blue," he told me. "I am true to the Blue."

We sat a while and talked. The sun bedazzled us from over the tops of western buildings; I barely followed the action. Derrick, though, picked out specific plays—when the Owls ran the trap, the sweep. Jack LaPlante still coached, and the offense, Derrick declared, was much the same as it had been more than ten years earlier.

Then he told me that a month or so before the reunion he was unpacking boxes and had come across some old clothes, among them his high school football jersey. Navy with sky blue lettering. Owls on each shoulder. "D. Walker" on the back, and "32" on both sides. It still fit.

What was it like, pulling it on again?

That jersey, he said, that stays. He couldn't quite describe the feeling associated with it. Going off to war with those guys. It was like the whole world rested in the moment.

He pointed out the cheerleading coach. She was here back then, he said. And the man announcing the game? An alum, two or three years older than Derrick. On the field silhouettes scuttled here and there. Derrick and I stayed until the end. The Pub—unrocked—won, 30–12.

We walked out together, pausing near the school building. Aloud, Derrick recalled the prom of 1990 and his friends, and he wondered who might make the reunion, named a few he hoped to see. Eric, of course, but others, too. He looked at the school building's rough edges, its rusted window frames, the scratched Plexiglas, the flaking paint.

"I was walking by this," he said, "and I wondered if it was like this when I came here, if it was this corroded. Maybe I was too young to notice."

After the game, I returned to Maple Avenue. This was my first trip back since deciding to make my household elsewhere, and the sense that I had broken faith with Hartford made the trip bittersweet. Worse, I knew there was nothing to be done about it.

As always my grandmother insisted I stay with them. Though I argued that I could afford a hotel room and though I worried that my visits burdened her, she was too frugal and proud to have her grandson pay for lodging while her house had available beds. In truth I was glad for her stubbornness. I remained enough of her little-boy grandchild to enjoy a peck on the cheek before she headed upstairs for bed.

During those quiet visits, my grandmother and I talked about so many things: updates on the lives of my cousins, my sister and brother; Hartford history; the characteristics of the different priests at St. Augustine's; whether I should pull the weed maples that populated their lawn ("If it's green and it lives," Grandma said, "it can stay"); what words might fit in five down and in sixty-two across; and their health. We always talked about their health. Grandpa's memory grew spottier each day, she said. He remembered me because he often looked at my photograph. I was the professor from Montana. Professor Mike. She always pronounced herself "all right," declared it with a shrug and the hint of a frown as if she had just described a stew without salt. I knew "all right" wasn't the case. She couldn't put on weight, and because she couldn't stomach most foods she lacked vigor. She was weary and irritable with my grandfather. She made no noisy complaints, but the house was bereft of the vitality and joy I recalled from my childhood. Even on sunny days, my grandparents lived in shadow.

When my grandmother needed to fix a meal or when she wanted to pursue another puzzle or just rest her arthritic joints, I occupied my grandfather. That day of the reunion, he and I strolled once around the block. Every few, halting steps he paused and with his cane pushed wind felled oak twigs to the edges of the sidewalk. Back home we perused family photo albums. He was a handsome man, my grandfather, and I told him that.

"Thank you," he said. "Coming from a discriminating judge like you, that means something."

I have a memory of my grandparents. I've just come off the front porch after working there, typing notes into my laptop. It's not that weekend of the reunion, some other time. It's a day when my grandfather's incapacities have demanded too much of my grandmother. She has to double-check everything: that he dresses himself properly, that he locks the doors to the porch after collecting the newspaper, that he takes his proper medications and the correct number of vitamins and avoids leafy green vegetables. Her words are kind in meaning ("Yes, honey; no, honey; I love you, too, Walt") but the delivery is clipped, hard as winter.

I've come from the porch, and as I look the length of the hall, I see in the kitchen my grandmother sitting at the table, sitting sideways, so her back is away from the chair back. Behind her, my grandfather leans, his cane hooked over the chair, and he rubs my grandmother's shoulders, her back, around her neck, down to her hips. Neither of them speaks. His hands, nine decades old, are big on her fragile bones, and strong, and gentle, and tireless.

On the evening of the reunion, my grandparents and I shared an early dinner. On the TV, men golfed in some part of the world where the sun still shined bright. In Hartford, it was the twilight of an unusually warm autumn evening, and the people of the city took advantage. They jogged trails through Goodwin Park and boys in long pants goofed around with a basketball. At the Maple Avenue Cafe and across the street at the First and Last Tavern, patrons enjoyed beers at tables streetside.

Downtown was its usual quiet after rush hour, all of its energy drained away by the weekend in the suburbs.

On Prospect Street, the BPOE Lodge No. 19 had its doors wide open to welcome the night air and the reunion of Hartford Public's class of 1990. The Elks' building—at least one hundred years old, according to the bartender inside—sits kitty-corner to the Traveler's Insurance tower with its searchlight bright and circling the Hartford sky. As I walked from my parking spot, I crossed paths with a half dozen or so older, white couples dressed in formal wear, heading for some party across the road at the Wadsworth Atheneum.

I arrived about twenty minutes before the scheduled start of the reunion, set for seven o'clock. Inside, Joshua attended to the final details as a disc jockey wired speakers and the bartender checked bottles. Helium-filled blue and white balloons and streamers adorned the ballroom. The turn-of-the-century chamber looked old as a pocket watch, pillared, and with cloth wallpaper embossed in gold and red. The floors were hardwood, and every bit of trim was a dark mahogany. Two fireplaces—each big enough to burn a redwood trunk—sat empty on either side of the long room. I almost expected to see white-haired men in tuxedos and pince-nez, smoking cigars and debating whether the U.S. should declare war against Spain.

Nah, look closely, the bartender told me. This place has aged hard. Stag parties and the like have left marks. He pointed to a painting with a couple of slashes in the canvas as if some drunk took a knife to it. Outside the door, stone busts of bull elk stood at attention, their antlers snapped off.

Joshua walked the room, adjusting a streamer, a tablecloth. All the tables were draped in white with sparkling confetti sprinkled at their centers. Eight chairs per table, twelve tables, seats for ninety-six people. Joshua re-arranged them. "All these tables might be a fantasy," he said.

By seven fifteen, Joshua had stepped out to Prospect Street, looked both ways and seen no one. He stuffed his hands in the pockets of his black trousers. He looked elegant there in his gray sport coat and collarless black jersey, even as he paced the sidewalk.

He had financed the whole show, and he needed at least fifty people to break even. If the reunion earned any cash beyond that, he planned to put it aside as seed money for another reunion. Maybe this one would even generate enough so that the organizers of the next reunion (fifteenth? twentieth?) could get a nicer place. The money—his investment—meant less to him than the momentum. He wanted the night to serve as a foundation, a success on which to build.

The tuxedo-and-black-dress Atheneum crowd continued to stride past. Now and then, one glanced at the Elks lodge where the disc jockey had cranked up his operation so music echoed out the doors, rapping up and down the otherwise silent street.

Finally, by seven thirty, a small crowd. A dozen maybe. Each person stopped at the registration desk to pay twenty dollars and offer up a name and an address. A dentist from Virginia. A cop from Wethersfield. From Rhode Island a specialist in the financing of affordable housing, who had played football at Boston College.

They took their nametags, Eric and his wife, Taren, and mingled. Then Taren found a seat, and Eric stood near the door talking with Joshua. Each at the same time saw Derrick come up the steps from the sidewalk.

Joshua said, "There's D-Nice."

"I know," said Eric. "I recognize that small head."

Derrick signed in at the registration table and chatted with the ladies—classmates—who put his money in the strongbox. "I could tackle him," Eric whispered, as much to himself as anyone. Then Derrick turned toward the room and Eric moved four or five steps to grab Derrick's hand. The two smiled, then embraced, and Joshua snapped a photograph. Eric and Derrick broke their clinch, spoke quietly, then hugged again.

Later into the night, after the two had talked a while, Eric took Derrick by the shoulders. "It's good to see you," he said and hugged him once more. "We gotta bury this hatchet."

Laughter and shouting. Eric—the leader, the vocal one, the take-charge-this-is-how-it-goes fella—held the attention of a small group. He was telling stories.

Okay. Eric and Derrick have this date with their girlfriends—a couple of Bulkeley girls. But they have to get across town. Two, three miles. Eric is sixteen, and he's just got his driver's license, and his aunt offers to loan him her car so he and Derrick can drive to the South End. "Eric, I trust you. You're the pride of the family, blah blah blah. I trust you with my car." So, Eric and Derrick buckle up. Key goes in the ignition. Eric looks down. "It's a stick, D," he says. "I don't know how to drive a stick." But there are girls waiting. Ladies. Lovely ladies. Says Derrick, "You better learn." So Eric cranks the ignition, and the two drive to the South End, the car herking and jerking and screeching the whole way. They make it. Yes, they make it. But the clutch doesn't. Sucker burns out by the time they park.

Later: football stories. So there's this game, Eric said, and I'm close to passing for two hundred yards. Just need four or five. Nothing big. Josh runs a little down and out, and I toss to him. He's four or five yards downfield. If he holds on to it, I've got a two-hundred-yard game! But Josh starts to bobble the ball, and the ball's going *backwards* through the air, and Josh is chasing it, and by the time he's got it caught, he's four or five yards *behind* the line of scrimmage, and he gets tackled. It was like Josh's only catch! And it cost me four yards!

Everyone at the table laughed, even Joshua. So another story. This one about Derrick, about a bad day Derrick had against Weaver, some Beaver receiver who kept beating him until LaPlante pulled Derrick off the field, benched him. Laughs again. But as people laughed, Derrick looked at Eric. He wasn't laughing. "I never got pulled out," he said. "I never got pulled out."

The DJ played Chubb Rock's "Treat 'Em Right," and other hits from the days when these alum were students, mixed those oldies with newer tunes. When the music was rap, no one danced. When it was salsa, the Hispanic alums found partners and overran the dance floor.

Then the music quieted and Joshua borrowed the DJ's microphone. He asked his classmates to remember all the alums who graduated in '90, especially those who had died. He asked them to remember, too, those who couldn't make it for other reasons, like the one who just received the blessing of a baby a week before. Then Joshua handed the microphone to a visitor, a representative of Hartford Public, who wanted to talk about the school, its history, its bad press of late, its struggle to take the blemish off its accreditation report, its restoration of a piano. The visitor spoke about the HPHS alumni organization, and how that group held a cocktail party to raise money for the school.

And he told them of Hartford Public's historic mementos that are kept in a vault near the principal's office ("I suppose some of you remember the principal's office for one reason or another. No? Yes?"). The school wants to buy display cases, he said, to show off those historic relics.

He talked a while, transforming the party—by his demeanor and his words—into a fifth-period class. The alums looked like high school students again, slumped in their chairs, chins resting on the heels of their hands.

Thirty-six. Joshua needed fifty. The evening had cost him nearly three hundred dollars.

Now the music was so loud people could hardly talk. Fewer of them mingled. Folks had broken into smaller, comfortable groups: Hiram and Derrick with their friends from the South Arsenal Neighborhood Development projects, Eric with Taren. Joshua sat alone at the registration table.

The inside of the Elks' Lodge was warm. To cool off, Hiram first shed his suit coat. Then he stepped out to the sidewalk, taking in the easy night air, talking real estate with a SAND buddy. He talked of how he planned to quit the job in East Hartford working with second-graders. The Litchfield company had offered to put Hiram in charge of a new halfway house in Bridgeport. He'd get to hire his own staff. It would be a little different situation. The new house was right there in the city, smaller than the one in Litchfield. It will serve only a dozen girls, who will also have to get jobs. Hiram had thought about it and figured the drive to Bridgeport—about an hour each way—won't seem so bad now that he'll only work one job. No, he won't move to Bridgeport. Push comes to shove, he'd still rather own a piece of Hartford.

Eric and Taren were among the first to leave. Three or four times, Eric and Derrick bid each other farewell, sincere in their affection. Derrick carried Eric's business card in his pocket, the Shorters' home address and phone number written on the back.

The party passed its crescendo, quieted, and now faced the finale. Outside, a street cat prowled past. Inside, the edges of nametags curled loose from suit coats and from blouses. Joshua has sat by the door, legs crossed, jaws working a piece of chewing gum, ever the good host, standing to greet people as they leave and thanking them for coming. Now only a dozen or so remained. One of them hit on an idea; the old classmates grabbed fistfuls of balloons and ran out onto Prospect Street, laughing and shouting, and they let the blues and whites go, let the balloons drift into the city-bright night, cheered the balloons on until they vanished. Joshua, though he looked tired, smiled, before heading back inside.

The DJ packed his equipment, and Joshua's father came by to help clean. It was just after midnight. Sunday morning. I thanked Joshua, then stepped outside to head to Maple Avenue. Some of the alums lingered on the sidewalk deciding where next to take their party. Hiram declined. He planned to get up early. Be at work by seven.

Just before I left, Derrick took me aside to say goodnight, then asked me to telephone him the next morning. He wanted to meet one more time before I drove to the airport.

The next day, I packed and left my grandparents, wondering, as I did each visit, whether this time would be the last.

I parked in front of Derrick's house a few minutes later; his mother's place was less than a mile from Maple Avenue. The day shined sunny and warm, and Derrick, a little tired with eyes a bit puffy, greeted me dressed in sweatpants and a University of Connecticut T-shirt neatly tucked into the waistband. Inside the house, curtains and some of the shades were drawn, and a cozy combination of sun and house lamps lit the rooms. A vase on the coffee table overflowed with pink silk roses. Derrick's mother and two of his sisters looked busy planning the family's Thanksgiving, an out-of-state gathering at the house of another sibling. Derrick led me out of the living room, and we settled in around a small, Formica-topped kitchen table.

"I definitely had a good feeling, seeing Eric," Derrick said. "We wish Harvey could've made it down. He was there in spirit."

He paused, and it was clear he meant Eric when he said, "He really doesn't like to come back here."

We talked some more about the evening. After the reunion the diehards moved the party to a downtown bar. When that broke up, Derrick went to his girlfriend's apartment where he stayed up late, sitting and meditating on the evening, on the pledge.

"Thinking about the guys," he said, "thinking about Eric, that I'm proud of him. And proud of him as a friend. I was thinking around all these things. It's more or less time for me to step up to the plate."

But was the pledge, he wondered, a strict thing or just a guide? Harvey and Eric didn't come home as they promised, but maybe that was okay, so long as they took the spirit of the pledge to wherever they landed and helped out there. That's what Eric had said, that it was important to contribute no matter where. Derrick wondered, too, whether it would have been different for them—for him—if they had all come back. Did the success of the pledge depend on them remaining close, feeding off each other's passion and dedication and friendship?

"Maybe as time goes on, we go to see Eric, we'll get our community back. Maybe we will get that feel, that zest for the statement we made."

Or maybe not. Maybe he could regain the sense of the pledge without Eric or the group. He'd been thinking about this all night. Once upon a time, they had been Owls, and they had been B-Side, "Brothers Striving Together, Independently Demonstrating Excellence." Maybe what he needed was a new pledge, one that focused less on the team and more on that independent demonstration of excellence. So the night before, as he sat through the dark morning hours, he arrived at an idea he hoped would spur him forward.

"Will the Walk. W.W. It is a willingness to make it, if you have obstacles, and they're keeping you from your goals, that first step, that first walk."

He noted that he would turn thirty on Valentine's Day. Four months away. It seemed a good time to mark change.

"An obstacle came my way," he said, "and I've been stuck in a standstill. Now I have to do it. I have to get that hunger again. Last night I was hungry again."

Before I left for the airport, I asked Derrick if I could photograph him and his mother. I wanted a snapshot should I need to remember how they looked. They sat together on the couch in the living room, Moms and Derrick, in front of lace curtains, and he put his arm around her. She shined in a bright floral print blouse, with petals as pink as those silk roses. They both smiled, and as I pressed the shutter button, Derrick's mother radiated contentment and confidence. It was as if she knew she had made something to last through her lifetime. A family. Ten children. Three of them—including her youngest—keeping her company, right here, right now, in her own big house near Wethersfield Avenue. Though she was older, growing older yet, her house remained full and robust. She smiled as if she knew these riches would always be hers, or as if this fact were beyond knowing, a thing certain and understood: some of her offspring, at least, would never stray far from home.

Epilogue

In January 2001 the Minnesota Vikings faced the New
York Giants for the NFC championship, the winner to head
to the Super Bowl. Harvey Kendall found the game on the
big-screen TV in his Kansas City town house, and he and
I sat to watch. Both of us had been Vikings' fans since
childhood, rewarded for our dedication—as all fans of
the purple and gold—with decades of spectacular frustration. Plenty of teams have never won a Super Bowl, Minnesota included, but no team has more often reached the
top only to lose. But today, said the oddsmakers: Vikes by
two.

In the Kendalls' town house on Kansas City's north side,
Harvey and I had talked for days about Hartford and his
life there, about a dead man's suede Converse high tops
and about Butch Braswell's creeds. ("You talked to Butch?"
Harvey asked. "Is he out? I had no clue. Nobody lets me
know anything anymore.") It was a cold, foggy weekend,
and Harvey's boys, Marshey and Maliek—then ages five

and three—played indoors. They were remarkably well behaved for kids cooped up that way, and now and then we'd enjoy their interruptions: requests for help to spin a top or to identify a marshmallow or for attention as one of the boys showed off a cowboy outfit worn over white briefs. Marshey, Harvey said, had inherited his smile. Maliek had his game face.

After college Harvey and his wife, Carma, had found jobs with a telecommunications giant in Raleigh, but better offers led them to change companies and move the family to the Midwest. It was clear there was no chance of moving to Hartford.

"Mr. Kendall knows—" (Carma often called her husband Mr. Kendall)—"there is no way on God's green earth—well, I won't say that." She composed herself. "I do not want to move to Hartford," she said.

Nor did Mr. Kendall. He felt bad for Hartford, regretted its decline, but was glad to keep his distance. The city felt too much like a losing cause. Not enough people cared. Not enough of the police, not enough of the schoolteachers, not enough of the politicians, not enough of the business leaders. The one person who did care? He got thrown in prison. Even if Harvey could imagine a move back, could imagine fulfilling his pledge, it would be quixotic, a fool's errand. He'd help a few people, but he'd put himself and his family in danger. All the promises in the world meant nothing if his wife and sons weren't healthy and happy. He had a better alternative: love your family; help others; aspire to kindness, humility and generosity; be positive.

But that last part was difficult for him when it came to Hartford. Harvey—like the others who made the pledge—had grown up with hope for Hartford's future.

Moreso than the others, he came finally to believe in the city's failure. If he couldn't be upbeat about Hartford, how could he be its champion? How could he live there? What would he have to offer?

So he gambled on a future elsewhere. In the months after I'd visited the Kendalls, their move to Kansas City took on the feel of permanence, and then permanence itself, as much as any such choice. Carma started and finished graduate school, receiving her degree in business management in May 2003. After that they bought a house in Missouri, one that's on the southern edge of Kansas City's sprawl, where the homes are affordable. "A good place to raise a family," Harvey said.

This plan holds one danger: the boys might grow up as Chiefs fans.

"No," Harvey says. But it's a joke. Just as he teases his co-workers when Minnesota beats Kansas City, he's only teasing when he tells his boys not to talk about the Chiefs around the house. Here's the truth: when a player for the home team signed autographs at a nearby mall, Harvey brought the boys to get a signature.

But the Vikings remain Harvey's team, just as they were on that foggy January weekend. So there we sat—the easy chair for Harvey, one end of the couch for me—taking a break from sad talk of Hartford to watch football. It was no more joyful. The game was three minutes young, and the Vikings had already surrendered two touchdowns. By halftime, they trailed, 34–0. No NFC championship game had ever been more lopsided.

A minute or two into the second half, after more Viking bumbling (a fumble, another Giants' touchdown), Harvey had seen enough. He left hapless Minnesota to lose while he sorted laundry. The boys needed clean clothes. Mr. Kendall had no time to waste watching another spectacular failure, another painful end.

When I visited Butch Braswell at his North End home on a sunny afternoon in July 2001, police cars cruised by five times in five minutes. The patrols had increased since the Fourth of July holiday, Butch told me, when seven-year-old Takira Gaston had been shot in the face. The shooting happened just the other side of the Spring Grove Cemetery from where Butch lived. Takira and her family had been outside enjoying a holiday picnic when rival drug dealers decided to kill each other. Takira, playing suddenly in a cross fire, suffered a bullet through the left cheek. Her jaw was wrecked. She lived but spent many painful days in the hospital. The *Courant* ran her nearly life-sized portrait on its front page: her cheeks and eyes swollen, tubes snaking into her nose, a larger tube at her throat pumping oxygen through a tracheal incision, her bottom lip split in half, a stitched scar on her left cheek. After the shooting, police mounted a North End crackdown. Hence the frequent patrols along Martin Street.

Butch looked in better shape than his neighborhood, better than he had before he'd gone to prison. He'd shaved clean, perhaps the thing that surprised me most. His arms were tight cords, and his shoulders filled out his T-shirt—one that advertised Hartford Public's annual track invitational. He was finding his way back into the track and field business, he told me, officiating the jumps at some meets and also coaching privately. He'd clipped a recent newspaper photo of a long jumper in flight at a recent track meet. In the background an out-of-focus Butch watched the jump.

To keep himself fit, he ran an hour each morning and

practiced martial arts. He also worked to maintain interest in his case. He found ways in conversation to drift back to the prosecutor, the informant, and from there to all the injustice of the world, to the ways the quality of mercy is thwarted by the exactitude of law.

He was consistent in his attitudes. When we talked about officiating, Butch, who once smuggled junk food to a hungry prisoner, told a story of a track and field judge who bragged that he had called a close foul against Olympic gold medalist Carl Lewis. Lewis had jumped twenty-nine feet nine inches in the long jump, a phenomenally good jump. But the judge believed Lewis had planted his take-off foot too far forward, a sliver or so past the legal mark. Calling such a foul on such an impressive jump, the judge said, took courage.

Butch saw it as the sin of pride.

"If a kid makes a slip like that, goes a fingernail off the mark, I'm not going to call a foul," he said. Then he repeated the instructions he gives jumpers before a meet. "'Here's what we're going to do, fellas. Stay on the board. I make the calls. I'm very fair. If there's a reasonable doubt, I'm going with the jumper. Anybody have a problem with that?' No, and that's it."

We talked more than an hour. The inside of Butch's house was poorly lit. Sheets covered the furniture. On the tv, cars squealed through some big city somewhere. Brakes. Music. Engines. Collisions. Hollywood cops and robbers.

When we finished, Butch walked me out to the curb. We chatted a bit more, but quit when a patrol car parked across the street. Two men, one in uniform, the other not, but both with handguns, stepped out of the car. They looked toward an outdoor gathering at a nearby apartment building, at people playing cards and grilling meat. Just like that, a couple of the guys playing cards broke away at a sprint. The cops followed.

Butch turned to me. "You never know what's going to happen," he said. "Better get while the going's good."

Eric Shorter drove away from his ten-year high school reunion satisfied by the news he'd heard there. Of the five friends who had pledged themselves to Hartford, all five lived. All five worked. All five loved. He was glad to see it. And if the pledge seemed a bit tattered, not wholly fulfilled, well, fine. He believed that time and reflection had changed the terms. Those forces might yet change the terms again, perhaps in Hartford's favor. For his part, he had plans that included the city. Not living there, no, not likely, but plans nonetheless.

Soon he would change jobs, and that was part of a long-term goal. He had learned about affordable housing. Time now to learn something else. So he would take a job with a national corporation that helped poor neighborhoods attract new businesses and build housing. Step-by-step, he was gaining the knowledge and connections that would allow him to form his own development company, one that could bring quality construction into inner-city neighborhoods. He had his eye on some sites back in Hartford, back on Sigourney Street, where people would benefit from windows that kept out drafts and toilets that flushed and pipes that never burst. No guarantees, but worth the work, worth a dream.

For living, there was Greater Providence. In what little spare time he had, he volunteered as a mentor to boys in state custody who were about six months from their release dates. Once returned to a world free of curfews and constant supervision, a world full of fast-food jobs and neighbors who do all their work with cell phones and baggies, the young men would need a reasonable soul to listen and help them sort through it all. That was Eric's role. He saw this as living the spirit, if not the letter, of the pledge. "I've always had a commitment to give back to a community similar to mine," he said. "My thing is this: do whatever it takes."

He held tight, too, to the dream of a cul-de-sac where he could watch from a front porch as his girls rode bicycles past the houses of neighbors they knew by name. But—like the pledge—the dream's details had gone fuzzy while the spirit held strong. The subdivision he'd once frequented, the one in the Rumford neighborhood of East Providence, had sold its last lot before he and Taren were ready to buy. There were other neighborhoods, though, and in the autumn of 2005 he and Taren moved into a new home in Swansea, a nearby Massachusetts town. A step up, yes, but if it didn't suit them in every way, there could always be another place, a better place.

"If you're not striving to get better, you're going to get worse," he said. "We're moving. We have a plan."

Hiram Harrington had been dating Sonji for more than a year when her housemate moved out, leaving her to pay her mortgage alone. She asked Hiram to move in. She knew he'd been looking for a new place. For Hiram six or so years at Billings Forge seemed long enough. Moreover, he had a pet now, an English bulldog named Dante, and dogs weren't allowed at Billings Forge. So Sonji asked him to move in to her three-bedroom ranch-style home in Bloomfield. He said yes. In the summer of 2003, he left Hartford.

In doing so he made himself part of a trend that has changed the face of the city and its neighboring suburbs. For nearly one hundred years each census had shown growth in Hartford's black population. The 2000 Census was the first to show a decline—by about eight thousand people. It is not the poor who are leaving. Instead, middle-class African-Americans have deserted Hartford for homes in bordering towns, especially in East Hartford, Windsor, and Bloomfield.

Hiram still worked for the company that ran the home for teenage girls in Litchfield, though the halfway house in Bridgeport faltered. "It was a bit too ghetto," Hiram said. The neighborhood's gunfire didn't help the girls change their bad habits. Now he traveled the state training others to be counselors. Things have changed. The girls committed crimes at a younger age, it seemed, as young as twelve. More of them came from Bridgeport. It used to be that most came from New Haven and Hartford. Not that Hartford was the best place to raise a teenage girl, but yeah, Hiram said, when compared with Bridgeport, Hartford seemed better for kids.

He chuckled when he said that, recognizing that he compared levels of despair and misery. "Better than Bridgeport" wasn't a quality to consider as he and Sonji talked about marriage and buying a house together. She said no to Hartford. Having lived in half a dozen Connecticut towns, she held no great loyalty to the Insurance City. In truth Hiram didn't much want Hartford, either. He liked the price of housing in the city, but not the other costs. Where the prices were low enough, he said, the crime was too high. Until the city cleaned itself up, he couldn't see buying there.

The clean air of North Carolina ended their search.

Both had ties to the Tar Heel State. Sonji graduated from a small college outside Charlotte, and Hiram had family who lived in the same area. His only brother, Herman, had died of a rare and incurable disease, leaving a wife and three children. Hiram visited whenever he could. "Support is everything," he said. On one of these trips, he and Sonji parked at a rest stop just inside the North Carolina border. Outside the car Hiram breathed deeply.

"Wow, smell that air!" he said.

So Sonji did. It smelled nothing like the air of Greater Hartford. Back and forth they bantered about the air until finally Hiram said, "It wouldn't be a bad idea if we moved down here." And Sonji agreed.

Months later—in Gastonia, North Carolina—Hiram stood with his nephew, Shaquor, in an empty lot of a housing development. This is where we'll live, Hiram told the boy, and our house will look like that one. He pointed to the model, a big house with columns, so big Shaquor asked, "Are you rich?"

Hiram laughed. "Absolutely not," he said.

They stood on the empty ground where one day a house would arise, a place where Shaquor and his siblings could sleep over and visit on holidays and weekends and birthdays and even, some day, where they could baby-sit their young cousins. But now, to prove he was not rich, Hiram talked about hard work and savings and the value of money and the value of any house at all. What matters most, he told Shaquor, is that we all have houses. Shaquor listened, then told his uncle that he would work hard in school, that he was motivated. Hiram thought, I'm having this conversation with a boy in a field and he understands what I'm talking about. This, Hiram thought, is why I'm supposed to be down here. This will make North Carolina my home.

Mortson Street and Putnam Heights are short—each one block long—with a history of misery to last a hundred miles. When new, their buildings—called "perfect sixes" —housed Hartford's turn-of-the-century immigrant factory workers, and six families could fit into one, hence their name. Nowhere in Hartford was there a greater concentration of that style of building: triple-decker apartments on either side, separated by a staircase. Though they housed immigrant laborers, they were built with an elegance lost to most of twentieth-century America's working-class housing. The buildings had brick façades. Front porches. High, wide bay windows on every floor. The two blocks—parallel, one alongside the other—hide a bit from the rest of the city, on a hill, caught between two busy roads and with nothing to draw drivers who live elsewhere. In the last decades of the twentieth century, as the buildings neared their hundred-year anniversaries, their neighborhood foundered from neglect and arson. Many perfect sixes had been burned, their insides gutted. The brick was discolored by soot, and some of it had been chipped away. Unsteady porches lacked steps or posts to support their roofs. Boards had replaced glass in the windows, and the wood was so old it had turned gray. Lawns lacked any landscaping—nary a bush—and grass had been trampled to weeds and dirt. The buildings seemed fit only for rats or cockroaches or feral cats. Homeless addicts snuck in and out.

Now, years later, what was once blighted has been, in part, recovered. Developers—some working for profit, others as nonprofits—joined with local corporations to invest in the two streets. They began to rebuild the perfect sixes, turning them into townhomes while adding new houses on the streets' vacant lots. Estimates put the investments at more than eleven million dollars. The company that now employs Eric Shorter had something to do with it; its Hartford branch championed a new Connecticut law that provides tax credits for developers willing to turn neglected, historic buildings into housing, and developers used those credits as they rebuilt Mortson and Putnam Heights. A city program has encouraged people to buy into this resurrection, to brave what remain dangerous neighborhoods, to become what some folks call "urban homesteaders."

Joshua Hall and his wife, Timcia, signed up. The down payment was low, and the city offered to finance eighty thousand dollars of the purchase price—nearly 70 percent. If the Halls stay seven years, the city will forgive the balance of the loan. By the time Joshua and Timcia married in August 2005, they had already committed to Hartford and their new neighborhood. They understood the risks.

"It's in a really, really, really bad neighborhood," Joshua said. "But that's the way to improve a neighborhood—to make opportunities for people. They're trying to get good, solid people in here by any means necessary."

Joshua and Timcia fit the profile of the city's ideal urban homesteaders. Born in Jamaica, raised in Hartford, Timcia worked in the office of a bank in one of Hartford's suburbs. Before she met Joshua, she had already invested in the city, buying a condominium near the South Green neighborhood. Joshua still taught at Weaver High School, now bringing to his work the extra qualification of a graduate degree in educational leadership. He had expanded his duties at the school. Afternoons in autumn he took up a whistle and became Coach Hall, leading the freshman football team and working with the junior varsity and varsity. Outside of football season, he tried to attend as many after school events as possible. At track meets he sometimes bumped into Aaron Fisher who knew someone on the team. Joshua's students called Aaron "The Hat Man" because he now owned a little shop—a hallway with shelves, really—on Albany Avenue where he sold hats and T-shirts. It was boring work, Aaron admitted, but better than the street life he knew in high school.

Now after school Joshua drives home to Putnam Heights, to a town house he and Timcia watched change beam by beam, wire by wire, from gutted shell into a home. Now many of the neighborhood's buildings are beautiful again, with arched windows and ornate porches, and bushes and grass, and the bricks a warm orange. Landlords keep properties clean. Neighbors agree that nights aren't so loud, that crime is less frequent and less severe. It's the kind of change that suggests Hartford might yet regain some of its old life, make the city attractive again, draw the middle and the professional classes back, and keep people like Joshua and Timcia Hall from leaving.

Not that they would consider such a move. A promise is a promise. Even now that he and Timcia expect their first child, the Halls' commitment to Putnam Heights and Hartford remains strong. They agreed to seven years, and for seven years they will stay. At the end of that time, who knows? Joshua dreams of one more move. Somewhere in the Blue Hills neighborhood, perhaps even on Canterbury Street, a house awaits.

A few months after the reunion, Derrick Walker moved in

300

with Mirasol, his girlfriend, and her three children in her apartment in East Hartford. Together, they lived as a family, and Derrick enjoyed her children. In the years that followed, he switched jobs a time or two, landing for a while at the elementary school that served the SAND projects where as a boy he played neighborhood football games. There he ran the computer lab, guiding students through tutorials that helped them learn reading and math. It was in Hartford, and it was working with Hartford's children, and he was glad for it. The work was part-time, and though he hoped it might lead to more, eventually the budget ran out. From there he moved onto a department store's distribution warehouse.

His mother, Emma Walker, died on Thanksgiving Day, 2003.

No one expected it. Even after her morning trip to the emergency room, even after the doctor's diagnosis of pneumonia, no one expected this, not even Moms. She sent her children and grandchildren on to their Thanksgiving dinner with instructions for the food she'd already prepared and left at home. As they often did, members of the clan gathered at a hall they'd rented for the occasion. They arranged the food on the table, sat down to eat and say the blessing, and it was just after the "Amen" that a cell phone chirped with the news that she had been moved into the hospital's intensive care unit. Kidney failure. She died that night.

Months later Derrick still felt the shock. His voice quavered when he talked about her. No, he didn't have bad days, he said; his mother had always taught that some days were good, others so-so, but there were no bad days. He missed her. He tried to concentrate on things she'd taught him: to be kind, gentle, and polite. She was, he said, an angel sent to earth. He recalled her willingness to help people, to help her children in their times of need. He recalled the church service where his family said their farewells. Friends came, too: Joshua, Hiram, and Eric. One of Derrick's brothers, Curtis, a minister, officiated. Despite Curtis's grief, he had to try to direct the ceremony, he had said, and if he tried God would help him through. It was, Derrick said, "a great homecoming service."

II

Students at the university sometimes asked me about my summers or my spring breaks, what I did to keep busy. Briefly, then, I told them about this book and about Eric and Derrick, Harvey, Hiram, and Joshua. I told them about my grandparents.

Jason listened more intently than most. So did Courtney.

Courtney grew up on a farm in a central Montana town of fewer than four hundred people. Every harvest season, it seemed, that number shrank as crop prices dropped and farmers sold their land. Though Courtney wanted to go home, though she even fantasized about raising her own children there, she believed it to be impossible. Though she loved the open plains, the horizon-long sunsets, and the sense of feeling so very small, she had no choice but to leave. Her town was dying, her home vanishing. Her parents had sold their farm. Nothing she could do—no martyrdom—would change that, no matter how great her sacrifice.

Jason felt it, too, the constant tug of *there*. He was Navajo, and he'd worked hard to become a good reporter at some of the country's best newspapers. But when adventuring in the world of journalism—in Portland, Oregon, in

New York City—he ached for his family and the New Mexico desert, the dry air, its smell like no other place (maybe because of the sage, maybe because of the absence of trees and their damp scents). Back home on visits, he missed city life: the music he could surround himself with in those other places, the concerts, bands like Korn coming to town; he missed his friends who knew who Korn was and with whom he could delight in talk of bad, campy movies over a sushi lunch.

We talked, Jason and I, Courtney and I, about our places and our people—the ones we gave up, the ones we kept, the necessity of choosing, the punishment for having chosen. We had none of us ever promised to go back, but we felt an unvoiced summons that had to do with love and loyalty, that required no oath to trouble us. Here or there. There or here. I couldn't tell them then, I can't tell them now, that there is one way, one answer. It is a problem to live through, a circumstance to suffer and enjoy. A decision to make and unmake.

In early August 2002, I received the phone call with the news that my grandmother was near death.

I arrived in Hartford on a Thursday. At the hospital we crowded into my grandmother's room in the hospice ward—all of her children, all of her grandchildren, spouses, even a couple of great-grandchildren. She delighted in the company; I'd not seen her looking healthier or happier in half a decade. She clapped her hands and told jokes.

The next day my grandmother sank into a morphine coma. In the ensuing days we spent long hours at the hospital, and when my mother and her sister decided to start staying overnight, I slept in their stead at my grandparents' house, keeping watch over my grandfather.

At times Grandma opened her eyes and stared at nothing. She flexed her feet and moaned. Without eyeglasses, without dentures, with her hair having lost its perm—swept back against the pillow—she looked already changed. We sponged her lips with water, and we whispered to her permissions, assured her that we were fine, that we would care for Grandpa and love him, that it was okay for her to go. My mother and aunt hardly left Grandma's bedside. They brushed her hair. They slept in hospital chairs. They prayed that she would die. Often she shuddered, and the nurse would declare that my grandmother's life appeared to be ending. But this was a woman who had lingered for years in her home on Maple Avenue, surviving, defiant and unwilling to surrender. In the hospice ward, Grandma held on.

It was late Sunday night, near midnight, when she died. I had driven home from the hospital just a few hours before to put my grandfather to bed. When he left her, as he always did, he stroked her hand and kissed her forehead. "My sweetie," he said. "Oh my sweetie."

Grandpa, before he was Grandpa, before his wedding in 1939, wrote to his future sister-in-law who had moved to Iowa for work. She had asked him in a previous letter how he was enjoying the run-up to the nuptials.

"My reading," he wrote back,

> is confined to a rather specialized field these days: *If I Have Four Apples, Personal Problems of Marriage, Budgetary Control (or The Classic Envelope System), How to Evade*

Dishwashing Tho' Hitched, classified rentals and kindred piffle-and-stuff.

I've doubled the quantity of socks, tripled my supply of shirts, increased my stock of pajamas, ties, and multiplied to a pile my kerchiefs. I've inventoried my shoes, refurbished my present wardrobe of suits, purchased two additional ones. I have ceased abruptly to act like a rational human being. Thoughtful furrows now etch normally placid brows, a film of conjecture beclouds an erstwhile clear optic, plump facial contours are retreating before angular gauntiness, the steadiness of extended hand takes on a palsied waver. Damn it, woman, draw your own conclusions.

I was in the living room as upstairs my Aunt Barbara told Grandpa that his wife was dead.

He dressed himself that morning with all the formality he could muster. When he came down he paused at the landing, steadying himself with one hand on the final post. He wore slacks and dress shoes and a gray sport coat. Underneath the coat, he wore a short-sleeve jersey decorated with Mickey Mouse over the left breast, a gift from one of his children, and he had attached a clip-on bow tie, crooked at the collar.

"We've lost Helen," he said.

The family moved my grandfather to Tucson to be near my mother. They decided Tucson was the best choice because it was warm and he'd have family nearby year-round. My brother and sister still live in Tucson, and they could also visit my grandfather if he moved there. It was the best thing to do, everyone agreed. So in October, my aunt brought Grandpa to the airport, and he flew with her to Tucson, leaving behind the city where he'd lived for ninety-three years, where his father had driven a livery wagon and his mother had called for beer on her death-bed, where he had flirted with young Helen Urbanik at the Pulaski Day parade, where he had owned a share of a downtown restaurant, sweated as he wrestled with bar-bells at the YMCA, prayed at St. Augustine's Church, given away two daughters at the end of a wedding aisle, golfed at Goodwin Park, drowned Japanese beetles in soapy wa-ter before they could destroy his rose bushes, led exercise classes at the South End Senior Citizens Center, chanted Polish rhymes to his grandchildren. He left the city where he had been at home for ninety-three years, where he had buried his wife.

My mother chose for him a pleasant assisted-living cen-ter, a clean and well-lit one-story building laid out as a dog-leg, with outside paths that meandered past green lawns, a bird house, a gazebo, and lawn statues of rabbits and frogs. The staff was professional and kind. In his room, which faced westward and caught the long afternoon sun, my mother hung a big clock on the wall and photos of his children. By his bedside, she set his wedding photo. Even so, he almost never mentioned my grandmother.

The first few months in Tucson were the worst. He nev-er grieved openly, but his health collapsed. He suffered tiny strokes that incapacitated him for minutes at a time. He was tired and disoriented and sometimes incontinent. He never stopped asking my mother, "Can I come home with you?"

A year later, though he still had bouts that sent him to the hospital, he seemed calm and relaxed, as if he had surrendered the idea, the hope, of ever again living with family or in Hartford.

Almost eight months after my grandmother died, my mother sent me an e-mail to say that the house on Maple Avenue had sold.

"A young couple with no children bought it," she wrote. "We are pleased that it didn't take too long."

On my last visit to Hartford, we placed my grandfather's body in the ground beside that of his wife. What I loved most in Hartford is gone, and the city feels strange to me. Indifferent. Unfamiliar. The house on Maple Avenue knows other voices. I could go back now and then to visit the graves, but what would be the point? Grandma and Grandpa aren't there. Their bodies are dust. Instead, I look at their pictures in frames around my house. I dream of them at night, and of Hartford, and of what I once knew was home.

Selected Bibliography

I list here by chapter the works I used either as source material or to provide me with context to better understand my subjects. It is not a complete list of my readings on Hartford.

PRACTICE

Downs, Mike. "Braswell Turns on Striders to Track Meets." *Hartford Courant*, August 14, 1989, 6/7 edition.

——. "City Champ: For Kendall, Achievements Begin at Home." *Hartford Courant*, June 20, 1990.

CHAPTER 1

Burgard, Matt. "Officer Is Cleared in Fatal Shooting." *Hartford Courant*, November 23, 2000, 6/7 edition.

Hartford Courant. "State Adding 2 Narcotics Squads to Expand Battle against 'Crack,'" September 6, 1986.

CHAPTER 2
Books

Griffis, William Elliot. *The Story of New Netherland: The Dutch in*

America. Boston: Houghton Mifflin, 1909.

Weaver, Glenn, and Mike Swift. *Hartford: Connecticut's Capital; An Illustrated History.* Sun Valley CA: American Historical Press, 2003.

Articles

Bothwell, Dick. "Warm? That's August . . . " *St. Petersburg Times,* August 4, 1973.

Documents

Deposition of Linda Shorter, recorded by Cowan, Cheryl B., court reporter, Circuit Court for Pinellas County, Florida, November 15, 1973.

State of Florida v. Robert Shorter. Sixth Circuit Court, Pinellas County, Florida, Case Number 73-3210, filed on August 5, 1973, judgment and sentence on February 8, 1974.

Web Sites

The City of St. Petersburg. "Lakewood Estates." City of St. Petersburg. http://www.stpete.org/nnlak.htm.

St. Petersburg Times. "Man Held in Slaying of Cousin," August 6, 1973.

CHAPTER 3

Books

Baldwin, Peter C. *Domesticating the Street: The Reform of Public Space in Hartford, 1850–1930.* Columbus: Ohio State University Press, 1999.

Beeching, Barbara, Lary Bloom, Garret Condon, Tom Condon, Steve Courtney, Jim Farrell, Anne Farrow et. al. *Twain's World: Essays on Hartford's Cultural Heritage.* Hartford: *Hartford Courant,* 1999.

Faude, Wilson H. *The Great Hartford Picture Book.* Norfolk VA: Donning, 1985.

Grant, Ellsworth S., and Marion H. Grant. *Passbook to a Proud Past and a Promising Future, 1819–1969.* Hartford CT: Society for Savings, 1969.

Grant, Marion Hepburn. *In and about Hartford: Tours and Tales.* Hartford CT: Connecticut Historical Society, 1978.

Twain, Mark. *Mark Twain's Speeches.* New York: Harper Brothers, 1910.

Articles

Barger, Theresa Sullivan. "Dental Records of Missing Hartford Youth, Victim Compared." *Hartford Courant*, October 25, 1988.

Barger, Theresa Sullivan, and Efrain Hernandez Jr. "Victim of Killing Identified." *Hartford Courant*, October 26, 1988.

Cain, Sherman. "Give Public Football Its Due." *Manchester Journal-Inquirer*, December 6, 1994.

Clark, Charles H. "The Charter Oak City." *Scribner's Monthly*, November 1876, 1–21.

Dempsey, Christine. "Board of Education Modifies C Rule." *Hartford Courant*, November 22, 1994, North final edition.

Downs, Mike. "The C Rule: Designed to Keep Athletes in School—And It's Working." *Hartford Courant*, March 31, 1992.

——. "City Champ: For Kendall, Achievements Begin at Home." *Hartford Courant*, June, 20 1990.

——. "Front and Center: Bobby Torres." *Hartford Courant*, May 22, 1990, 6/7 edition.

——. "Team of Two Enough for HPHS." *Hartford Courant*, June 6, 1990, Final edition.

Doyle, Paul. "HPHS Duo Stars Again in New England." *Hartford Courant*, June 10, 1990.

Hathaway, William. "Hartford Feeling Impact of Orphaned Real Estate." *Hartford Courant*, April 4, 1993.

Rodriguez, Joseph. "Witnesses Say Cruiser Rams Youth Mistaken for Suspect." *Hartford Courant*, June 6, 1984.

CHAPTER 4

Documents

State of Connecticut, Bureau of Vital Statistics. Medical Certificate of Death: Teodor Petrykowski. City of Hartford, Connecticut. July 17, 1917.

Web Sites

The International Website of Phi Beta Sigma Fraternity, Inc. http://
www.pbs1914.org.

Norfolk State University. http://www.nsu.edu.

Virginia State University. http://www.vsu.edu.

CHAPTER 5

Books

Néret, Gilles. *August Rodin: Sculptures and Drawings.* Translated by
Chris Miller. Koln: Benedikt Taschen, 1994.

Pinet, Helene. *Rodin: The Hands of a Genius.* London: Thames and
Hudson, 1992.

Rilke, Rainer Marie. *Rodin.* New York: Haskell Booksellers, 1974.

Seward, Desmond. *The Hundred Years War: The English in France,
1337–1453.* New York: Macmillan, 1978.

Tuchman, Barbara W. *A Distant Mirror.* New York: Alfred A. Knopf,
1978.

Varnedoe, Kirk, Rachael Blackburn, Aida Audeh, Antoinette Le
Normand-Romain, Mary L. Levkoff, Daniel Rosenfeld, and
Jacques Vilain. *Rodin: A Magnificent Obsession.* London: Merrell,
2001.

Yeats, William Butler. "Easter 1916." In *The Norton Anthology of
Poetry,* edited by Alexander W. W. Allison, Arthur M. Eastman,
Arthur J. Carr, Herbert Barrows, and Caesar R. Blake. 3rd ed.
New York: W. W. Norton, 1983.

Articles

Brisgone, Gina. "Teen Killed, Man Injured in Shooting." *Hartford
Courant,* December 31, 1991.

Burgard, Matt. "Protestors Demand Better Policing." *Hartford Courant,* February 6, 2002.

Julien, Andrew. "A Life of Creativity Ends All Too Quickly: Young
Artist, Who Tried to Depict City Life, Falls Victim to Its Violence." *Hartford Courant,* January 4, 1992.

Kauffman, Matthew. "Teen Gets 33 Years in Death of Artist."
Hartford Courant, May 20, 1993.

Nakashima, Ellen. "Gang Violence Led to Doubling of Hartford's Homicide Rate." *Hartford Courant*, January 2, 1994.

Puleo, Tom. "Teen Killed by Gunshots." *Hartford Courant*, September 1, 2001.

Quintanilla, Blanca M. "16-Year-Old City Boy Charged with Murder of High School Student." *Hartford Courant*, January 1, 1992.

Documents

List or Manifest of Alien Immigrants for the Commissioner of Immigration. ss Amsterdam, Holland-America Line, from Rotterdam to New York, March 9, 1903. http://www.ellisislandrecords.org/.

Web sites

"Królik Polski," translated by Michael Downs and Magda Chaney. http://www.rymanow.pl/miejscowosci1_5.htm (accessed March 2002; site now discontinued).

CHAPTER 6

Articles

Condon, Tom. "Sheriff System Constitutes a Clear Case of Rot." *Hartford Courant*, January 17, 1993.

Gorman, Kathleen. "Racial Checks Routine, Ex-Avon Officer Says." *Hartford Courant*, April 17, 1994.

Halloran, Liz. "Aquan Case Tests Mettle of 2 Men." *Hartford Courant*, September 26, 1999.

Leavenworth, Jesse. "M. Donald Cardwell." *Hartford Courant*, August 3, 2002, 6/7 edition.

Rivera, Hector L. "'Butch' Braswell Faces Another Tough Hurdle." *Metro Bridge*, February 18, 1993.

Trotta, Brian M. "Report: Avon Police Targeted Minorities." *Hartford Courant*, November 22, 1994.

Documents

State of Connecticut v. Melvin D. "Butch" Braswell. Superior Court, Judicial District of Hartford/New Britain, Connecticut, Case Number 434149. Transcript reported by Patricia L. Masi, April 4, 1994.

CHAPTER 7

Books

Leccese, Michael, and Kathleen McCormick, eds. *Charter of the New Urbanism*. New York: McGraw-Hill, 2000.

Articles

Greenberg, Alan. "Studying the Moves of Shorter." *Hartford Courant*, December 15, 1994.

Hart, Andy. "City Legislators Voice Concern over Downtown Revitalization Panel." *Hartford News*, August 19, 1998, Internet edition. http://www.townusa.com/southsidemedia/819city.html.

Lott, William F. et. al. *The Economic Impact of Complementary Components of Adriaen's Landing: A Dynamic Impact Analysis*. Connecticut Center for Economic Analysis, Department of Economics, University of Connecticut. February 24, 2000. http://www.lib.uconn.edu/ccea.

Puleo, Tom. "Adriaen's Retail Component Shrinks." *Hartford Courant*, January 18, 2003, 6/7 sports final edition.

———. "How Much Is Too Much Housing?" *Hartford Courant*, February 7, 2003, Sports final edition.

Spencer, Mark. "The Dream Factory." *Northeast Magazine*, July 8, 2001.

Swift, Mike. "As Adriaen's Rises, So Does Public Bill." *Hartford Courant*, February 8, 2004, Sports final edition.

Vega, Michael. "Shorter BC's Strong (Minded) Safety." *Boston Globe*, August 28, 1994.

Zielbauer Paul, "Poverty in a Land of Plenty: Can Hartford Ever Recover?" *New York Times*, August 26, 2002, National edition.

Documents

Office of the State Comptroller. *Comprehensive Annual Financial Report of the State of Connecticut for FY 1999–2000*. By Mark Ojakian. Hartford, 2000.

State of Connecticut, Executive Chambers. "Governor Rowland Offers Plan to Promote the Redevelopment of Hartford: Plan Identifies Six Pillars of Progress, Calls for Tight Management of State Investment." Hartford, March 19, 1998, http://www. state.ct.us/governor/news/980319.htm.

Web Sites

Boston College. "Boston College Football." Boston College Official Athletic Site. http://bceagles.ocsn.com/sports/m-footbl/bc-m-footbl-body.html.

Capital City Economic Development Authority Board of Directors. "Adriaen's Landing." Capital City Economic Development Authority. http://www.cceda.state.ct.us/adriaen.

Flood, Kevin. "Who the Heck is Adriaen?" Hartford History. http://www.hartfordhistory.net/heck.html.

CHAPTER 8

Books

King, Martin Luther, Jr. *A Call to Conscience: The Landmark Speeches of Dr. Martin Luther King, Jr.* Edited by Clayborne Carson and Kris Shepard. New York: Warner, 2001.

X, Malcolm, and Alex Haley. *The Autobiography of Malcolm X.* New York: Ballantine, 1992.

Articles

Archer, Jeff. "Connecticut: State Takeover and a Desegregation Ruling Result in a Hands-On Approach to Urban Reform in Connecticut." *Education Week on the Web.* http://www.edweek.org/sreports/qc98/states/ct-n.htm.

Cordero, Nick. "Loss of Accreditation Pitches Hartford High into Uncertainty." *Metro Bridge,* April 1997.

Dee, Jane Ellen. "Honoring a Home of Historic Achievement: He and His Family Helped Change Us All." *Hartford Courant,* February 22, 1995.

Frahm, Robert A., and Rick Green. "Hartford's Woes Detailed as Desegregation Suit Opens." *Hartford Courant,* December 17, 1992.

———. "Plaintiffs Rest in Sheff Case." *Hartford Courant,* January 29, 1993.

Green, Rick. "Teaching with Heart." *Hartford Courant*, August 29, 1999.

Hamilton, Anne M., and Lisa Chedekel. "High School Draft Report Says Work Is Still Needed; Progress Reported at Hartford Public." *Hartford Courant*, February 25, 1998.

Hartford Courant. "Blacks Say Disturbances Not Organized," June 13, 1969.

———. "Businesses Still Tallying Up Cost of North End Marauding," June 11, 1969.

———. "Curfew Stops Violence," June 7, 1969.

———. "Disturbances Add to Costly Total," June 10, 1969.

———. "Police Arrest 100 During 2d Curfew," June 8, 1969.

———. "Shots Fired in North End Violence," June 5, 1969.

———. "Two Wounded By Police as N. End Erupts Anew," June 6, 1969.

Janick, Herbert F. "Racial Violence of the 1960s." Connecticut Heritage Gateway. http://www.ctheritage.org/encyclopedia/ctsince1929/racialviolence.htm.

Kuczkowski, Michael. "It's Takeover Time: How Bitter Infighting and a Lack of Leadership Forced the State to Take Control of Hartford Schools." *Hartford Advocate*, April 17, 1997.

Lee, Mary Jane. "How *Sheff* Revives *Brown*: Reconsidering Desegregation's Role in Creating Equal Education Opportunity." *New York University Law Review* 74, no. 2 (May 1999): 485–528.

Miller, Julie, A. "Connecticut: Back in Court." Education Week on the Web. http://www.edweek.org/sreports/qc99/states/policy/ct-up.htm.

Prestamo, Cecelia. "Honoring a Home of Historic Achievement." *Hartford Courant*, February 22, 1995.

Sheridan, Chris. "Desegregation Lawsuit Fails." *Hartford Courant*, April 13, 1995.

Westerman, Gayl Shaw. "The Promise of State Constitutionalism: Can It Be Fulfilled in *Sheff v. O'Neill*?" *Hastings Constitutional Law Quarterly* 23, no. 2 (Winter 1996): 351–406.

Documents

Connecticut General Assembly, Legislative Program Review and Investigations Committee. *Staff Briefing: State Board of Trustees for the Hartford Public Schools.* Hartford, September 9, 1999.

Connecticut General Assembly, Legislative Program Review and Investigations Committee. *State Board of Trustees for the Hartford Public Schools: Final Report.* Hartford, December 14, 1999.

Connecticut State Board of Education. *Quarterly Progress Report on Hartford Public Schools.* Hartford, May 2002.

New England Association of Schools and Colleges, Commission on Secondary Schools. Letter to Amado G. Cruz, principal, Hartford Public High School. February 21, 1997.

New England Association of Schools and Colleges, Commission on Secondary Schools. *Report of the Visiting Committee: Hartford Public High School.* Bedford, October 6, 1996.

Sheff v. O'Neill, 238 Conn. 1, 678 A.2d 1267 (1996).

Web Sites

William Caspar Graustein Memorial Fund. "Hartford." The Children First Initiative. http://www.wcgmf.org/CFI/Hartford.html.

EPILOGUE

Articles

Brown, Tina A. "Takira's Scars Are Healing." *Hartford Courant*, July 4, 2003.

Budoff, Carrie. "Drawn to the City." *Hartford Courant*, January 31, 2004.

Swift, Mike. "City Loses Blacks to Suburbs: Hartford's African American Population Drops for First Time in Century." *Hartford Courant*, March 21, 2001.

Documents

Capital City Economic Development Authority, "$11 Million Community Revitalization Project Reaches Major Milestone." Press release, Capital City Economic Development Authority.

http://www.cceda.state.ct.us/news/releases/Mortson_Putnam_062101.htm.

Web Sites

Hartford LISC. "Featured Stories: Mortson Street." Hartford LISC. http://www.liscnet.org/hartford/partners/featured_6414.shtml#Mortson.

UNIVERSITY OF NEBRASKA PRESS